STOLEN FIELDS:

**A Story of Eminent Domain and
the Death of the American Dream**

STOLEN FIELDS:

A Story of Eminent Domain and the Death of the American Dream

By Jean Boggio

STOLEN FIELDS: A Story of Eminent Domain and
the Death of the American Dream

Colerith Press
175 Dickey Mill Rd.
Belmont, ME 04952 USA

Orders @ Colerith Press; http://www.jeanboggio.com or
http://www.colerithpress.com

Copyright © 2008 by Jean Boggio

ISBN-13 978-0-9799330-4-2

First Colerith Press printing 2008

LCCN # 2008900057

Author Photo courtesy of Julia Boggio Photography
Cover and interior design: 1106 Design

Publisher's Cataloging-in-Publication
(Provided by Quality Books, Inc.)

Boggio, Jean.
     Stolen fields : a story of eminent domain and the
death of the American dream / by Jean Boggio. — 1st ed.
     p. cm.
     ISBN-13: 978-0-9799330-4-2
     ISBN-10: 0-9799330-4-8

     1. Boggio, Jean. 2. Boggio, Jean—Family. 3. Cole
family. 4. Eminent domain—Pennsylvania—Neville Island
—History. 5. Loss (Psychology)   I. Title.

CT275.B5826A3 2008   974.8′03′092
                            QBI07-600349

DISCLAIMER

Every effort has been made to make this book as complete and accurate as possible. However, it is based on the memories of me and my cousins and memories are imperfect. Where possible, information has been taken from family documents and accounts in various periodicals for the time before our memories began. Events that occurred within the scope of our memories are portrayed as we have perceived them, or according to stories that have been handed down in our respective families, varying from one to the other. Our feelings about these memories have also been presented as honestly as possible.

A few names have been changed to protect the innocent. Others have been changed to protect the guilty.

Table of Contents

List of Photographs

Descendants of Unknown Cole

Unknown Cole — Unknown

- James Cole
- Rufus Cole
- George W. Cole — Dorcas Bragdon
  - Mary Ann Dickson
    - Augustus Porter Cole
    - Emerson Porter Cole — Helen Henderson
- Ivery Cole
- William Cole
  - Caroline Cole
  - George Henry Cole
  - Henrietta Cole
  - Milton P. Cole

James A. Cole — Agnes

Marie — Robert Augustus Cole

Jeanne Tenney

- Lucretia Cole
- Frank Cole
- Gladys Mae Cole — Arthur Bernhoft
  - Marian Bernhoft
  - Marilyn Bernhoft
  - Robert Bernhoft
  - Donald Bernhoft
- Norine Cole
- Mersha Cole
- Roberta Cole
- Helen Cole
- Keith Cole

Corinne Elizabeth Cole — John Frith

- Ella Jean Frith — Ugo Boggio
  - Julia Elizabeth Boggio
  - James Derbyshire
  - Sarah Catherine Boggio
- Nancy Carol Frith

Ned McCaughtry Cole — Evelyn Murrin Cassidy

- Evelyn Cole
- Ned M. Cole (Tucker)
- Darlene Elizabeth Cole

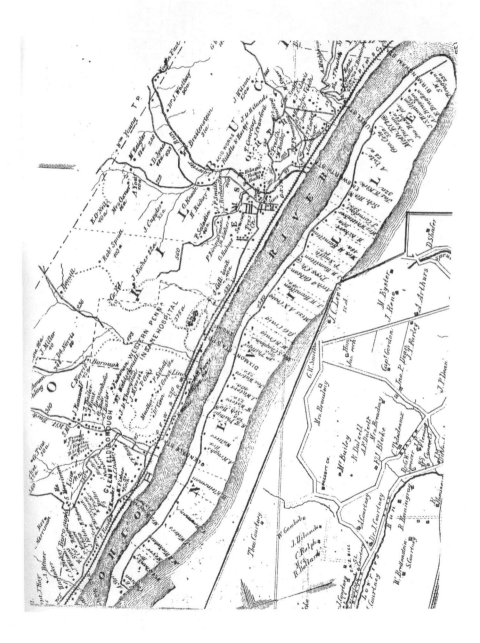

Dedication

To my cousin, Darlene, who believed in me, and to my sister, Nancy, without whom I might have grown up a different person.

Prologue

My mother never tried to either stab or shoot my father, but her father — my Grandpa Cole — once threatened to ventilate the sheriff's deputies, who brought the eviction notice, with the two guns he wore on his hips.

Grandpa Cole's farm grew the best asparagus on the East Coast. Some of it was shipped all the way to New York City to the Waldorf-Astoria Hotel, where it was served a la Neville Island. The farm also grew strawberries and tomatoes, and my grandfather grew and processed his own horseradish.

The loss of the farm grew other things as well. It grew hatred, bitterness, greed, ambition and lust. It fed on zealous religion proclaimed with fire and brimstone, but that said little of love or Christian charity. In later generations, those who left, thrived. Those who stayed, struggled with the lives they endured. Some of them found solace in the very religion that was the source of their suffering.

All our lives are affected by things that happened to shape our parents. Family traits are handed down; attitudes are either perpetuated or discarded. Sometimes the younger generation rebels against a rigid attitude on the part of the parents. This rebellion can either be a complete about-face, such as when my cousin, Tucker, turned his back on religion after his father over-reacted to his questioning of God, or it can be a silent, gradual change, as it was with me and my sister.

My mother grew up under the influence of the family's loss of the Neville Island farm in Pittsburgh and I grew up under the influence of her dreams, her regrets and her obsessions — all of which fed her determination to leave the new farm in Sandy Lake. She would spend much of her life trying to reclaim her lost status as a Cole of Neville Island.

I benefited from the benign neglect I sometimes enjoyed while my mother was busy with her various pursuits, as it counterbalanced the times she focused her attention on me. This attention was caught by what she perceived as negatives in my character that bore correction, and her remedy involved references to how I was shaming her and the whole Cole line, by not living up to her image of what they were, and what I had the ability to be. Her grandmother, Mary Ann Cole, was the image before my mother's eyes, and my mother had seldom found favor herself with that lady. When I heard the litany, "What will people think?" that meant, "What would my Grandmother Cole think?" As much as my mother loved living in Sandy Lake, and expressed happiness at the move from Neville Island, the influence of her early days there, and Mary Ann's fiery pride in the family's status, had an even stronger influence on her outlook.

Perhaps if I had been mentally deficient, she would have let me live quietly in a corner, or borne me proudly as her cross. But I had a good mind and was expected to follow the path she had conceived for me. I did not. Her big mistake was allowing me to go to the movies weekly during most of my formative years.

Some things carried over. I shared her interest in elegant houses, and the underlying drive to have one remained with me. She liked the theatre, but I carried that interest beyond what my mother considered acceptable. When it counted, I did well in school, but my performance usually matched my level of interest in the subject matter. I somehow developed a stronger sense of injustice and sympathy for the underdog that surpassed her surface recognition that the world was not perfect.

From my grandfather, I inherited my love of animals that sometimes clashed with my mother's more practical attitude toward them, acquired from her life on the farm. She never hesitated to do away with one if she found it expedient. She would then burden me with her remorse, like the time she flushed the mother mouse and her babies, although the tiny, brave creature refused to leave her young to save herself. My mother told me about it after the fact, and left me the legacy of haunting mental images of those defenseless animals, looking to her for mercy, drowning in the septic system. I would have released them outdoors.

My life did not follow a straight path, but twisted and turned to navigate the maze of influences on it. More than my own life, this is the story of what happened long ago, of the event that changed the direction of the family, of how my generation survived the effects of that event, and the influence of the strong personalities that made up the family psyche. Greed grew in a higher place than the farm, wrapped its tentacles around my mother's generation, and affected those of us who came after.

This is what happened to our family — my aunts and uncles, me, my sister and my cousins. Their voices were the cadences of my youth, their western Pennsylvania accents as familiar as that of my New Jersey neighbors.

The family's loss of the Neville Island farm certainly affected my mother's generation, leaving feelings of bitterness in three out of the four siblings. The effect on the lives of my generation was more subtle, but became part of the fabric of which we were made. Some of us have accomplished what we did because of that loss. Others, responding to the reactions of our parents, and perhaps the actions of our grandparents, achieved success in spite of it. But it did affect us. It was always there, lurking in the background of family stories. There is not one of us in this family today who is ignorant of the events of 1918 to 1921, who does not know that we collectively fell from a certain height and were left to pick ourselves up as best we could.

Neville Island is who we were — who we are. Those events shaped our parents. As water ripples out from a pebble thrown into it, so is my generation shaped in the next ring. Whatever our present names, we are the Coles of Neville Island.

CHAPTER 1

I Begin

My mother was Corinne Elizabeth Cole Frith, third child of Everson and Helen Henderson Cole. I was named for my Great-Aunt Ella Kirk, who was Great-Grandmother Lucretia Henderson's sister.

My mother hoped that Aunt Ella, who was wealthy, and who shortened her name from Kirkpatrick when she tired of writing her whole name, would leave me some money in her will. She did not. However, she did leave me a Currier and Ives framed print of *Little Ella* sitting in a railroad car, her feet resting on a hatbox. The Ella of the print was a saucy little miss with long, thick golden ringlets and a pert, fine-featured face. She didn't look like me with my dark, sullen expression.

Meanwhile, because of my mother's little avarice, I was saddled with a name I hated. My family could have called me El or Ellie — I might have liked that — but they didn't. They called me Ella Jean. My father's name was John; Jean means John in French, and my mother was a French teacher. It's surprising the number of things Ella Jean can rhyme with on the playground.

All my life I have been the spitting image of Grandma Cole at the same ages and stages, and I have her dark brown hair and dark eyes. I am grateful for that as I would not have wanted to look like my Grandfather Cole with his aquiline nose and corpulent physique. Grandma was small and lithe, even when she was old and I knew her. I don't know what I inherited from my father's side of the family — perhaps a little more gentleness and patience to my nature than the Coles had, a little less of the killer instinct, although when pushed to the limit, my patience thins.

Introducing my Mother

My mother, Corinne, was a child of Neville Island. The direction of her life was determined by the family and events that shaped her earlier years. She broke away from much of the life she had known on either farm, harboring some resentment toward her father for making it necessary to find her own way. But she had goals, and she set out to achieve them with a strong and determined will to make her dreams a reality. She made her life very different from that of her mother.

Like her father, who spent the rest of his life trying to obtain satisfaction from the government for what it took from him, my mother spent hers trying to regain what she saw as her rightful place in society. She was not fixated on the money, being content with our own modest house in an upscale town. Instead, the way she viewed others, and the way she perceived their view of her, carried back to her childhood as the daughter of one of the first families of Neville Island. Our lives were ruled by what the neighbors might think and her unsuccessful struggle to be accepted into the inner circle of the social elite.

As the younger daughter on a busy farm, Mom had grown up to be independent. She often attributed her upbringing to her older sister, Gladys, but as she grew older, Gladys was seldom at home. Mom loved her mother, perhaps out of a sense of duty, but my grandmother was taken up with the chores of the farm and didn't develop a close relationship with her younger daughter. When Mom was a child, her mother told her she was ugly. So who was her role model for motherhood? She designed her future based on what she gained from books and her dreams. That future surely included children, but she never got past the idea of children in order to grasp the reality once we were there. In her mind, her dream children followed her design. They were one-dimensional.

A romantic, she dreamed of faraway places and a faraway life. She had spent her girlhood seeing Gladys, her Grandmother Cole's favorite, getting all the advantages: the good school, the clothes, the piano lessons. Struggling through her sister's books, Mom taught herself to play the piano. She adored Gladys but felt the unfairness of the situation. With her father's aquiline nose, Mom was not a beauty, but she had a forceful personality, and a certain attractiveness, like Mary Ann Cole in many ways. She had determination. Her father squandered her inheritance, and she harbored some resentment, as did her sister, but my mother would make her own way.

Mom — Houghton and Cornell

Gladys went off to Houghton College with tuition paid for by her grandmother. Since her father had lost her education money, Mom had given up her plans to follow Gladys to Houghton, and was preparing to settle for a career in nursing at Mercer County Hospital. She had arrived there to prepare for her first term. She was no sooner settled than she had a visit from an admissions representative from Houghton, who offered her the opportunity to attend college with a scholarship and a job taking care of the dean's children. She immediately left Mercer and headed north to the Genesee Valley.

Now my mother pursued her interest in foreign languages and dove into the study of French and Latin. She attempted a course in German, but hated the guttural sounds and masculine orientation. The sounds were not romantic. By comparison, French was everything she dreamed of; the musical cadences of the language, the romance and color of the culture, and the literature that enthralled her. Latin was a practical "also ran." She became proficient in both and vowed to become an expert on French language and culture. She took a second major in religion, influenced by her early life. She graduated as salutatorian of her class and had been valedictorian of her high school class of six in Sandy Lake.

She didn't stop there. She went on to a graduate program at Cornell University and obtained a scholarship that financed a summer studying in France. Gladys's husband, Arthur, had become the principal of the Tompkins Cove High School in Rockland County, New York, and had an opening for a French and Latin teacher. Being more than qualified, Mom was summoned from Cornell to fill the slot. She was also required to teach a course in math, her weak area, but her joy at the opportunity overshadowed that detail. She would worry about the math when the time came. Gladys and Arthur had room for her in their house, along with their small children, so the matter was settled and she transferred to Columbia University in New York City, to complete her master's degree.

Mom and me

It's odd that Mom, who had a major in religion that she kept in close touch with all her life, and a master's degree in Latin, who was traveled and cultured, believed in ghosts. She passed this down to her daughters. When we were young, we would go by Spook Rock on our way to visit our Grandmother Frith in Haverstraw — at least monthly — and we would wait until we came to it, then stare avidly as we passed, hoping to see some wraith flitting around. We never did, not even on the way home in the dark.

Mom said that ghosts can't hurt you, being spirits that are just restless over some unresolved facet of their lives. She cautioned that you could hurt yourself with fear of them, however, and that some ghosts, less cordial than others, might try to cause you to do that. None of us ever saw any ghosts, but we don't know. We just don't know...

Romance Finds my Mother

Soon after her move, Mom discovered a French restaurant in Haverstraw, a larger town on the Hudson River near Tompkins Cove, and she became acquainted with the chef. She often went there to practice her French conversation in the evening after her friend's workload had slackened. There was a young man who had the same habit, but on a different evening. He had studied French in college and wanted to polish his conversational skills. The romantic chef arranged for them to come on the same evening and my mother met John Frith, an engineer with AT&T in New York City.

After a whirlwind romance, my parents were married in the living room of Gladys and Arthur's house. Mom had vowed never to have my grandmother prepare a wedding meal for her after remarks made following Aunt Gladys's wedding to Arthur. In her memoir, my mother described her wedding to my father:

"An intense courtship preceded our wedding on December 28 (1937). The Christmas holiday seemed a good time to take a honeymoon at the Cole farm where John could meet my family.

"John's relatives and friends gathered in the living room where the ceremony was to be performed. Unknown to John and me, my brother-in-law had invited a few of my students to watch the ceremony. The students had gathered quietly on the front porch.

"Reverend Oliver stood up as a signal for the bride and groom and their attendants to take their places. As they did so, the best man took the place next to the bride. John, suffering, no doubt, from the usual attack of nerves for the groom, did not immediately take a hand in the situation. The bride was left to deal with the terrifying fear of being married to the wrong man. The pastor stepped forward and laid a hand on an arm of the offender, while John took the other arm. They calmly moved the best man into place, leaving space for John to slip over next to his bride.

"The ceremony proceeded without further incident. The time came for the bride to toss her bouquet. As she took her position on the stairs, Arthur opened the door for the students to come into the hall. My two nieces and the students stood eagerly awaiting the toss. Inevitably, the bouquet was caught by one of the students.

"There was time for visiting and congratulations while food was put on the table for a sit-down dinner. Gladys very competently carried out that part of the reception. I was glad that Mother did not have that responsibility as I remembered her reaction after my sister's wedding.

"By 9:00 on that dark, cold winter's night, John and I had said our goodbyes to the wedding party. We got into his Buick and off we went on our trip to the Cole farm to introduce their new son-in-law to my parents and two brothers — the wedding was a deed, 'deja fact.'"

Nancy and I Arrive

My parents moved briefly to an apartment in New York City near my father's office on Canal Street, but they soon bought a new house across the Hudson River in Ridgewood, New Jersey. We lived at 33 East Glen Avenue, and our phone number was Ridgewood 6-0489. There were no area codes or zip codes then. My sister and I were both born while our parents lived there, although I was born at St. Luke's Women's Hospital in New York City, and Nancy was born in Hackensack, New Jersey.

Dad the year I was born

My Father and Nancy

My father was a very sweet-natured man, quiet and unassuming. He had a spinal curvature from a teenage biking accident when he was thrown over the handlebars while delivering groceries after school. Dad put up with my mother and her social climbing ambitions, and her imperious ways, and with me and my creative imagination that sometimes led me down dangerous paths. When I was older, Nancy told me he worried that once I was off on my own, I would become a drug addict or worse. I don't know why he thought this as I had no leanings in that direction while I was still at home. He did tend to be an excessive worrier, and some of his worrying might have had a basis in reality, but a potential for drug addiction wasn't one of them.

I had really liked being an only child, but that came to a crashing halt once my sister arrived on the scene. Not only did I have to put up with this creature and share my parents' attention with her, but I was forced to give up my cat, Angel. My mother held the old-fashioned belief that cats sucked the breath of babies and she wasn't taking any chances with Nancy. Angel was wrenched from my life, taken to my father's sister's farm, and released — never to be seen again.

As a child, Nancy, three years younger than I, had a round face and long blond hair, that my mother would brush into corkscrew curls. Everyone was always saying how cute she was. I wondered what that made me. I had wanted a brother — I could have tolerated that better. Nancy considered herself a tomboy as a child, but as she grew older she became more like my father's side of the family — practical and something of a doubter.

One thing stands out in Nancy's mind. "Grandma really knew how to spit. I remember her walking me to the dentist's when I was in first grade. She could spit through her teeth farther than any of the boys I played with." Nancy has remained aloof from Cole intrigues. She denies taking any particular pride in being descended from the Cole line, but, by whatever means, pride of family that Mary Ann Cole personified, nonetheless permeated her being. Nancy caught the feeling that she needed to present a certain face to the world. I suppose I had that, too, as I got older.

Reflection

It occurs to me that if things had turned out differently, if Grandpa Cole hadn't lost the farm and the family had remained on Neville Island, Aunt Gladys would not have heard about Houghton College and would have continued to attend Margaret Morrison, the women's division at Carnegie Tech, as Mary Ann Cole planned for her. She would not have met Arthur Bernhoft, married him and moved to Tompkins Cove, New York. As a result, my mother would not have gone to Houghton, would not have gone to live with Gladys and Arthur, and would not have visited the French chef in Haverstraw who introduced her to my father. I would not exist. For that reason, I look with mixed feelings on the life-changing event that befell my family — the loss of the Neville Island farm and the move to Sandy Lake.

This was my family when I was young. We were always a little closer to the edge of normalcy than other families, but never went too far over. My mother was ahead of her time in some ways, but living in the past in others. I certainly never fit into the mainstream socially. We had our idiosyncrasies that made us odd, but not bizarre.

During these years, our bedtime stories often consisted of tales of Mom's family origins. Nancy and I clamored for stories of when she was a little girl on Neville Island. She always obliged. Many of our cousins heard the same stories — or the versions as experienced by my aunt and two uncles.

When I was older, some of my cousins and cousins' children began to research the facts. They searched archives and interviewed the last generation who still remembered the island and what happened there. What follows begins the Cole saga.

CHAPTER 2

Early Coles

I stood high on a bank of the vast Ohio River as it swirled past Neville Island, its waters turbulent, and murky gray. In the distance I could see the far shore. The sun made little flashes of diamonds skipping across the surface and a soft breeze was blowing. But no fragrance wafted from the locust grove on the riverbank. The locust grove was gone.

A few hundred yards downriver is the place where the house once stood. It was the house my great-great-grandfather George built for his wife, Dorcas — an elegant house with thirteen rooms. My great-grandfather, my grandfather and my mother were all born in that house.

There's no house there now. It disappeared, along with the locust grove, at the time of the First World War, razed to the ground to make way for a giant munitions factory that was never built. When the war ended, Carnegie Steel erected its structures, part of its giant steel-producing complex. The eastern end of the island is now covered with factories and other businesses. The once fertile soil, formerly known as the "Market Basket of Pittsburgh," is paved over. Only the hardiest weed dare drill its way through to the surface.

At present, the only church on the island is the Neville Island Presbyterian Church, which was built in 1917. However, the congregation was first formed in 1848 and my Dickson ancestors, my great-great-grandparents, were instrumental in founding that original church that stood on the site of the Long Island Presbyterian Cemetery. The island now claims the cemetery as its most important historic site.

When we were in our sixties — I was pushing seventy with a short stick — my cousin, Darlene, her husband, Craig, and I, climbed the locked fence that closed off the road to the Presbyterian Cemetery. Craig drove the rented car up just under the fence. We climbed onto the hood to get a good toehold, then hoisted ourselves over the top. We gained another foothold on the other side and jumped to the ground. We walked up to the cemetery, looked around, took pictures, and were about to turn back to the road and the car. Craig called back over his shoulder, "there's a cop writing me a ticket."

We headed back toward the road as quickly as we could, smiling, and the cop gave us a gruff greeting. "We had a call that there were three young kids that climbed the fence and were drinking and pulling down tombstones in the cemetery."

We laughed and explained our mission, that some of our ancestors were buried there. The cop tried to maintain a straight face. "Well, you know that climbing over a locked fence is criminal trespass. I could arrest you all and take you down to the county jail." He hadn't understood our right to be in that cemetery.

I laughed and told him, "If you don't, I'll mention you in my book."

At that, he could no longer hold his straight face and the trace of a smile pulled up the corners of his lips. His colleague drove up then, having been sent to obtain the padlock key from the church. He had been unable to locate anyone and had returned empty-handed. We could have told them there was no one at the church — it was locked up. Concerned now for our safety, they offered to help us back over the fence.

We were grateful for the assistance, as going back over seemed more difficult than the initial climb. The cop, whose name was Kevin, of the Ohio Township Police, checked our identification, directed us to other sources of information, and wished us well. I told him to watch for the movie version. We proceeded on our way, imagining the tale that would be told back at the station house.

Four generations of Coles, spanning over one hundred years, lived on the bank of this river, watching it flow past their front door. They cleared forest and planted crops. They built a comfortable and prosperous way of life, fulfilling the American Dream. This is the story of what happened to the Coles and their dream.

It Began in the Year 1814 in Maine...

Many of the early émigrés from Scotland settled along the northeast coast of the New World because of its similarity to home. It was and is, a craggy, wild coastline where waves break over rocks, sending white froth spewing high into the air. The sharp, rocky hills and cliffs of the headlands, sometimes form canyons around the intruding sea. There are few sandy beaches; most are rocky, or pebbly at best. Summers are short and frantic with nature's need to crowd all the exuberant growing into a few short months.

They came to Prince Edward Island, Nova Scotia, and Maine. Bangor was a town at the head of the Penobscot Bay, along the Penobscot River and many were drawn there. The river and bay were named after the Penobscot Indian tribe that made its home in Maine's mid-coast region. Coles, Hendersons and Bradgons, among others, peopled this outpost of civilization. My family records go back only as far as the five Cole brothers who left Maine in 1814 to settle in Allegheny City, Pennsylvania, now Pittsburgh. Those of my cousins who have already done some research discovered that the records of our ancestors were reportedly lost in a courthouse fire in Bangor. We know that George Washington Cole was sixteen at the time of the brothers' departure from Maine, as he was born in 1798. During that time in history, many children were named for General Washington, and we conclude from my ancestor's name that the elder Cole might have fought in the Revolutionary War. The other brothers were James, Rufus, Ivery and William, the youngest, born in 1801. There is also the possibility that they may have been cousins rather than brothers.

By piecing it together, I found that the family lived in Maine for at least twenty-three years before the boys left, since James Cole, the eldest, was born there in 1791. They headed west, crossed Lake Erie by boat, then traveled down to Pittsburgh by wagon. It was an arduous journey as they passed through hostile, as well as friendly, Indian territories on the way. They faced other wilderness dangers as well, but they survived. The parents of the boys, names unknown, were not with them. Did they succumb to some end, be it disease, harsh winters or savage attacks? Or did the boys decide to strike out on their own to see what they could see, and make their fortunes, leaving their parents behind? Maine was — and still is — mostly wilderness, with a few settlements hugging the coast. Pittsburgh, on the other hand, known at the time as Allegheny City, was an up-and-coming place, a bustling trade center on the banks of the Ohio River. It offered many opportunities to industrious young men.

My great-great-grandfather, George Washington Cole, and his brothers came to Neville Island, which was named for General John Neville, an excise officer in the Whiskey Rebellion. Neville purchased it in 1763 when it was still known as Montour's Island. The first owner was Henry Montour, and the name Montour's Island dates from 1628. He was either an Indian owner and Chief of the Shawnee, or an Indian interpreter of French and Indian descent. The records are unclear on that point. After General Neville bought the island, he had it surveyed in 1776, just after the American Revolution. The island, then covered with forest, was approximately five miles long, 2,000 feet wide and made up of 1,200 acres. Depth to bedrock at that time was reported to be sixty-five to eighty feet.

The Cole brothers bought 150 acres of heavily timbered land at the upper, eastern end after their arrival in the early 1800s. Once that was paid for, they bought 150 more acres. They now owned the whole eastern end, roughly one-fourth, of the island. Their goal, like that of the other new owners on the island, was to garden. The timber — oak, locust and maple — was cleared and cut into cordwood, then sold to the steamboats that plied the Ohio River. This was the first great environmental change in land use.

George began gardening on his portion. (The term "gardening" at that time referred to small farming.) The soil was rich, having developed from alluvial deposits. It would one day be known as the best farming land in the county. It hadn't been flooded since the Ice Age, as it sat high above the river. The front and back rivers were low at that time, and there were twenty-foot-wide sandy beaches all the way around the island.

Today, the topography of the island has changed. It is deep with industrial fill materials — coal, slag, ash — that aren't obvious to the casual observer. Public information has it that the chemical elements present beneath the ground range from inert to severely contaminated. Two of the biggest offenders are the Dravo Light Metals Plant, near the I-79 interchange, and Neville Chemical, along the back river channel.

Archibald Hamilton had already settled there in 1795, and his descendants would eventually become the most numerous on the island and later appear in the Cole family tree. His granddaughter, Mary Hamilton, would marry James Dickson, and produce Mary Ann Dickson, who would become the wife of Augustus, the eldest son of George W. Cole. Neville Craig, grandson of General Neville, was born on the island in 1793, and the Craigs continued to live there, as neighbors of the Coles. The Cole brothers sold off some of their land to other families who came and settled at the tip of the island, including the Bragdons, who had also come from Maine.

Somewhere along the line, George found the time to court and marry Dorcas Bragdon, twelve years his junior. Together they produced five children: Augustus Porter; Carrie, who died young; George Henry; Henrietta; and Milton P., who would eventually go west to Wisconsin to seek his fortune in logging.

The latter met and married Lillian Mae Wood Wilcox in 1872 (she had been married before, and there was some question about his role in her divorce). That marriage took place in Iowa, but three of their four children were born in Allegheny County, Pennsylvania during the 1870s, according to the 1880 census. Those children were: George Milton Cole, Frank Ellis Cole and Austin Samuel Cole. Claude Louis Cole, the youngest was born in Wisconsin in 1884 after the family moved back there. When Milton died, after being hit on the head by a falling limb while felling a tree at the logging camp, no Cole from Neville Island would claim his body when they were notified. His remains lie in a grave at Glenwood Cemetery in Wisconsin, the logging company having paid for his funeral.

Augustus, my great-grandfather, was the eldest of George and Dorcas's children, and he was a handsome man. He attended Mount Union College in Ohio, then returned to help on the farm. When the Civil War broke out, he served nine months with the Army of the Potomac, 123rd Company K, Pennsylvania volunteers, from 1862 to 1863. He fought at Fredricksburg, Antietam and Chancellorville. At Fredricksburg, he was wounded during a charge and sent a letter home informing his family about it, assuring them that he was all right. He continued on to say that he would not tell them where he was wounded as they would then know what direction he was heading at the time.

When Augustus's service was up, he headed back to the farm where he remained, taking over gardening after his father's death in 1875. His father lived long enough to see Augustus married in 1870 to Mary Ann Dickson, daughter of their neighbor, James Dickson, and his wife, Mary Hamilton Dickson. Mary Ann's father had come to Neville Island from Prince Edward Island, where his father, William, had landed when he emigrated from Scotland. Mary Ann strengthened the genes for stubbornness and other strong qualities that ran in the family blood.

Meanwhile, Augustus's brother, George Henry, had also returned to gardening at the request of his father, and owned the farm next to Augustus. And although Augustus inherited the livery stable that his father had acquired in 1823 in Pittsburgh, he devoted most of his efforts to his own farm.

The brothers improved their farms and expanded their houses. Augustus's house had thirteen rooms and faced the sweep of the Ohio River. The interior was elegant colonial in style. This was to have a lasting effect on my mother, who would later grow up in that house, and on other descendants as well. The white exterior was without adornment except for a little gingerbread that graced the upper corners of the side porch and green shutters on large windows. Mary Ann liked to sit on the wide porch that spanned the front of the house and watch the passing boats on the river in her few moments of leisure.

She did this to her dying breath, although by that time there was no river within her view.

The ten-foot-high tin ceilings had intricate designs that Mary Ann had painted in different colors to make them stand out. The rooms were spacious, and there were eight fireplaces. A big, black, coal-burning stove for cooking dominated the kitchen. In the entrance hall, a curving balustrade wound up to a landing, then to the wide halls of the upper floor. My uncles and my mother would later enjoy sliding down that balustrade. The front stairs were carpeted, and there was a back staircase, too. The furnishings throughout were of the finest quality. In the best parlor, it was green mohair stuffed with horsehair, with mahogany wood, in the Victorian style. This furniture would outlast the house. There were no bathrooms, but there were sinks. Mary Ann bathed every Saturday night in a large tub in her kitchen. An outhouse sufficed for other bodily functions.

The *Burgettstown Home Monthly*, a periodical, in its October 1900 issue, featured an article about the wealth of the early farmers on Neville Island and their large, pretentious homes that were the most beautiful and comfortable in the Pittsburgh vicinity. It referred to Neville Island as the "gem of the Ohio."

Industrial expansion insinuated itself into the island as early as 1872, when the Pittsburgh and Lake Erie Railroad was planned to connect the island to the mainland. By 1884 a railroad bed had been prepared along the south bank and construction of a bridge was begun. By the 1890s there were seventy families on the island, and bridges had been completed.

The two brothers, Augustus and George Henry, added outbuildings to their farms. On Augustus's farm this included a large greenhouse covering two acres, and a shed that they called "the pickle house," where they boiled the horseradish and bunched the asparagus that were their main crops. These were then wholesaled in Pittsburgh, although some of the asparagus was shipped to New York City, where it was served at the Waldorf Astoria Hotel as Asparagus a la Neville Island. The finest hotels and restaurants in Pittsburgh also featured this delicacy.

There was a large barn to house machinery on the ground floor, and men in the rooms above during the growing season. The brothers were active in local politics, and each in turn held most public offices on the island at one time or another.

Augustus and Mary Ann had two children: James A., who inherited Augustus's good looks, and Everson Porter, who inherited his looks from the Dickson side of the family. James left the farm to become a train engineer and settled with his family in McKee's Rocks across the river. After some early adventures, Everson Porter settled on the farm with his parents and took a wife. It was he who would face the crushing machinery of eminent domain and the unbridled greed of big business interests and the robber barons who controlled them.

Everson Porter Cole – age 4 (my grandfather)

Everson's character was a mass of contradictions. To his son, Ned, he would be a warm, loving father, and a loving grandfather to Ned's son, Tucker (Ned, Jr.). To his son, Robert, Everson would become the focus of resentment and bitterness for fortunes and opportunities lost. His daughters would also harbor resentment toward him, but they would overcome the losses and build lives by their own skills and intelligence. His daughters and granddaughters would also see Everson's dark side, which his wife, ever vigilant, would try to hide.

Everson Porter and Helen

As a young man, Everson Porter, my grandfather, was an enterprising youth with high spirits and a sense of adventure. His father, Augustus Cole, offered him a college education but he declined. He wanted to be a gardener. But before settling down to that life, he had some wild oats to sow. He took himself on a tour of the European continent, the trip financed by collecting debts owed to his father. There are two versions of this story: one told by his daughter, Corinne (my mother), and one that he himself told to his grandson, Tucker.

Grandpa (Everson) told Tucker that, for his twenty-first birthday, his dad gave him all his late and uncollectible invoices for various of his produce customers in Pittsburgh. According to Grandpa, his father told him he could keep all the money he collected, and this was enough to finance the trip to Europe. According to the version that was told in Corinne's household, Grandpa took it upon himself to collect the debts — unbeknownst to his father until after the ship had sailed! The Dickson men, Mary Ann's brothers, were neighbors of the Coles, and were Grandpa's uncles. They always held this adventure against him. My mother said, when telling the story. "They held it without mercy with no thought of forgiveness...They thought that was an awful thing to do." That lends more credence to the second version.

On another occasion Grandpa traveled to Spain and, although he spoke often about it to his sons, no written record of what he did there was passed down, nor did my uncles tell the rest of the family. Grandpa also went west to Colorado to try his hand at mining. As with everything he undertook, he worked hard at it, but, "He never quite made it at mining," according to his son, my Uncle Ned.

Tucker heard directly from Grandpa about his adventures in Mexico. Tucker has a 1901 model .38-caliber Colt revolver that Grandpa carried with him during that time. Grandpa and a buddy were roaming around Mexico in the early 1900s, prospecting for copper, and the gun was necessary defense against Pancho Villa's men and other dangerous marauders. Grandpa was sitting on a knoll waiting for his buddy when he heard the crack of a shot and the ping of a bullet as it struck near him. His buddy had shot a rattlesnake that had slithered up close to Grandpa. That was enough to prompt their decision to pull up stakes and head for home.

Grandpa's mind was sharp and ideas flowed for ways to improve the farm and his fortune. He invented tools, devised processes and applied for patents, but did not manage to sell them. It is said in the family that he gave away the family's secret catsup recipe to his wholesale garden customer, H. J. Heinz.

He tried his hand at investing when he received an $11,000 inheritance from his father, Augustus, and put some money into the oil fields at Titusville, Pennsylvania. By that time, the fields had already started to dry up, and he invested more money to save the first. He ignored the axiom, "Don't throw good money after bad." The Titusville oil fields failed.

Grandpa's best investment was in the farm and other land parcels in surrounding areas. The existence of the latter wasn't known until long after his death but they had already disappeared along the way — sold by him and the proceeds again unwisely invested. He was always looking for "just one more turnover."

Grandpa's mother, Mary Ann Dickson Cole, was a stern, forbidding woman when she chose to be. She ran a tight ship and developed into an imposing matriarchal figure. She also had her soft side, doting on her son, my grandfather, and later, some of her grandchildren.

Helen Henderson, my grandmother, was the only daughter of Lucretia and Harvey Henderson of Hendersonville and Sandy Lake, Pennsylvania. Helen had six older brothers and was adored by all of them. Uncle Ned liked to say that Harvey ran off with an Indian squaw to get away from home, and it is true that he was absent most of the time. He made periodic returns long enough to procreate, then left again.

I learned more about Harvey Henderson's life from my cousin, Tucker, who heard it from Chuck Henderson, a relative of Harvey's. According to Chuck, who remembered him, Harvey was a happy-go-lucky young man at the beginning of the Civil War. He was an accomplished musician, who entertained and played for his friends throughout the Hendersonville area. He enlisted in the Union army and found a place in the army band. In those days the band had two jobs; one was to play as the troops went into battle, and the other was to collect and bury the dead when the battle ended.

Harvey was in several battles during that war, including Little Round Top at Gettysburg, where his name is on the Pennsylvania memorial. He also fought at Fredericksburg, Virginia. The Union army was ordered several times to charge across open ground up to a stone wall where, from above on a ridge, the Confederates poured murderous fire. Harvey was ordered up to the stone wall where he and other members of the band crouched throughout the day and night.

Union troops died by the thousands, burying Harvey under mounds of dead, sometimes six or seven deep. When the battle was over, Harvey and the rest of the grave detail went forward over the wall to gather up the thousands of dead and dying Union soldiers.

Harvey remained in the army for most of the Civil War and returned sometime during 1864 or early 1865 to Hendersonville. When he returned home, he was a deeply disturbed young man. Today we would call this Post Traumatic Stress Disorder. Gone was the carefree, happy-go-lucky boy. He married the young and beautiful Lucretia Kirk, partly in an attempt to restart his shattered life. The war experience continued to haunt him. To put the horrors of war behind, Harvey traveled to the West, as did so many veterans who were trying to rebuild their lives. He settled in Taylor, North Dakota and worked as a shoemaker in Dickinson, a small town nearby.

Harvey also had a small ranch on which he raised cattle. Regularly, Harvey sent money back to his family and encouraged them to join him in North Dakota. His wife refused. He made trips back East to visit his family and again entreated them to come with him. When he died, he left all that he had to his wife and had arranged for her to receive a Civil War veterans' pension.

The story told of Harvey Henderson by his wife, and handed down to later generations, was much different. She told of a worthless man who abandoned his family and left them in poverty. From the records of Chuck Henderson, the memories of the old folks of Taylor, North Dakota, the records in the county seat at Dickinson, and other records that somehow survived, Chuck Henderson's version appears to be more truthful.

Frank, one of my grandmother's brothers, left home as well, but we know he returned often to bring gifts from the Far East: ivory figurines and a painted china umbrella stand, an elephant with ivory tusks, and a ship in a bottle, among others. The family still has his old passport with stampings from his trip to India. Frank worked for one of the oil companies as an oil driller — possibly Standard Oil — and this took him to many parts of the world. His nephew, my Uncle Ned, was one of Frank's favorites and at one time Frank gave him a .25-caliber Colt revolver.

As a child, Tucker visited Uncle Frank many times in his later years, when he lived in the old Sandy Lake Hotel. Another cousin, Marian Bernhoft who was older, remembers visits to him at his law office in Sandy Lake. She and Tucker both recall that he kept little pieces of candy for children who visited, and loved teasing them by making them wait while they stared intently at the candy jar. Money for ice cream was another perk of a visit to Uncle Frank. My cousins have only fond memories of their great-uncle. I do not remember meeting him, but it's possible that I did when I was very small. I would not have seen him often, as I lived such a great distance away in New Jersey.

Frank never married. There is a rumor in the family, supported by a photograph of him on a beach with another young man, that he was a homosexual. They are gazing at each other with expressions that might be interpreted as going beyond friendship. Whatever his sexual leaning, it is evident that he was a kind and sensitive man.

Near the end of his life, he moved into the Sandy Lake farm and slept in the front parlor. He died there.

Despite the absences of the men, the Henderson household was a cheerful one. Lucretia and her daughter, my grandmother, loved to laugh and be gay. Helen was an excellent seamstress and earned her living at sewing as a young woman. She was also very beautiful, with her thick dark hair, snapping brown eyes, and lithe figure, and young men clustered around her at the gatherings she often attended at Aunt Rhoda Henderson Bragdon's in Avalon, across the river from Neville Island. It was here that she met the earnest and imposing Everson Porter Cole, a relative of Aunt Rhoda's husband. Everson was tall and slim with dark hair and a bushy mustache. He was also a well-to-do landowner.

By now, Neville Island was known as the "Market Basket of Pittsburgh," and the Cole farm was prospering. The soil was the richest in the county, and both the wholesale and retail businesses flourished. My grandfather's main crops were asparagus and horseradish, but he also grew tomatoes, rhubarb, and lettuce. The Pittsburgh market was only an hour away by wagon. He was growing the family fortune.

Mary Ann expected her son to marry well. Her displeasure was great when he introduced the pretty little seamstress from Sandy Lake. Helen was an artist with her needlework, being a dressmaker, an expert quilter and crocheter. Mary Ann did what she could to discourage the relationship but her son was as stubborn as she, and the marriage took place in June 1901, the same year that Augustus died.

My grandparents' younger daughter, Corinne, my mother, wrote in a memoir, "My father and mother had a highly respectable wedding in the homestead on Neville Island. After the ceremony there was a sit-down dinner prepared by the cook and served by the maids."

Helen moved into the big house on Neville Island, on the banks of the Ohio River. She tended to be frivolous and her gaiety irritated her austere mother-in-law. Mary Ann also suspected that Helen did not adore her son as much as he adored her. Helen, according to my mother, was considered to be one of the beauties of her day, and was more dazzled by the fact that she had landed a man who was said to be a "good catch" than by any deep feelings for him — at least initially.

Uncle Ned said to his niece, Marian, "At times I couldn't understand everything. My dad really loved my mother, my mother really loved my dad, but I don't think she really loved my dad as much as he loved her. Don't misunderstand me. My mother was a very good woman...I had a very good mother and my dad was always good to me."

Of the relationship between Mary Ann Cole and Helen, he said, "it was not too good though I never heard them squabble — but even as a child I could feel a little something there. They lived in the same house but it was divided. They each had their own side of the house and each kept their side quite well." A division of the house was the only solution to save Helen from Mary Ann's constant carping. The house was partitioned, and Mary Ann lived in front, up and down, and the young family lived in the back, up and down.

The situation was further complicated because the Coles were Presbyterian, while Helen was Methodist and would have preferred to continue practicing that religion. When she first arrived on the island as a young bride, only the Presbyterian church existed, however, so the whole family attended services there.

Everson Porter and Helen had six children. One, Lucretia, who would have been the youngest, named for Helen's mother, was stillborn, and young Frank, named for Helen's brother, died of diphtheria at age three. Gladys Mae was the eldest of the four surviving children. Her sister, Corinne Elizabeth, when in her nineties, remembered Gladys as clever at memorizing and reciting, as well as "very nice looking."

Corinne, when asked if Gladys was well-behaved, replied, "Yes, I can't remember having any problems ever with her. And I loved her. I loved her to pieces. I would creep up in back of her if she happened to be sitting so that I could get in back of her and put my arms around her neck. Then she would fuss around about that. She didn't like it particularly, but I liked to do that. I was very fond of her. I think she was fond of me, too."

Robert, my Uncle Bob, was next. My mother remembered him as "quite an efficient boy. He would do things around the place. I can remember him being busy working at various things…he never just sat around."

Corinne was the third of those who survived — high-spirited, a mischievous tomboy in contrast to the clever and refined Gladys, the serious and industrious Robert, and the baby darling of the household, Ned McCaughtry Cole. Throughout their lives, Corinne was always close to her younger brother and said of him, "Ned was a baby then, and he was everybody's pet. He was cute. Never got over it. He was always cute."

That was the family unit on Neville Island. Mary Ann Cole ruled imperiously in her part of the house, and Everson Porter and his wife, Helen, with their four children lived happily, not at all daunted by Mary Ann's majesty, in theirs.

I have presented my grandparents as accurately as I can, given the distance of time. My grandfather's adventuresome spirit, combined with his love of the land, his sons, and his grandsons, made up the positive aspects to his character, but he developed some flaws as well.

My grandmother, on the surface, was the weaker vessel. In her youth she was lighthearted and fun loving. But, as the reed bends with the wind, so did she, rebounding to take ascendance later in her life over my grandfather and older uncle. My grandmother studied her mother-in-law's methods well, made them part of herself, and turned them on her children and grandchildren. She, too, would have her favorites and would show them only the sunniest side of her nature. To the less favored, she ranged from indifferent to cruel.

CHAPTER 3

Life on Neville Island

One year before his death in 1901, my great-grandfather, Augustus Cole sold twenty-five acres of his land to American Steel and Wire Co., which had just become a subsidiary of the newly formed U. S. Steel Corporation under the guidance of J. P. Morgan. The deal was handled by the American Land Company. He received approximately $2,000 per acre — the average price that the buyer paid to all the farmers involved in the deal for a total of 182 acres. American Steel and Wire paid a total of $382,202. Other plots were previously bought by the company. This information is according to *The Pittsburgh Tribune*, February 8, 1900. This still left the Cole family with sufficient acreage for their farm, plus the house and outbuildings — enough to continue prosperity.

A municipal history of Neville Island reports that, in addition to the American Steel and Wire plant, real estate interests purchased three large farms and planned to build Neville Island City, promoted as the "9th Wonder of the World." The promoters began the sale of lots on April 25, 1900 at a base price of $500 per lot. They advertised two water works, a gas well and smoke-free air, as the winds over the project were westerly, thus avoiding the mills. The air would be pure and wholesome.

In 1901 the Dravo Mechling Corporation, owned by Francis Dravo, had established its foothold on the island. This company eventually operated the largest inland boat works in the United States. It also repaired and maintained river boats. The company built locks and dams, making the river navigable. It later branched into manufacturing concrete for construction. A 1906 map showed the railroad and a mill complex at the east end of the island, not far from my great-grandfather's farm. Grand Avenue ran down the middle of the island.

My mother, Corinne, and my uncles, Robert and Ned, three of Everson and Helen's four children, were interviewed at various times during their later years by younger relatives, and my mother wrote pieces of a memoir in her eighties. What follows borrows from their memories. Aunt Gladys died of cancer without leaving a written record, so we could only piece together memories about her.

When she was in her nineties, I interviewed my mother for a short booklet of her memories that I was preparing for a family reunion. She was quite forgetful by then, but she remembered the divided house of her Grandmother Cole — divided to enable mother and daughter-in-law to live amicably. "I remember lots of things about the house. I remember it had thirteen rooms — a big house — so you could divide it without any hardship...[in the entrance hall] there was a beautiful, heavy balustrade to steps going up to the second floor. I used to slide down it from the second floor and down around. We took the back part of the house which was convenient because we had to go back quite a ways to get to the streetcar line. It was the only way we could get to places because we didn't have any automobile for ourselves. We did have an automobile, but my father drove it and he wasn't about to be a chauffeur for the kids."

When she was in her nineties, my mother lived in an assisted-living facility and one of her activities was a memoir class. I came across several anecdotes that she wrote at that time. One was about an accident that she witnessed on one of the streetcars as a schoolgirl:

Cole house on Neville Island

"Frances Hurda, who was my age, ten years, got on the trolley car with us after school one day. She lived near the school but was going to visit her aunt up north on the island.

"The conductor on the car was Farvar, a favorite with the school kids. It was nothing unusual to see Frances and Farvar talking together at the back of the car. It was Farvar's responsibility to see that all the school kids were seated and stayed put. But this day he left Frances standing alone while he hurried forward to talk to the motorman about something urgent.

"Frances was going to get off soon. As the car approached her stop she stepped down one step, holding carefully onto the sidebar. As the car lurched around a sharp bend, it made Frances lose her hold, throwing her off the step onto the ground beside the track.

"A couple of the kids in my bunch screamed. Farvar came racing back. He signaled the motorman to come to the back of the car after stopping as gradually as possible, and bring the equipment necessary in order to return to the spot where Frances was lying quietly beside the track.

"We kids all flew to the windows to watch as the conductor and the motorman stopped over Frances. At this point the motorman stood up and pulled some sort of phone from his pocket to call headquarters. All traffic on the line had to be stopped until the ambulance arrived.

"It only took a few minutes until we heard a shrill horn blaring to clear the road. The driver and a woman nurse examined Frances closely before laying a white sheet over her, lifting her carefully, and carrying her to the ambulance. There was a short conference that delayed Farvar and the motorman.

"The kids all kept very subdued as the car delivered the Cole kids at their stop. Bob, Ned and I jumped off and ran to the house, where we all excitedly told Mother what had happened.

"The next day at school my teacher told us that Frances was dead. Her mother, Mrs. Hurda, had called to invite the whole class to come to the Hurda home, where our little classmate was laid out in the living room. We all walked in sad silence from school to the house of mourning.

"I never saw Farvar again. The rumor was that he had been transferred to a line where he wasn't responsible for school children."

In another piece, my mother described her early memories of Carnegie Steel during its early foothold on the island:

"Neville Island was the base for several great industries among which were Carnegie Steel and Dravo's. Carnegie Steel was at the northern end of the island about five miles from the homestead. Frequently, the dumping of melted slag made a glorious, crimson hue for miles around the sky, an unearthly spectacle which entertained the people who happened to be outdoors.

"A certain Mr. Louden came to be superintendent of the Carnegie Steel plant some years before 1917, bringing with him his family: Mary, his wife, and three sons, Keith, Donald and Malcolm. It happened that the Louden family and the Cole family became intimate friends due to the compatibility of Mary Louden and my mother, Helen Cole. And especially due to the fact that Keith's birthday fell on the same day as mine.

"Of course my family...along with parents, shared birthday parties over a number of years until a frightful accident caused the death of Mr. Louden. As superintendent of the steel works, it was his responsibility to check the quality of the steel and everything that affected it in the process of development as it was smelted in the vast vats. There was a catwalk over the vats from which regular inspection was made. On an inspection walk, Mr. Louden lost his balance and toppled into a red hot vat of smelted steel.

"Needless to say, the body that was retrieved could not be recognized. The terrible shock and sorrow sadly affected the two families and many friends. As a result of that accident the two families were separated. Mary Louden took the boys to her family in Ohio. Desultory visits and correspondence kept the friendship alive over several years, but the memories are still vivid.

"Keith Louden's birthday fell on the same day as mine, so the families celebrated the occasion together. Keith was two years older than me, Donald was the same age and Malcolm was the same age as my brother Ned. My brother Robert and Keith were the ring leaders." In later life, Robert named his only son Keith.

Mom spoke of arguments between her father and Grandmother Cole. "The bulk of Grandpa's [Augustus's] money and investments had been left to her for safekeeping. She guarded the trust faithfully, not to say fiercely. Sometimes she and Dad went at each other with angry yells because Dad wanted her to loosen up enough money to put a bathroom in the homestead, or to buy some needed equipment for his business."

My mother continued with her picture of Mary Ann. "I can see the Ohio River so clearly. It was at the front. And, of course,...there was a back river. That wasn't so deep and fast as the front one. But there was a lot of commercial traffic on the river, and there were steamboats that would have several floors. We could see them coming and going for miles. The front porch was Grandmother Cole's vantage point for watching river traffic, and she sat and rocked in one of the wicker rockers by the hour. Her portly figure, clad in a long and full, ruffled black sateen skirt, and a long-sleeved shirtwaist blouse, could be seen there.

"It was a very pleasant life. We had quite a big lawn between the house and the barn, where we had a horse and a cow. There was a big building with two floors, with farm equipment on the ground floor, and rooms upstairs for the hired men. It was a big place to take care of and we had at least one hired man that lived there year-round. Plain food was served — meat, potatoes and vegetables. And always lots of pies.

"There was a side porch to that part of the house — you'd come out from our living room onto that side porch. People never used that when they came to visit us. They always came to the kitchen door and walked through the kitchen to the living room. There was an entrance from the side porch into what we called an entry. It was a small room…when they (the hired men) came in to eat, sometimes we set up a table for them in that little room. I remember mostly the one hired man that was there year-round, ate at the table with us in the kitchen.

"Once I was playing school teacher, sitting at the table in the dining room, and when I had everything in place, all treated me with great respect, as if teaching school. One day Dad came through and slammed something down on the table and made me so mad I slammed something on the table, too. Then I was so mad I threw it on the floor and he said, 'if you don't want it, I'll take it back.' It was the rack for the books."

My mother told Nancy, my younger sister, about the time she was in a church program and forgot her lines. When she got on stage, her mouth wouldn't work. My grandfather was sitting in the audience and got up from his seat, went to the stage, and whispered in her ear, "I will see no evil…" and she was able to speak and got through the program.

My mother further described the farm. "There was a building on the farm that was used for washing and grinding horseradish and for bunching asparagus — all could work at that, even the kids whose hands weren't so big. I was too little to bunch asparagus, but Mother did. There was a small house across the courtyard from our kitchen door, which housed hired men, those who stayed all winter. There was another dormitory to house six men over the garage. The farm also had a large greenhouse and many sash structures (cold frames) for seedlings.

"Doing the washing required the service of a regular washer-woman who also did the ironing. Seasonally, a seamstress came in and stayed a week or more at a time — this in addition to the sewing that Mother did. Mother was a gifted seamstress. There was always at least one live-in maid, Mrs. Morgan, to do cooking and cleaning. We had no refrigerator. The cold earth of the cellar floor, reached from the side porch, was the only means of cooling. Here were the big pans of rich milk set out for the cream to rise. I used to love to dip a finger in those pans on the sly.

"There were four brothers [Mary Ann's Dickson brothers]: John, Gerney, Finlay and Wilson. They all lived in a row — like a street row — and there were ashes — so that it was dry, even in wet weather. You could walk there without getting into mud. John was the first one right next to us. Then there was Gerney. His name was a long name — Algernon. Uncle Finlay…he was another one…he had a business in garden things. They were Dad's uncles."

"I was inclined to be sassy with Grandma Cole [Mary Ann] because I knew that she didn't like my beloved mother who, she thought, was on a lower social level. I was snippy so she didn't like me. I brought it on myself, I'm sure. She did have a soft spot in her heart for the four grandchildren living in the same house with her…but Grandma Cole had her favorite grandchild, my older sister, Gladys, whom she sent to Margaret Morrison in Pittsburgh for a year."

I asked my mother about Christmas on Neville Island, and her memories of that were vivid. "We went to bed early. It gave them time to decorate the tree. We knew the tree was there, but they didn't decorate it until we had gone off to bed. It was always set up in the big living room — our front room. This was in the middle of the house. We had all sorts of presents. One December my Grandmother Henderson came by train from Sandy Lake to spend Christmas with us. She and Mother spent time making doll clothes for my dolls, and particularly for the one given to me that Christmas named Crenedbee — Cre from my Grandmother, Lucretia (Henderson), and a cousin, Bertie, and her husband, Ned. These three people had given me the beautiful golden-haired doll. Mother and Grandma worked at this while I was in school, keeping their work carefully hidden from me.

Grandma and Grandpa Cole with baby Gladys and toddler Frank

"When I was home from school with my older sister, Gladys, and two brothers, we all made things for the Christmas tree. We popped and strung popcorn with corn colored and sweetened in red sugar boiled in water [glaze]. What fun it was to chew all the corn off the string behind the tree when no adults were around.

"My father took one of the horses to cut down a hemlock that was the right size and dragged it to the house the day before Christmas. Dad set the tree up after we children were in bed. Then the adults got to work trimming it. Even the maid joined in but the overseer was not called in from his house across the courtyard. Mother and Bob [brother, Robert] had brought the ornaments down from the attic while Dad was getting the tree. The same lovely angel stood in its special place at the top. Tinsel, colorful glass ornaments, and icicles made the tree sparkle. The children's four homemade stockings gave a festive air as they hung around the fireplace in the living room. We had the fun of hanging them before going to bed.

"When we came down on Christmas morning, it was wonderful to see the tree alight with burning candles. We were cautioned to be very careful not to touch them for fire offered a real hazard. We were so happy to have Grandma Henderson with us. Our Grandma Cole lived with us but she did not enter into the spirit of the season. She did like to make suet pudding for us children. She did this every once in awhile.

"It gave Grandmother Henderson pleasure to watch us with our bulging stockings or later as we opened presents with shrieks of excitement. We did not go to church on Christmas Eve, but we did gather around the piano to sing Christmas carols as Mother played.

"For a week, Mother, Grandma, and the maid, who also did most of the cooking, made the house redolent with a spicy fragrance. We enjoyed the luscious tidbits at every turn and at every chance. We had plum pudding and the various things you usually associate with Christmas. We always had turkey."

My mother remembered another story. "I liked to play with the cat and Mother gave me some baby clothes that she didn't plan to use anymore. They were very nice — all of them. I think she could

Helen Henderson Cole (my grandmother) and her brother, Frank

have done something with them — you know, sold them second hand…and got some money for them.

"My big brother, Bob, was no whiz at school but his abilities and skills took him many places where I could not even imagine going. One of my early-life memories takes me back to Neville Island when I was eight years old and Bob was nine and a half.

"It was a sunny spring morning. I was busy dressing our cat, Mouser, in the lovely baby clothes that Mom had given me to play with. Mama said that after six babies she had no further use for the baby clothes. So it was great fun for me to pretend that Mouser was a real baby although she [the cat] objected in no uncertain terms.

"At last she was dressed, even with a bonnet and a light coat. Then a big silk scarf bound her firmly into the doll carriage for a walk along the river road. Ned, my younger brother, four years old, came along. We strolled along, watching the rolling water of the Ohio with its frequent turbulent swirls where the sand barges had left deep holes. This day we paid little attention to what was going on across the river, at least a mile away but clearly visible. Ned and I had set a goal for our stroll with Mouser. On the river bank there was a thick stand of black locust trees which perfumed the air with their white blossoms. I was eager to see them again and to breathe in their delicious fragrance.

"Having arrived at the point where Ned and I had a clear view and had enjoyed some deep breaths, inhaling the fragrance, I decided to take Mouser out of the carriage to let her have a closer look. The ungrateful creature leaped out of my hands and jumped over the bank. She scrambled up the first tree she came to, and crept out onto an overhanging branch where she perched in great self-satisfaction. But when she decided to move on, she found that she was firmly stuck — her dress had caught on a twig. No matter how much she struggled and squirmed, she could not free herself.

"There was only one solution — to get Bob as fast as possible. Ned started back to the house, his little legs flying. He soon found Bob and they both came dashing to the rescue.

"To negotiate the steep bank and the overhanging branch took the stuff that heroes are made of. But Bob was equal to the demand.

He freed the dress and Mouser, put the cat under his arm, which served as a vise, and clambered safely back up the bank."

When she was re-telling the story to me in her nineties, after she had reached the end with the cat's safe return, another memory struck her. "Wait! I'll tell you something. There was a corpse came floating down the river. We kids saw it. Of course, the river was a mile across, but we could see that there was something there and we notified the men folks around and they got into a rowboat and went out and brought the corpse in. I can't remember what they did except they must have phoned to some agency who came down with an ambulance and took the corpse."

I asked, "So you never found out who it was?"

"No, we didn't...I was around ten."

Uncle Ned was in his seventies when he was interviewed by Gladys's oldest daughter, Marian Bernhoft Morse. He remembered other aspects of his grandmother's personality when asked if Mary Ann Cole had been a loving person. "No, Grandma was not a mean person but she wasn't a real outgoing person. She'd hold herself a little too stiff and reserved. She was very reserved."

When Marian asked if Mary Ann Cole had a good relationship with her husband who was long dead by the time his grandchildren arrived, Uncle Ned replied, "I think they did from what I heard. Grandma...was always a proud woman. After we'd moved up to Sandy Lake she started getting hairs on her chin and [she] would give me a penny a hair for pulling those hairs out."

Marian interjected, "You must have made a lot of money."

Uncle Ned replied, laughing, "Oh, no! But Grandma would always give me money on the side...The children could go over to her side of the house anytime we wanted and she was always real good to me.

"As I remember, she was a rather stately woman and always liked to wear expensive clothes. She lived in one part of the house — I remember going into that other part of the house to eat breakfast with her. She used to make suet pudding — all of us kids liked it. I can remember the raisins. It was a treat to go in there. Every afternoon I'd get the eggs, I'd take Grandma a brown egg. Every morning for breakfast she'd have this brown egg. Sitting near her dining room-kitchen table was a gas stove with a beautiful hearth made out of blue tile.

"She was tall, held herself very straight, not necessarily beautiful, but you never had to be ashamed of my grandmother — either her looks or her dress. You'd be proud of her if you walked down the street with her."

Concerning the absence of bathrooms, Marian asked Uncle Ned, "How did she [Mary Ann] keep herself so clean in those days?"

I can picture Uncle Ned replying with a straight face but laughter in his eyes, "Tell you the truth, I never went in to see how Grandma took her bath. At that time, there were very few bathrooms and we didn't have one, but Grandma, I know, took her bath every Saturday night in a tub. And the same with us kids. After we got a little dirty in between. I remember that if my mother would give my brother or sister a bath then want me to get into the tub but using the same water, I did not want to do it. If she put me in the tub *with* my brother, I wouldn't mind. We had sinks but no regular bathtubs as we know them today. We also had to make use of an outhouse at that time."

"Would you say your parents were well-to-do people? Did you think of yourselves as rich kids?"

"Yes, they were well-to-do. Not rich, but well-to-do. I did appreciate the beauty [of their home and lifestyle]. I never considered myself rich. I never figured our folks had as much as they had. They were a little better off. What I can't understand is why didn't we have inside bathrooms in a beautiful house? Grandma's part of the house was beautiful, our part was nice. The Dicksons had toilets — inside bathrooms."

At this point, Uncle Bob, who was also being interviewed, interjected that the Coles weren't that dirty so they didn't need them — a flash of pride.

The family attended the Presbyterian church that they had helped to establish on the island. In his interview, Uncle Ned gave an example of their almost puritan lifestyle when it came to religion. "In those days, if you had kindling wood to be brought in at home, it had to be on Saturday night because you did not do anything that was not absolutely necessary on Sunday...we went over to the Presbyterian church as long as I can remember. We were always brought up in the church...when I was small, I can remember pictures taken when I was three or four years old…and I remember the Christmas plays there and that's why yesterday, when I went down to the island, there were a lot of visions in my head of what I was seeing from way back."

Marian returned to the subject of the farm. "What do you remember about the truck garden? What did they raise? How did a day go?"

"It was really nice to get up in the morning and look across when the produce was coming on because they raised asparagus and horse-radish to grind and sell and they raised tomatoes and rhubarb, but my father always kept his fields so clean. He hired four [men] who stayed all the time in the rooms he had in our buildings and then he hired extra hands during the busy season. I can still picture them out there with their hoes. There may have been up to nine fellows in a row hoeing across the fields. Those who were not there year-round were called foreigners. They ate at a table out in the entryway.

"Dad, I'd say, was a rich truck gardener. At that time, Dad would get up at 4:00 in the morning, load up his wagon, and he kept beauti-ful horses, with harnesses all shined up and the brass and leather all oiled. I can still see this large green-sided high wagon and that's what Dad would take his produce in up to the market in town [Pittsburgh]. Most of it would be sold wholesale, and then he would go to retail off the wagon up in the bottoms of McKees Rocks and around the Pittsburgh area.

About the bridges that provided access to either end of the island from Pittsburgh, Uncle Ned said, "I don't know when they were built. There was one at the head of the island we called 'the Park Bridge,' then at the other end was the Coraopolis bridge. Those were across the back river. There was no bridge across the front river. We always went the back way to get to the mainland.

"The trolley cars came from Pittsburgh to the head of the island and down the middle at that time and then across the Coraopolis bridge at the lower end to Coraopolis and that's where they turned around and ran back up. We had good trolley service then. The one year I went to school, I rode the street car."

Uncle Bob was asked about his perspective on Grandmother Cole. "Grandma was a large woman. She wasn't fat but she was big. She wore black silk most of the time — occasionally a white shirt-waist — shoe-topper skirts. You could hear Grandma coming clear around the corner of the house with her silks swishing. She was friendly and warm, a whole lot like my mother. She was law. She ran the show, and she was asked for advice by a great many people on the island."

"Did you feel better off than most of the folks on the island?"

"We had a lot of excitement — more than they had by far. Yeah, but we had good food. Dad was a good provider always."

"Did you go to market with him?"

"Only to the stand in Pittsburgh — up in Smallman Street. The vegetables went by wagon and later by truck. We had special wagons with a five-inch steel tire — special make. We had big Clydesdale horses — the driver took care of the wagon and when they'd get up on the wagon, they'd snap themselves on — that is, two straps so they couldn't fall off from the seat, which was up over the wagon. The horses were educated so when streetcars would come along in back and gong the bell a half dozen times, the horses would cross off to the side where there was room.

"We had special racks for the tomatoes and they were put on shelves that would go between cross boards — you could pile them closer that way. We'd have as high as seven tiers of tomatoes. Then cabbage and sweet corn we could just pile on top of each other. We'd take that in the early morning so it would be there before the stores would open up. Sometimes one buyer would purchase for five or six stores, so we had to be there before or we'd just be out of luck. We were the wholesaler. There were two sets of them. One stop would be Smallman Street where we unloaded the produce. Someone like H. J. Heinz would take as high as two or three full loads. There would be as many as ninety bushels of corn on, and they would go eight tiers high.

"One wagon we weren't allowed to use. They cut us off on account of safety. They said that when it would be raining, one of the men might get electrocuted. Now this is far-fetched. Sometimes the rain would run down the trolley from the hill, and there'd be a steady stream of water, and maybe, just maybe, they'd get grounded on the streetcar tracks. The tires on the wagon were steel. So we had to abandon that wagon."

Uncle Bob went on about the horses used on the farm. "They would provide a kind of rehabilitation service for the horses by swapping with different department stores whose horses' feet had become damaged walking on the cobblestones in the city. On the farm they would 'cure' them or let them go. The horses would improve walking on the soil of the farm.

"We had the fourth truck that was in Allegheny County. Dad or John Eckert usually drove the truck in. John used to be our good man [foreman]. He finally went berserk. He was going to kill Uncle Finlay — gonna' shoot him. Dad stopped him. That was some fight, I'm telling you, when a person goes crazy in a time of fire or something like that, you're at least twice as strong as you ordinarily are. Dad almost didn't make it. John was going to shoot him. Just the mercies of God, that's all."

The conversation switched to health issues in those times, particularly when Grandma [Helen] had an operation. She herself had spoken of that time to me and my sister, Nancy, when we were young, saying that she had died and come back. She described her near-death experience to us, saying that she saw a great, bright light, and then an angel. "God just wasn't ready for me yet," she would say. When we were young, we believed every word, but later we chalked it up to her strict beliefs. She also used to tell us that she had one kidney held up by wire. We thought that was quite amazing! We believed that part of the story, even as we got older, because of the comparatively primitive surgical procedures used at that time.

Uncle Bob remembered about the operation in more detail. "I don't know the reason for the operation over in Sewickley, but she was in for hours. There were five doctors. After Mother was brought home we didn't think she'd live. They had her on the meat cart at the old Sewickley Hospital. They thought she was dead. Mother was on the cart that was against the wall. They had a black robe [sheet] on her waiting for the meat grinder to come. One of the nurses went by and she thought she saw the blanket move and she turned around and it fell to the floor. Well, she screamed and fainted. That was before they embalmed.

"[Mother] was the chief cook and bottle washer, took care of the kids. We had hired help for the pickle house. We grew corn and tomatoes and at one time, eggplants, pattipans — never looked for regular squash, though. Asparagus was our major. Five and one-half acres on the island. We double planted — two rows instead of one row, which was equivalent to eleven acres. Neville Island asparagus was very well liked. The soil on the island was the tops in vegetable-growing ground. The top soil was anywhere from one and one-half feet deep to four feet deep."

Marian asked, "Do you remember the names of the boats that went down the river?"

"*Iron City* was a commercial boat, *P.M. Piffle, Sunshine* was the only side-wheeler, and *The Homer Smith* was a stern-wheeler. And they brought another one in there that didn't have any name. It was a boot-leg boat, so they said, and it didn't have a license." One of the boats was named *The Aliquippa*. My great-grandmother Mary Ann often watched it from her vantage point on the front porch, along with the other boats.

Uncle Ned's son, Tucker, had another story about the boats, told to him by Grandpa. There was a law that boats in distress could tie up to anything on the riverbank. However, the boatmen sometimes abused the law and tied up with long ropes to the fruit trees that Grandpa had planted there, causing damage to the trees. The boats were in no distress, their crews just wanting to tie up for the night and party. One night Grandpa went out to the riverbank with his rifle and spotted a boat tied up to his trees. He fired a warning shot across the bow of the boat and, using an axe, cut the rope. The boat went off, spinning down the river. He did not have any trouble with the boatmen after that.

Marian asked Uncle Ned what he remembered about world events while they lived on Neville Island. "World War I. I can remember my parents getting the paper, and that is one of the first things they'd do — go down across the names of the ones that had been killed, and watching 'cause I had cousins and different relatives in the war. And as luck would have it, I can't recall any of our relatives being killed. And I remember the Armistice — the first [report] was false and I believe…the next day [was] the true Armistice, and the bells — I could hear them ringing from over across the river."

CHAPTER 4

Eminent Domain

The bucolic tranquility of my family's life was about to be shattered. The U. S. government was nearing the end of the war with the German Kaiser, and the biggest thorn in the side of the U. S. military was the mighty Krupps Works in Essen, Germany, that provided the munitions for the German juggernaut. The U. S. government developed a plan to rival that plant, and U. S. Steel Corporation was designated to be the engine that drove that plan to reality.

Government officials proposed the perfect locality in the midst of a hilly territory — a small, flat island in a fast-moving, major river. The island was made up of alluvial deposits and had never been flooded. It was the richest farming spot in the county. Wharves could be built all around the island to easily transport the war supplies to the Gulf to be loaded on ships for the front in Europe. There was just one problem. The island was inhabited by wealthy farmers who owned most of the land. Furthermore, it was known as the "Market Basket of Pittsburgh," because the land was extremely fertile and provided much of Pittsburgh's fresh produce.

An account in the Massachusetts newspaper, the *Fitchburg Daily Sentinel*, on March 12, 1919, told the story of what had transpired. U. S. Steel, a company created by John Pierpont Morgan in 1901, had been chosen to build and operate the plant for the government. The plan was for railroad bridges to be built over the north and back channels of the Ohio River. This plant would produce guns, rifles, coast defense weapons and siege artillery. These weapons would be bigger, longer, and stronger than those made by Bethlehem Steel in Pennsylvania, the Washington Naval Yard or the Watervliet Arsenal. Production would extend beyond the war to store munitions for any future eventuality. This country would be prepared for anything the Hun, or any other aggressor, might plan.

Once this was accomplished, the government planned to continue to utilize this behemoth plant, turning it over to heavy industrialization, and building and repairing railroad equipment. A government takeover of the nation's railroad industry was anticipated. No thought was given to the impact the loss of this superior food supply would have on the people and businesses of Pittsburgh, or to the people of the island whose lives would be uprooted. This was not a poor, deteriorating community that the government planned to eradicate. It was made up of wealthy farmers and landowners, some of whom had lived on Neville Island for generations.

Six months before Armistice, eight months before the Paris Peace Conference and thirteen months before the Treaty of Versailles was signed, a meeting was held of the industrialist committee that had been formed by U. S. Steel to engineer the project. Col. C. W. Watson of the government Ordinance Department met with the members on May 17, 1918. John Oursler of U. S. Steel was to oversee the construction.

An illustrious group of players was present at this meeting. John Reis of New York, vice president of Carnegie Steel, was chairman of the committee. Carnegie Steel had been sold in 1901 by Andrew Carnegie to J. P. Morgan for $480,000,000. That had made Carnegie the richest man in the world at that time. J. P. Morgan had gone on to create U. S. Steel. Other Carnegie Steel vice presidents in attendance were William Filbert and William Whigham. Mr. Whigham was based in Pittsburgh and would play a prominent role in future events.

Committee members also included: Taylor Allderdice, vice president and W. B. Schiller, president of National Tube Company in Pittsburgh, a division of U. S. Steel; August Zeisling, president of American Bridge Company in Pittsburgh, a subsidiary of U. S. Steel; George G. Thorpe, vice president of Indiana Steel Company in Chicago, a subsidiary of U. S. Steel; George G. Crawford, president of Tennessee Coal, Iron and Railroad Company of Birmingham, Alabama, a subsidiary of U. S. Steel; and C. L. Miller, vice president and general manager of American Steel and Wire Company of Pittsburgh, a subsidiary of U. S. Steel. This company already had a foothold on the island with land purchased in 1900 from my great-grandfather, Augustus Cole and other farmers. These players had more than altruistic plans in mind for Neville Island.

Col. Watson had several announcements for this powerful group: first, the government would likely need the entire island for the factory due to its size, second, U.S. Steel would not be involved in the negotiations with the property owners for their land — this would be handled by department agents of the government, and third, the properties had been appraised by the Pittsburgh Real Estate Board. The scope of the proposed project was outlined to the committee, the massive size of which was to be an indicator of its permanence. The budget was $70,000,000. In addition, roadways would be built by the project and maintained by the city of Pittsburgh, and a new bridge was recommended. Model housing with garden plots was proposed for the workers.

The government officials solved the problem of obtaining the necessary properties by invoking the process of eminent domain. Under this process the government can seize private property for public use to serve the public good. Time and again, it has been used by local and state governments to force people off their land for various reasons, sometimes hiding ulterior motives for plans that would benefit other interest groups. The government determines what it considers to be the fair market value. Court cases and news stories have kept this practice in the public eye over the years, but it still goes on. Politicians speak against it when running for office, and investigative reporters expose it from time to time, but on it goes. In

1918 there were even fewer restraints involved in its use, and opportunity for misuse by outside parties was readily available.

Patriotism ran high. The war effort came before all other considerations. Who could argue that such incredible defense weapons would serve the greater good? The U. S. government invoked eminent domain to build a better war machine. With the war fever as its impetus, the government rushed its plan through to get the current owners out as quickly as possible.

The government wasted no time in serving the eviction notices and pressuring the owners to leave. In many cases, the deals with the owners were not even settled before steam shovels and other heavy equipment arrived to level their homes and lay the groundwork for the mighty munitions plant. Ten million dollars was already invested for the steel for the groundwork alone.

The descendants of the Hamilton family were the most numerous on the island at this time and figured in our family tree. Mary Ann's mother was a Hamilton. H. T. Hamilton, son of Archibald, the first Hamilton settler, and the oldest member of the Hamilton family still farming on the island, said in the *Fitchburg Sentinel* article, "I thought the people will be allowed to get the last crop out before the government takes over the garden plots." They were only two weeks away from harvest. The government did not allow even that consideration, backing up the eviction notices with pressure, and sometimes scare tactics, as soon as, or even before, agreements were reached with the owners, and after paying them far less than the properties were worth. The government was spurred on by its military goal of rivaling Krupps and crushing the Kaiser's troops.

All of the farmers protested and attempted to dissuade the government from taking their land. But in the end, most capitulated, packed up and left. The Cole family, my family, held out. U. S. Steel began the work of preparing for the building of the factory while some families were still there. Work crews dug into the river banks to lay tracks for a private railroad that would carry the goods from the factory to the wharves that other crews were building. By early 1919, my grandmother and the younger children had been sent north to Sandy Lake to stay with Grandma Henderson, my other great-grandmother. Mary Ann, my grandfather and Robert, age seventeen, remained on Neville Island to defend and protect what had been their family's homestead for over a hundred years, from the invaders.

The interviews that my cousin, Marian, conducted revealed the memories of my mother and my two uncles about this time. For the most part, these memories were still vivid in their minds as they had experienced the uncertainty, anger and fear generated by the events.

Corinne was first. "Before I left, the steel company had dug out for several miles along the front river bank to install railroad tracks. Instead of the quiet country road and the locust-covered river bank, trains came in, spewing smoke and noise. We could no longer step out of our front gate.

"Probably the reason I was sent away was the fire. Fire broke out in the pickle house in the middle of the night. Fortunately, the bright light shone through the window where Gladys was sleeping, and woke her. She spread the alarm so the house was saved — a miracle because the corner of the house was no more than six feet from one corner of the burning building. Firemen arrived quickly."

Uncle Ned also remembered the incident. "It [the trouble] started when I was five years old and my first recollection was during the...First World War. Several men came and notified my father that he had to vacate, and my father wasn't about to lose the place, but the government was condemning it to put up a munitions plant. Then the next thing — we had what was called the pickle house where they boiled the horseradish and bunched the asparagus that my dad sold wholesale. That was set on fire and it was very close to the house. As luck would have it, my mother, father, and sister were sleeping with me in one big bedroom at that time...anyhow, my dad always figured that the pickle house was deliberately set on fire...it was a terrible night.

"Next thing I could remember, they came in with an old-type steam shovel and started digging out for a dinky railroad in front of the house and they took the front steps off the house while we were still in it. Then one morning a rap came at the back door and at this time I, my brother, my father, my mother, and Corinne were there. There were two men in uniform sitting on horses, and I can still see my father standing in front, and my mother just back of his shoulder. Bob was there, and I was hanging onto my mother's skirt looking at these men. Corinne was standing alongside my mother, too.

"But these fellas told my dad again to be out by a certain date. At that time my dad wore a gun on his hip and he said, 'Well, gentlemen, when you come to throw me out just remember this.' And I'll never forget it — it was really burned into my mind. 'The first man up, the first man down.' And directly the men left.

"Well, my father went out to one of the buildings and got an old wash tub. He stood real close to it and just shot six holes in a circle in the bottom of the tub and he took it back along the driveway and set the tub up. He took a handful of cartridges, went back a reasonable distance, and put the pile of shells right down to show them, when they came back, where he'd shot the bottom out of the tub and that's what he'd do to them. Dad really wouldn't hurt a flea but they didn't know it."

Marian asked if the men did come back. "No...but they made things so miserable. I couldn't go to school anyhow in the long run. Dad sent all of us, except his mother and Robert, up to Sandy Lake, and they stayed there and patrolled. During the last few months we were there, every night we closed the shutters and my father, my grandmother, and Robert took turns patrolling around the house because we actually were afraid of the house being set on fire...But they finally pushed us out, and the government took over."

Marian asked about the reaction of the neighbors who were also being evicted. "They had bargained some — they didn't want to give up their land either, but because it was so much trouble, they couldn't take it any longer and they left. They took what the government offered because they couldn't stand the harassment — and we were harassed. They left, and there wasn't a neighbor above us or below us for at least half a mile or more. We were just there by ourselves. And the whole thing was, Dad was just trying to get a fair price out of the land that he had there. That's all he was asking and he never did get it."

Dashed Hopes

The government finally succeeded in driving out the last of the holdouts. U. S. Steel started its preparations for building the giant munitions plant. The groundwork began to the tune of $10,000,000. The ideal industrial community — Neville Island City — was on the drawing board, including the little houses with gardens for the workers.

Then came November 11, 1918 and Armistice. The bells rang out — the bells that Uncle Ned remembered hearing. The war was over. The farmers were ecstatic. Now they wouldn't have to leave their homes and crops. Eagerly, they approached the government to negotiate — to beg, if need be. They would be happy to return the pittance they had been paid; some had been paid nothing yet.

Their joy was short-lived. Government agents informed them they would be welcome to bid for the land, but it was going up for public auction now that the government no longer needed it. The farmers could not just return and pick up their lives.

Many of the old farmers were vocal about their view that they considered any so-called purchasers to be "squatters," and said they would deal with them accordingly. However, most were willing to simply make the exchange and go back to their homes. A group of six farmers went to Washington, D.C., to make a direct appeal to the Secretary of War to have their land returned. They felt that since the government had no further need of it, and they were willing to pay back the money, the problem should be solved.

The farmers soon learned the true seriousness, scope and complexity of the situation. Not only would they not be allowed to make a simple exchange, but they also would have to bid in order to attempt to get their land back. The final blow came when they learned the identity of their primary opponent. They would be bidding against Carnegie Steel, now a subsidiary of U. S. Steel, and other companies founded by men to whom history has referred as the robber barons. Some farmers felt that bidding on their own properties was the same as agreeing that they no longer owned them, but all were unanimous in their intention to cause difficulties for anyone trying to take over their homes.

Uncle Bob told his recollections to Marian, starting with the eviction when he was seventeen. "Yes, I was there. The police backed up about four steps, mounted police came to our back door, rapped on it, and handed the eviction papers. Dad says, 'I'm not takin' that and I'll give you this.' He pulled out two guns. So Lawrence, he was the chief, left and said, 'boys, you take care of it'. They never did."

Marian asked, "Did you leave soon after that?"

"Oh, no. It must have been at least three or four months. I toted a rifle for about a year, lost a year at school, didn't go anywhere. Didn't do us any good, two attorneys that we had, court costs, nearly everything was gone before we left."

"Who were your attorneys?"

"Replogle was one from Pittsburgh and there was one from California. They took one-third plus and took the plus first.

"They were cutting a path along the river and they came with steam shovels right up to our front porch. They went down to Uncle [Tom] Hamilton's that was about one-half mile below our place and that's where they ended it. What they did, they knew was wrong. But they were just after their $10,000,000." That's the figure quoted by the newspapers that it cost the government to begin laying the groundwork for the plant. "It was to lay the foundations for the power house. It was a ninety-foot drop. Ginnys from West Virginia, and Mexicans, were on this long ladder and the ladder broke and covered a lot of them up."

Marian asked, "Was your house the only one left at that time?"

Robert replied, "Yes, we were holding the fort. On Dickson Avenue in Avalon, Uncle Gerney built six houses. The Dicksons scattered around. Uncle Finley went to Crafts, Uncle Wilson went to Coraopolis and Uncle John — I think he was dead. Dad stayed on the island and was foreman on the Emsworth Dam for about two years."

During that time, the Coles entered into some sabotage activities. "They used a machine to drill test holes — they drilled ninety or one hundred of them. They went down about eighty feet. Well, this was the last day that this fella freely used this equipment. Used to be an old bathtub, and there were about five acres of pattipans [squash].

One side of the field was surplus, and they were half rotten. Me and my friend, Jack Myers took and piled dozens of them in this tub of water, and threw it into the machine. It gummed everything up. [The fellows] were here about a week. When we'd go down past it, they were saying 'oh, I wish we knew who did that!' Well, they knew. All those fellows around there were on our side, definitely…what we used to do…we'd have been put in jail if it had been anyplace else. They were one hundred percent for us. We two kids had lots of fun.

"There were five dump carts [steam engines] that were used to make that cut in front of the house on the island. They were cut down to three. When they quit their work at night there would still be 'fire up' in the engines. The fellas would just chop the old thing and pull the throttles back and set the brakes, and then jump off and go home. Jack and I would jump on, take the blocks out and pull the throttle back, and they'd go over to the end, and fall down into the hole. That would slow them up another day or two. We'd pull her back and jump off and away she'd go." He grinned at the memory.

"[There were] holes that bored in underneath and around two water mains that went from the upper end of the island down where the steel companies had their thousand Mexicans that were doing the work on the island. We'd go down there and shut the water off."

Marian asked, "Did your mother know you were doing these things?" His mother, my grandmother, was in Sandy Lake, ninety miles north of Pittsburgh at this time. Uncle Bob and Grandpa were still on Neville Island.

Uncle Bob replied, "She didn't know we were doing a thing. She wouldn't have stopped us — she was just as provoked. The steam engine had a chain on it for four days. Dad defied them. We left in the long run, finally, because it was twenty feet right off the front of the house into the trench, and they bulldozed right through the barn and took it down."

The farmers knew they could not win, but they went anyway on the morning of December 16, 1921, to the Moose Temple. Army officers were directing the sale. In that day's edition of the *Chronicle Telegraph* newspaper, an interview was conducted after the auction, with Clarence H. Hamilton, son of H. T. (Uncle Tom) Hamilton, as spokesman for the farmers. "The condemnation procedures forced many families to leave their homes before they could find shelter as the army took the homes for officers and employees of the government and U. S. Steel."

Mr. Hamilton went on to recount the events surrounding the eviction two years earlier. He told how their wagons and farm equipment were sold or destroyed before they could remove them. He hoped at the time that the government would accept his offer to let it use his property for free, to aid the war effort, but his offer was rejected. He and his father could not afford an attorney and had no alternative but to trust the honesty of the government and U. S. Steel.

The government and U. S. Steel had their way. Mr. Hamilton and his father were forced out and lost their livelihood. At this time, housing prices were greatly inflated, and they could find nothing they could afford. To compound the problem, the money wasn't even paid until two years later. When they did receive it, the counsel employed by the government to oversee the litigation, Mr. David Starr, went to the bank with Mr. Hamilton to collect $78.70 in taxes that had accrued in the interim. Mr. Hamilton was appalled by the pettiness of this act.

Mr. Hamilton went on with his story about the eviction. He told reporters that before they were forced to leave, he and his father had spent six months working at preparing their crops. They had to abandon them due to the government's precipitous eviction, losing nearly a year's income. The government also took his sashes (hotbeds) and sold them for more than $1,000, as well as his wagons, farm implements, and water system. The government agents tore out his water pumps, leaving him and his father with no drinking or cooking water. The greenhouses were burned. The Hamiltons were promised a hearing, but didn't get it until after the Treaty of Versailles was signed. The end result was that the property was taken.

On the day of the sale there were 134 acres to be auctioned off. The resulting sale produced an average price per acre of $4,260, but that average was increased because one bidder pushed the bidding up far beyond that for her land before she had to give up when her opponent surpassed her capacity. The primary bidders were William Whigham, vice president of Carnegie Steel, and A. J. Kelly, of Commonwealth Real Estate Company, representing an unnamed party.

The *Chronicle Telegraph* reported the pathos of the small, elderly woman dressed in black silk, sitting in the front row. This was my great-grandmother, Mary Ann Dickson Cole. She didn't speak, but nodded her bids, at $25 increments as she drove the bidding up. In the end, Carnegie Steel paid the government $7,700 per acre for her land — an enormous sum for the time, and far beyond what she had been paid by the government. Mary Ann was now seventy-seven years old. My great-grandmother fought the giants. She could not get her land back, but she made Carnegie Steel dig deep for it. Mary Ann Cole had lived on the island all her life, and her family had lived there for over one hundred years. She could not compete with the deep pockets of Carnegie Steel, and she lost.

Mary Ann Cole (my great-grandmother)

The year 1918 was considered to be the end of Neville Island as an agricultural community. The government had seized 134 acres near the Gulf Terminal (Mellon had big interests in Gulf Oil), including my grandfather's farm. By 1938, the whole eastern end of the island was industrialized.

In 1979, the island gained notoriety when its Ohio River Park was returned to the Hillman Company that had donated the land in a public relations gesture. Toxic wastes had been discovered in the soil of the property, and it acquired the epithet "Poison Park."

Uncle Ned continued his narrative. "This was early in 1919 when we went to Sandy Lake and lived with my Grandmother Henderson for awhile, and then Dad bought the farm. Finally, in 1921 he built a new house up there. He had enough money to buy a farm and build a house."

He told how it was with Mary Ann, in her final years. "My grandmother was brought up to the farm at Sandy Lake after the trouble on the island. Both my grandmother and my father stayed down trying to more or less guard the place after Dad sent the rest of us to Sandy Lake. I think this kind of affected her some, because she really loved it when she lived on the island. My mother looked after her, but my grandmother could still see the boats going down the river. There was no river and no boats because this was out in the country. She'd lie in bed and she'd say 'Oh, Ned, there goes *The Homer Smith*.' or 'Oh, Ned, don't you see *The Aliquippa* going down?' They were paddle wheelers pushing barges and she imagined...then I'd kinda' go along with her and she'd be satisfied..." Mary Ann Cole was eighty-eight when she died in the little back bedroom at Sandy Lake.

5
CHAPTER

Sandy Lake

Most of the family lived with Grandmother Henderson for about two years before the auction in 1921. My grandfather and Uncle Bob remained in the Pittsburgh area while Grandpa worked on the Emsworth Dam. They still had hopes of getting the Neville Island farm back, so they wanted to be close by.

My mother, Uncle Bob and Uncle Ned shared their memories of Sandy Lake.

My mother, in her nineties, remembered what happened when the trouble came. "They sent me away — I went to live with my Grandmother Henderson in Sandy Lake. They called her Crish — her name was Lucretia. She rented from Mr. Nelson who owned a men's tailoring business, and Ned McCaughtry worked for him. That's where my brother Ned got his name." When asked why Uncle Ned was named after this man, my mother did not recall, but I later learned that he was a cousin of Grandma's.

"Tell me about when your family bought the farm in Sandy Lake," I prompted her.

"That's when they were trying to take our property away from us, and there were all these men down there — wandering around. We didn't know them. They [her parents] decided it wasn't safe for me to be there because they couldn't keep me by their side all the time. So they decided I should go up and live with Grandma Henderson. Eventually, my mother and my brother, Ned, joined me there.

"What happened when the rest of the family came up there to live?"

"Dad looked around for a property. He wanted a small farm and that's what he got…a very nice property. We could see the main highway from the house. I liked that house — a pretty place with porches around two sides, and a big porch swing where three people could sit together. I spent a good deal of time sitting out there. That was in the front of the house and looked out over the front yard. The road that ran by had quite a bit of traffic, considering. It wasn't a lonesome place.

"What do you remember about Gladys at Sandy Lake?"

My mother – age 16

"I don't remember much because she was five years older than I was, and she spent a great deal of time with our cousin, Katherine Cole, who lived in McKees Rocks." My mother told my sister, Nancy, that when Katherine was in her twenties, she went on a trip to Florida and committed suicide while she was there. No reason was mentioned. James Cole, her father, was a handsome man. Relationships in the Cole family could become involuted.

"I know that, as a teenager, I envied Gladys's smooth, clear skin. My pimply skin bothered me greatly, at times causing unhappiness and a rebellious attitude. It did not seem fair that Gladys had a good complexion, while mine was the bane of my life.

"When she went to college at Margaret Morrison, the women's division of Carnegie Tech, she lived with Aunt Emma Parker in Avalon during the week, but came home to Sandy Lake on weekends. Sometimes she brought a girlfriend home with her, and those were delightful occasions. Both girls urged me to join them in singing, and they took turns accompanying us on the piano.

"Grandmother Cole had her favorite grandchild...Gladys... and had intended to send her to school for the next three years through graduation." But fate intervened. "Gladys came to Grandma Henderson's house in Sandy Lake for the summer vacation. Mother, my two brothers, and I were already there, waiting for Dad to settle things in Neville Island and join us. Gladys was attending the Wesleyan Methodist church in the village with the rest of the family, where she learned about Houghton College in New York State, near Buffalo. Gladys had a choice to make — Margaret Morrison was a prestigious college whereas Houghton was very small and little known. She opted for Houghton, where life was simpler and far less overwhelming than at Margaret Morrison. She applied and was accepted for her sophomore year."

The account goes on to tell what happened one evening when Gladys was with the family at Grandmother Henderson's over her summer break

"We were about to sit down to the supper table...when there came a knock at the front door. Gladys went to answer it. Instead of returning to the table, she stepped out onto the porch, closing the door after her. We could hear sounds of surprise in her voice answered by a man's deeper voice. Excitement ran through their conversation.

"At last, Gladys led a fine-looking young fellow into the dining room and introduced Arthur Bernhoft to the family. An extra place was set for him and he joined us for dinner. Questions and answers flew back and forth. Grandma Henderson's house, though comfortable, was too small to accommodate one more person. Therefore, Arthur spent the night in the Sandy Lake Hotel, after assuring us that he would have time to visit again the next day before taking a late-morning train home to Olean, New York.

"Arthur's family owned a large farm in the Little Valley area near Houghton. He and his sister, Dorothy, were still living on the farm although they both had different careers; Dorothy was teaching in a country elementary school while Arthur was a sophomore at Houghton College preparing to teach high school.

"The next morning, Gladys and Arthur sat for a long time on the porch swing. There seemed to be no lack of things for them to talk about. Time was getting short before Arthur would have to leave to catch his train, and he and Gladys came into the house so he could say goodbye. But there was more that he had to announce. He and Gladys would like to get married before summer was over — they could both attend the junior class at Houghton.

"Mother was fairly well acquainted with Arthur through letters from Gladys throughout the year, and, of course, through Gladys's constant talk about the 'wonderful' young man in her class, and she graciously welcomed him into the family.

"It was decided that Gladys would go for a visit to the Bernhoft farm in the very near future and, wonder of wonders, she would take me with her. What an unexpected pleasure that would be! The only 'fly in the ointment' was that I suffered from sharp jealousy when Gladys and Dorothy got together, and seemed to want no one else to hear [them].

"When my sister Gladys was married, we no longer lived in the homestead which had fallen into the possession of Carnegie Steel. The Cole family had moved to Sandy Lake to be near Grandma Henderson. My father had bought a small farm — 60 acres and

60 perches — about one mile from the town. He had the existing house remodeled, making changes and additions to make space and convenience for his family of five.

"The wedding was performed that summer in the parlor of the Cole farm. There was no formal reception, only a noon-day lunch served in the dining room. I had helped to prepare the food and a neighbor served the meal.

"After the guests and the bride and groom had left, Mother and I found ourselves alone in the kitchen. I was struck dumb by my mother's reaction to the whole occasion which was summed up in her exclamation, 'I never want to go through that again!' Puzzled and saddened by such a reaction, then and there I vowed that I would never ask her to go through it again for me."

I asked my mother what she remembered about her older brother, Robert, who was next in the family after Gladys. An example of his bullying came to mind. "He got his nose broken at school. He got into a fight with Elmer Dixon, who was a big boy. Robert started it, but Elmer hauled off and whammed him on the nose, and it broke. We had to take him to the doctor — up at McKees Rocks. He [the doctor] took care of it, but he didn't put it back into shape, so he [Bob] had a sort of trough there all his life, which didn't do anything for his looks! Otherwise he would have been quite handsome. It was too bad."

I later heard from my sister that the schoolyard wasn't the only arena where Uncle Bob used his fists and his bulk to bully. His brother, my Uncle Ned, was younger and smaller, slight of frame like his mother, Helen. It was easy for the burly Robert to push him around. Perhaps he was jealous of the affection that was showered on Uncle Ned. The day would come when Ned would have enough, and prevail over his tormenter.

Fun in Sandy Lake was simple, according to my mother. "We went to church...we had horses and cows, a dog and chickens. We belonged to a church that had prayer meetings. One night when the prayer meeting was at our house, I was kneeling by the window in the front room — a large room with windows on three sides. One of them looked out toward the chicken coop. I happened to lift my head and look out there and the chicken coop was on fire. Evidently, one of the chickens had knocked over the thing they had set up to keep the coop warm enough for them. The whole coop was on fire. I got up off my knees in a hurry and yelled. Everybody went out to take care of it."

"Did they save any of the chickens?"

"They saved all the chickens. They were smart enough to stay as far away from the fire as they could get.

"Social life was very simple — an occasional function at church, a trip to Pittsburgh to see the movie, *Birth of a Nation*, to hear Sousa's band or to visit the zoo. Gladys had a flair for drama. Sometimes she prepared and coached an evening's entertainment, which she put on in our big dining room.

"The children spent as much time outdoors as weather permitted. In the evenings we played running games like Red Light, Prisoner's Base, Hide and Seek, and Run Sheepie Run. It was a good place to grow up."

Marian's interviews with both uncles provided more insights into the Sandy Lake years. It seemed that our grandfather had various ideas about where the family would relocate. While our grandmother wanted to be near her mother and the area where she grew up, he was considering other options.

Uncle Bob mentioned one aborted plan. "Dad bought a plantation down in Virginia but it was a swindle. He'd already bought mules, he'd bought hogs, and was going to move down there. He even bought a boxcar load of furniture. He was gonna' send 'em down there. This fellow named John E. Walker came up to our place. I remember him, and he turned out to be a swindler, and it fell through. Mom was happy, we moved to Sandy Lake. So, I guess the old folks did have a little money. Well, I think I know where the balance went — nothing against Dad — the final line — lost it all. Just one more turnover."

Uncle Ned echoed, "just one more turnover." They looked at each other and shook their heads. They had heard that phrase often enough.

Uncle Ned continued, "Dad bought this farm and was going to remodel the house. I recall one day Dad got disgusted and he said,

'Tear it down. Just save the kitchen.' So they tore the whole thing down and started from scratch. Well, when the neighbors around there saw the house my dad was building, they said, 'Boy, that guy's rich!' — and they thought he was. He wasn't, but he got along alright.

"Anyhow, we were the first folks to have electricity, running water, and a bathroom in the house. That was something that very few people had in those days. Our uncles had bathrooms in their houses on Neville Island, but Grandmother Cole hadn't allowed Dad to put one in ours. We bought a new car and a new truck. It was a nice farm, but Dad would pick out things to raise that had a lot of work to them like seven acres of asparagus, a lot of cabbage and anywhere from twelve to twenty acres of potatoes, and they all had to be hoed at that time.

"Mother never did like the island — her heart was always around Titusville, Sandy Lake and Hendersonville, named after her relatives. She was born in Titusville. My mother was always trying to pull back toward Sandy Lake. In the long run, Mother was glad to leave the island, while my father and grandmother weren't. That's where their roots were.

"Dad provided well for us during the Depression. There wasn't as much money at that time because he had lost heavily in the stock market. [But] there was never a time that we weren't well-filled and had good clothes to wear."

Marian asked if Grandpa Cole had been a quiet person.

Uncle Ned replied, "Well, I do remember Dad was mad about something. I don't know what it was over but he was down at the barn. There was one horse that would playfully take a hold of him. Jim, the horse, took a hold of Dad's arm and got a little bit of skin when he did it. Dad turned around and swore at him, and then actually kicked the horse, which I never before had seen him do. 'Dad!' I said. 'I remember you firing a guy down on the island for kicking a horse.' Dad didn't say anything and I walked out of the barn. For some reason, a little later, I returned to the barn and there was Dad, with his arm up over the horse's neck, talking to the horse and telling him how sorry he was."

Marian asked, "Did your dad ever spank you?"

"Not as a general rule. I remember the only time he whipped me was with an ear of corn with the husk pulled back up, and he sent me back into the house. That was for lying about stealing two ears of corn from a neighbor, whose cornfield I'd been told to stay out of."

"How about your mother?"

Uncle Ned laughed. "Oh, she gave it to me every time I needed it, and that was quite often, I'd say. I remember Mom licking me at different times. Then she'd put her arms around me and cry because she'd licked me."

"Did she have a temper?"

Uncle Ned replied, "Mother always controlled her temper. There is only once that I ever saw my mother — well, she didn't lose her temper. Anyhow, I had a dog that had run away. This dog was tied outside, and I'd done something that had really upset my mom — this was up at the farm — Mom went out and turned my dog loose, and for Mom to do something like that was mean for her, because she just didn't do things like that, and that one time I thought Mom had lost her religion — 'cause Mom was a Wesleyan Methodist. Must have been on a Wednesday that I thought she'd lost her religion, 'cause I ran all the way down to prayer meeting and told 'em Mom had lost her religion and would they pray for her, and they got the biggest kick out of that.

"To show you what my dad was like — when we moved to Sandy Lake, he set up a chicken farm along with the other farming. I can't say how many hens he had — perhaps a thousand. He got top prices in Pittsburgh for the eggs — he sold them by the case. Every egg was candled — that was to look through to see if there was any spot on them, and every egg was stamped with the date. He got top prices from McCanns, and they took all the eggs he could produce. Finally in the fall, the coop burned. We never knew what happened." This was the fire that my mother had remembered on the night of the prayer meeting.

Marian asked Uncle Ned why he didn't stay in farming. "I really liked the food that was produced on the farm, but I didn't like the hoeing used to produce it. I could stand it just so long, and then I would take off for awhile. Eventually, I came back. My heart just wasn't in it. At one time, I was interested in starting a beef and hog farm because we had a good combination, but no one wanted to go along. So I figured the best thing to do was to work for the railroad. I ended up in train service, whereas Uncle Jim, Dad's brother, was in engine service. I'm really glad I did — I had a good life on the railroad and a good home life.

"I just found some papers — back in 1900, in comparison to today's $10,000, what do you think this would be worth now? When Grandpa [Augustus] Cole died, he left Grandma [Mary Ann] Cole $11,130.87. He left James P. Cole $11,000 and Everson Cole, our dad, $11,100 and some dollars. At least $33,000 altogether."

Uncle Ned had some more information, recently learned about the family fortunes. In 1917 there were over 950 acres of land owned by the Cole family — but what had happened to them was a question. The Lehigh Valley railroad was on some of the land, but the Coles didn't own it now. After he and Uncle Bob chewed that question over for awhile, Uncle Ned went on to other deals gone sour.

Uncle Ned and Uncle Bob were now focusing on the stock market crash. Uncle Ned began, "Dad went down and stayed down in Pittsburgh in 1929. He was going down for one last turnover, 'cause Dad knew it was coming. But he took that one last gamble and he lost it — all on the margin. Make it big and lose it big."

Marian interjected, "He must have been doing well at that time."

Uncle Bob replied, "He was, but what good did it do us?"

Uncle Ned chimed in, smiling, "I had a lot of fun going up to Stoneboro picking out a new car, 'cause Dad had told me he'd get it for me when he came back. He lost it."

Marian inquired, "How did he act when he came home?"

Uncle Ned answered, "Oh, — [we] couldn't leave him alone."

"Afraid he might shoot himself?"

"Yup — [we] stayed right with him."

Uncle Bob added, "He was berserk, mercies of God, that's all — that and prayer."

And Uncle Ned said, "Dad realized that he didn't only do it with his money, but he lost money that should have gone to other people. I don't hold it against Dad. If Dad had made it, we would have had it. We never had a day hungry — always had good clothes."

Marian observed, "Those are the fortunes of war."

Uncle Ned remarked, "Many jumped out of windows."

Uncle Bob contributed a bleak memory. "One time when I was taking produce down to Pittsburgh — maybe you never heard of High Level Bridge — I saw a man jump off, and all he had left on, when he hit the cobblestones, was just shoes."

For the rest of his life, Everson Porter Cole, my grandfather, pursued the government through the courts, trying to get financial satisfaction for the loss of the Neville Island homestead, but it was a snail's pursuit. The case never seemed to move along. Although he spent time on little inventions, he never sold the ideas. He continued making little deals, always looking for "just one more turnover."

Although the lifestyle of the Cole family had been simple, it had a quality of elegance to it. Female education was encouraged. It's interesting to note that although Everson did not go to college, both of his daughters did, but his sons did not. When the Cole family moved to Sandy Lake, it was to a house not quite so large, and a community where the family members were newcomers. They were, however, considered to be rich by local standards. After their hopes of regaining their Neville Island home withered, the family had made the final move north and looked to the future — all except Grandpa, who kept looking back.

As teenagers, Gladys and Corinne left the family home to live with relatives, both girls spending some time living with their mother's Aunt Ella Kirk, for whom I was named. Why they left home, is a question to be considered. The girls had broader dreams than the boys, wanting to control their destinies. In later years, my grandmother would throw their success up to her son, Robert, creating tensions on the farm.

The move to Sandy Lake changed everything for the family, and, ultimately, for me. It changed not only the course of their lives, but their attitudes. It broadened opportunities for my mother and Uncle Ned, and Gladys was able to choose her own direction and get out from under her grandmother's thumb. Uncle Bob and my grandfather just crouched down and crawled into themselves, each nurturing his own bitterness. My grandmother was happy for a time, but became embittered herself when she saw her hopes for her favorite son dwindle to nothing as she observed the farm deteriorate.

As Grandpa's children became adults, each had to make a decision about his or her future. Aunt Gladys's future was secured by Mary Ann Cole's legacy, which financed her college years.

Any money that might have been earmarked for my mother's education had been squandered by her father, looking for "one more turnover." She would have to make her own way.

Uncle Bob would remain on the Sandy Lake farm. He didn't really have other options.

When he was a young man, Uncle Ned ventured out into the world on a motorcycle to make his fortune. He returned with a wife.

It could have worked out well. The farm my grandfather bought was much bigger than the one on Neville Island, although farther from the market. Still, life could have been good. They were together and they had their health. They still had some money. The community considered them wealthy, so they still had some degree of status. If only my grandfather hadn't kept looking back. If only he had given his eldest son some recognition for his efforts. If only the family had taken root in its new surroundings. If only...

CHAPTER 6

I Remember Sandy Lake and Grandma

Traveling to the Farm

I never knew the Neville Island farm. My earliest memories of the farm in Sandy Lake begin with the journey to get there. When I was young, we made the trip every August at harvest time so my mother could help with the task of feeding the crews that came in to work. We lived in northern New Jersey, and it was a full day's job to get to western Pennsylvania with no four- or six-lane highways. They were not yet even on the drawing board. Our route took us over country roads, and I still remember the Mail Pouch Tobacco signs in huge letters that decorated the sides of barns, and the little signs staked into the ground with a rhyme, the ending of which recommended, "Burma Shave."

My parents packed the green Buick the night before, then went to bed early. Before dawn, my sister and I were lifted from our beds, still asleep, and placed in either direction on the back seat. We were made as comfortable as possible, with our pillows and blankets tucked around us, then we would set out through the dark, Nancy and I sleeping fitfully until dawn.

Cole farm in Sandy Lake

Nancy continued to sleep, but I loved seeing the first hesitant light, the dim brightening in the east. I sat up and pressed my nose and forehead to the cold glass of the window, taking myself out of the car and into the passing scene, becoming part of it. I watched lights come on in houses and imagined people rising from their beds, stumbling around in half-sleep in the early light. Where lights were already on, I imagined people at breakfast. I saw them as cozy, and eating storybook food like porridge, clotted cream and fresh-made bread with butter and jam. Gradually, outlines of buildings and trees, horses and cows, took shape through early morning mist as we passed through farmland and small villages. It's a feeling I still savor fleetingly on the rare occasions that I travel early by car, but now I'm usually the driver and can only glance as I pass.

When it was fully light, we stopped at the next town large enough to have a luncheonette or diner. Breakfast en route was a treat, and we were allowed to order whatever we wanted. Seldom were porridge or clotted cream on the menu so I chose our traditional Sunday breakfast of bacon, eggs and toast.

Ahead of us stretched another ten hours. We asked, "When are we going to get there? How much longer?" From breakfast it was straight through with a brief roadside lunch stop of sandwiches from home, and toilet breaks. There were no big rest stops with multiple toilets and a restaurant. It was usually a small unisex bathroom at a gas station, some better kept than others. We were well-instructed to cover the seat with toilet paper before sitting.

Our mother prepared little bags of things with which we could amuse ourselves along the way, and keep ourselves occupied intermittently. Sometimes we played the alphabet game, the winner being the first to have seen all the letters. Q was hard, but you looked for a gas station that sold Quaker State Motor Oil. Z was even harder, and you usually hoped to see it on a license plate or a sign for Pennzoil.

One time, when I was a little older, maybe ten or eleven, my mother gave me a book with the innocuous title being a girl's name. It was not a new book and it wasn't from her own library so was probably hastily picked out of a used book bin somewhere. Apparently, my mother never opened the cover. As I began to read, I barely looked up, even at rest stops, as I followed the tale of the girl's sexual experiences. When my mother commented about how I seemed to be enjoying the book, I tried to keep my face impassive, only to dive back into the story once her head was turned.

Finally, after an endless day, we descended the long winding hill into Franklin, Pennsylvania to stop at Uncle Ned's for the night. Our cousins, Snooky, Tucker (Ned, Jr.) and Darlene, were close to our age, and we looked forward to seeing them and to the dinner that Aunt Evelyn would have waiting. Snooky was a year older than I, and she was kind enough to allow me to tag along with her on her various stops to see her friends after dinner. Nancy joined Darlene on her rovings. When Snooky had completed her rounds, encompassing every girl her age in the neighborhood, we would walk home through the August dusk to the sounds of other children still at play, trying to squeeze every last moment of pleasure out of day's end.

During those early years at their house, there were times when the younger cousins, as children often do, took advantage of our being there to exceed the usual boundaries. I would stand sheepishly by when punishment was meted out, especially for Tucker, who was the most flagrant offender, being mischievous by nature. Physical punishment was not usually involved. I was let off with a gentle reprimand because I didn't know the rules — and I was the daughter of Uncle Ned's beloved sister, Corinne.

In the early years, Uncle Ned's family lived in a small bungalow on McCalmont Street in Rocky Grove, just outside of Franklin. Ned and Evelyn were a magnet to the neighborhood kids, good-humored, and willing to help a neighbor or a neighbor's child. They eventually built a larger house on the next block with Ned doing most of the work himself. They remained in that house for the rest of their lives.

Nancy and I loved Uncle Ned — he was always good to us and we endured his good-natured teasing. He played games with us and took us and our cousins around with him in the car on errands. With his railroad work, he would be on layover for a number of days in a row, and he would plan these to coincide with our visit. As we rode around, he carried on a joking commentary about the passing scene that would have us laughing and nudging each other. One of our big treats was to drive through the grounds of Polk State School and see the elderly ladies carrying their baby dolls. We thought this the funniest sight. Of course, all of us would find this sad now, rather than amusing. I have worked extensively with Alzheimer's patients, as a nurse, as well as gero-psychiatric cases. I am embarrassed to think of those episodes when we were children, but at least we kept our amusement to the confines of the car and the objects of our merriment were never aware of it.

Uncle Ned maintained strict rules of behavior based on his fundamental Wesleyan Methodist beliefs, and my cousins found ways to rebel — particularly Tucker in those days, and Darlene later on — but Nancy and I were moderately well-behaved while at his house. We did not want to displease him, although when at home, we had no qualms about displeasing our parents.

The Farm

The next day we headed for Grandma and Grandpa's farm, a half-hour's ride. As Uncle Ned's family would be there for a visit soon, the farewells were short. Once past the tiny village of Sandy Lake, we kept a sharp eye out for the turnoff since it was less than a mile outside of town on the right. The farmhouse sat on the corner of two dirt roads, downhill and a half-mile back from the country highway. Now those roads are paved, and Grandma and Grandpa's road is named Cole Road.

Once out of the car and the obligatory hugs over, we carried our things to our rooms on the second floor, where Nancy and I would share a small bedroom overlooking the barn and chicken coop. Our parents were in the room next door. Uncle Bob's room during his bachelor years, was across the hall at the other side of the house, and my grandparents shared the larger bedroom across the front. Later, when Bob married, they switched rooms. Grandpa took Bob's old room, and Grandma moved downstairs to the small room near the kitchen. There was one bathroom. That had been a major victory for Grandpa when he bought and renovated the farmhouse. By then, bathrooms had become more common in cities and towns, but less so in the country, and Mary Ann Cole, who believed bathrooms were frivolous, was still living with the family when they moved in.

At the foot of the stairs was a large sitting-dining room with linoleum on the floor. When not working, my grandfather sat there in his rocker, his spittoon handy, reading the paper and listening to the news, particularly the stock market reports. He met interruptions with silent but fierce glares. In future years, he would delight in rocking over the fingers of Uncle Bob's young children who lived at the farm.

A formal living room with green, horsehair-stuffed Victorian pieces and a piano, brought from Neville Island, faced the road at the front of the house. Children were not allowed in unless accompanied by an adult, but an exception was made for me so I could practice on the piano when ordered, and play for my proud grandparents. At no other time and for no other purpose was I to cross the threshold.

Behind the stairs, the small room in which Mary Ann Cole, had died was now my grandmother's own special room for sewing where she made family clothing and quilts. This is the room that later became Grandma's bedroom. When she married, every girl in the family wanted and expected a quilt from Grandma Cole. When I was in my thirties and finally received my quilt, I could recognize bits of clothing, some mine, from past years in the pieces. The colors of the quilt she made for me, the primary being an odd shade of bright blue, never fit into the décor of any room I had.

A big kitchen dominated the back of the house. Between the large black woodstove and the modern range, it got fiercely hot in summer with all the cooking for farm workers. In the cool of early morning, however, the kitchen smelled of fresh, raw milk that had been brought up in big containers from the day's milking. The milk was set in the pantry for the cream to rise to the top, then Grandma skimmed some off to use to make butter in the electric churn, saving the rest in a pitcher. There was always a large bowl of fresh eggs from Grandma's chickens.

Refrigeration was provided by placing food in the cool earth-floored cellar as it had been on Neville Island for a century before. Eggs that were soon to be used, were not put down there but were left handy in the pantry. In later years, a refrigerator was installed.

The mudroom inside the back door smelled of fresh manure and hay. This was where Grandpa and Uncle Bob would leave their dirty boots and wash up for meals. Off the back of the kitchen was a large, glassed-in porch. When the cooking was done, my mother and grandmother liked to sit out there, where there was often a cool breeze with all the windows open, and chat, sometimes shelling peas or performing some other mindless task as they talked. I remember one year sorting elderberries for jam. There were bushels and bushels of them lined up on the porch for us to pull the tiny berry clusters off the stems and put them into big basins — enough to make pies for an army.

Life didn't stop just because we were visiting. It was threshing time, and the threshers would be there for several days and noon dinner was expected. Today, it would take one man with a machine only one afternoon to harvest the same amount of grain that Grandpa and the threshers took several days to harvest in the 1940s. When we visited, my mother was expected to help prepare the meals. My father's job was to keep us out of the way, but he spent a lot of his time reading and relaxing, and kept only a loose eye on us. It was his vacation and he wasn't much of a farmer.

I remember going down to the barn after the threshers had packed up their equipment and gone. There was a very small pile of grain on the floor in the middle of the upper section where they had been working, maybe half a bushel. I looked at it and tasted a few grains. It had a nice nutty flavor. I thought, "What a lot of work for such a small return." I didn't realize that the grain had already been packed into bags and taken away to be sold or stored for winter and this was only the sweepings.

Downstairs in the barn, which was built against the side of a gentle slope, were the animals. There were several milk cows on one side, and chickens wandered in. Out behind the barn was a pig sty, sometimes with a pig in residence. We weren't allowed near the pig unaccompanied, and Grandpa wouldn't let us near the cows to milk them for fear we would do them some harm — not that they would harm us. He was protective of his animals.

Grandma allowed me to go with her to the hen house to gather eggs. This building replaced the one that my mother saw burning many years before during the prayer meeting. I learned to push a hen to one side to check for eggs under her warm feathers, and to quickly snatch my hand back if she made a sudden move. The coop smelled of warm chickens, hay, and dried manure. I wasn't allowed there alone, as I might startle the chickens and disturb their laying pattern. Grandma was training me to be of help, not to create more work. She had overall responsibility for the chickens, including butchering, a fact of which I was innocently unaware at the time.

Church in Sandy Lake

When visiting the farm, we attended the little Wesleyan Methodist church in Sandy Lake, after scrubbing well and dressing in our Sunday best. The church was plain inside with hard pews, the walls were stark and white. There were no stained glass windows — that would signify pride — and the organ was parlor-sized. The hymnals smelled old and musty.

Our church at home in New Jersey was mainstream Methodist with beautiful, big, stained glass windows, thickly padded pews, and rich mahogany woodwork. A great organ with massive pipes and four rows of keys pealed out our Sunday hymns. An elegantly gowned choir sat in the loft, directed by the Juilliard-trained organist who was also my piano teacher, Miss Hudgins. She directed both the chancel choir and the junior choir, of which I was a member.

This little country church in Sandy Lake was a far cry from what I knew. There was nothing to look at and the preacher droned. The wooden bench where I sat grew harder by the minute on my boney bottom. It was hot. Ladies moved the air in a desultory manner with their Chautauqua fans.

In New Jersey I could let my gaze drift to the beautiful mural of Jesus sitting in what looked like the mouth of a cave or grotto, speaking with a group of supplicants. In my mind, I made up stories about the scene to pass the time. The church itself was always cool, even on the hottest Sunday.

In the Sandy Lake church, even the hymns were not familiar with no complex harmonies to create interest. They all sounded pretty much the same. I thought the service would never end, and of course, I was expected to be on my best behavior in front of Grandma. Squirming was definitely forbidden. What would people think?

Mary Ann's Influence on Mom — Concern about the Neighbors' Thoughts

We attended the Ridgewood Methodist Church. So did the Parkers; Mr. Parker was then the President of AT&T, where my father worked. They lived in a large, elegant house on the upper side of the railroad tracks, high on the hill with other large elegant houses, and a distant view of the New York City skyline. There was no wrong side of the tracks in Ridgewood, but there was the good side and the better side. The Parkers were definitely on the better side. Our house was not far from the railroad tracks on the good side, but in status, my mother saw a vast gap.

My mother had attended church women's club teas at the Parker house and was in awe of Mrs. Parker. Mrs. Parker, herself, was actually a gracious lady and might have been embarrassed had she been aware of my mother's awe. One Wednesday afternoon, which was piano lesson and food-shopping day, I met my mother in the A&P parking lot for the ride home. She was all in a dither with joy. Mrs. Parker had been shopping there as well, and had helped my mother carry her bundles to the car. For a week Mom raved about how wonderful Mrs. Parker was, how kind, how Christian.

Mrs. Parker's democratic and benevolent attitude notwithstanding, my mother was still determined that the revered lady should view us as the perfect Methodist AT&T family. They sat two pews behind us in church. Once I was old enough to attend the services rather than go to the children's hour held in the Sunday School rooms — I had pushed that escape for as long as I could — I was expected to sit like a perfect lady, and God help me if I squirmed or rattled papers.

There was an apple tree that grew in our side yard at home and my mother kept a stripped, thin switch from that tree on top of the china closet in the dining room, out of my reach. If I fidgeted and/or made any noise in church, thus casting shame on the family in Mrs. Parker's eyes (so my mother thought), I would be switched when we got home, with self-righteous vigor, but never above the knees. My lower legs would be covered with red welts. The more serious the infraction, the more red welts there would be. I think Mrs. Parker would have been horrified if she knew to what lengths my mother went to ensure her peaceful enjoyment of the sermon. I think I would have had to do a lot worse than rattle a few papers to annoy that kind woman.

Back at the Farm

After an agonizing hour that seemed like two in the Sandy Lake church, it was over. I restrained myself from fleeing through the door. However, we were required to file out sedately, shake the pastor's hand and be introduced with great pride by Grandma. Then there were neighbors to be met. At last, we made it to the car.

A blast of hot air hit us as we opened the doors and stepped back to let the steam dissipate before we could chance getting in. We opened all the windows for the drive back to the farm. Once there, I was allowed to put on comfortable, modest, play clothes with skirts. No shorts.

My birthday usually fell during our farm visits. On the occasion that stands out in my mind, it was on Sunday. Uncle Ned's family was coming over after church for the noon dinner. The thing that added to my restlessness in church this particular Sunday was not only the anticipated visit from my cousins, but the strong desire to check out the creek that meandered out from a spring behind the house. I had been told that there was soda pop in it. (That's what they call it in western Pennsylvania — soda pop.) At first I did not believe it, but I was assured by Uncle Bob that it was true. I jumped out of the car as it pulled to a stop, and ran out to where the stream cut the backyard in two. I expected to see soda bubbling out of the spring and fizzing along the water course. Instead, several large bottles of soda were lying in the spring water to keep cold.

When Uncle Ned's family arrived, Snooky and I paired off as did Nancy and Darlene, the youngest. That left Tucker to head for the barn to see what trouble he could get into. Snooky and I followed him down and climbed around in the hayloft for awhile, but we soon tired of this and left him to it. We sauntered back behind the house.

"Let's play doctor," said Snooky.

"How do you do that?"

"Lie down on the cellar door and pull up your shirt, and I'll examine your tummy."

I had just obliged and Snooky was sprinkling dirt on my abdomen as cure for some rare ailment, when our mothers and Grandma rounded the corner of the house.

"What are you doing?" came their scandalized cries.

"Nothing." We suddenly felt very guilty although our game had been quite innocent.

I don't remember what my punishment was, but Snooky, who was older, got a whipping. For me, the guilt and embarrassment were worse.

Alberta

Sometimes during our visits, my mother would take me with her to visit her girlhood friends who still lived in their family homes nearby. One such was Alberta Mahle who was just down the road. She was a few years older than my mother. Alberta never married and had continued to live on in her parents' house after their deaths.

I remember two incidents involving her. The first was a visit at her house one evening. I must have been very young because I have only a vague sensory memory of the house and the living room where we sat. I remember that, after examining my surroundings, I grew bored, and disliked the musty, old-house smell. The two women chatted on and on while I became aware that it was getting harder to see as the sun was going down. I expected the lights to be turned on at any minute, but the minutes passed with no move on Alberta's part to throw a light switch. My discomfort increased as I peered through the gloom. Finally, when it was almost dark and shapes could barely be made out, Alberta got up and went to a side table. There she lit an oil lamp. The acrid-sweet smell of the burning oil-soaked wick began to permeate the room.

Living by the light of oil lamps was a novelty, as I had never seen such a thing in actual use outside of the movies, and it kept my interest for the next few minutes until the good-byes were said at last, and we were out the door. I realized that this woman still lived in "olden times," and my curiosity was piqued. But we were on our way home to Grandma's, and my mother and I walked there in the brighter twilight of the outdoors.

The following fall, Alberta made the trip east to visit us. One day while she was there, my mother went out grocery shopping, and left Alberta in charge. By now it was late fall, and days were short. I always liked the cozy feeling of the early fall twilight when we were warm and safe at home, but twilight deepened and Alberta would not allow us to switch on the lights. At first it was a game, running with Nancy through the house in the dusk, screaming and laughing, but it grew uncomfortably dark before Alberta gave permission for the lights. It was scary, and Nancy was crying. I didn't have much sympathy for her tears, but I felt close to them myself.

Now we raced through the house flipping switches, relieved to see everything familiar and safe at last in the brightness of the electric light. The delay was caused by Alberta's habit of economizing, this time electricity instead of oil. It was a disparity in our cultures.

Even now, during early fall, I continue to find comfort in the shortening days, with a feeling of coziness and warmth inside my house. I sometimes prolong the moment before turning on the lights, recapturing the initial fun of that long-ago evening, running excitedly through the darkening rooms and savoring the certainty that brightness is a switch flick away. That dusky, twilit moment holds a comfort all its own — a magic time. It evokes a mood, a prelude to whatever the evening will hold.

Another pleasure that I believe grew out of that evening is that of catching a glimpse inside other people's houses as they are lit up when I'm driving by. It's not to pry into their lives, but to experience, for a fleeting moment, the comfort or beauty of a lived-in place. When traveling a familiar road, I anticipate which windows I know will offer a pleasing vignette, a fragment of an attractive arrangement of lamp and chair, bookcases beckoning the reader, a kitchen busy with meal preparation. What are they making? Imagined fragrances add to the warm scenario.

Religion and Family Visits

My mother had been raised first in a strict Presbyterian church on Neville Island, then later in the Wesleyan Methodist church in Sandy Lake, equally as strict. My aunts and uncles still retained their fundamentalist beliefs and way of life. Once away from the parental and Houghton College influences, my mother acquiesced to her far more liberal leanings. Her exposure to French culture had taught her other views. My sister and I took piano lessons, which had been denied my mother but provided for Gladys by Mary Ann.

From there on, we were in deep waters as far as cultural life at our house was concerned. I took dancing lessons at the Betty Fletcher Dance Studio after some begging and pleading, once I had seen enough Fred Astaire and Ginger Rogers movies. I went to the movies every Saturday afternoon from the age of seven on — first with Addie Orr, the girl up the street who was five years older, then alone, then dragging Nancy with me. I planned to be a movie star and wear a filmy, floating dress as I danced over to Fred Astaire like Ann Miller in *Easter Parade* (before he ended up with Judy Garland). We wore shorts in summer.

My mother was risqué in comparison with her family standards. Our modern Methodist church was far more liberal in its cultural position than the stark Sandy Lake version. Mom played cards (she was in a bridge club), she had an occasional cocktail and wine or sherry on holidays (and not just for her stomach's sake), and she didn't hesitate to use wine in cooking if it was called for. When in the company of some of her friends, she would have a cigarette. She did not inhale. The result was that the clandestine pack would sit in the drawer, hidden for months at a time. This made for very stale cigarettes, as I discovered when I got older, and went exploring, and experimenting.

We never had to worry about a visit from Uncle Bob, or from him and his family once he had married. They never came.

Uncle Ned would forgive his adored sister anything, and although he might not condone such wild habits, he would look the other way if he stumbled upon them. He was probably not aware of the smoking and drinking, such as they were, as none of that would occur during his visit. But he most likely knew about the dancing lessons and might have known about the cards. He would smile indulgently.

The only criticism of Corinne that I have heard of Uncle Ned making was about some story writing she did in her younger years. Darlene told me that, during a conversation she had with Uncle Ned where the subject of her aunt's stories came up, Ned shook his head sadly and said, "I wonder how she could write such things." We can only guess what she wrote that shocked him so, but I'm sure it would be tame by today's standards.

When Aunt Gladys and Uncle Arthur visited, and most strictly when Grandma and Grandpa Cole visited, we were carefully instructed not to mention anything about our wild, comparatively depraved lifestyle. All trace of cards and alcohol was hidden away in the backs of closets and drawers. Dancing was a forbidden topic, and I had to suspend my movie-going during their stay. That was a real hardship for me. If I had a dancing lesson scheduled, I would be sent on the sly because it was paid for, but would not be allowed to say where I'd been. Of course, if it was summer, Nancy and I had to make do with skirts. No shorts or pants for girls. We enjoyed the visits but hated the restrictions. I learned that when he was grown with a family, my cousin Tucker continued the practice of hiding the liquor when Ned and Evelyn visited. Darlene did not hide the liquor which she could blame on her spouse. She hid only the cigarettes.

Grandma and Alec

Across the street from our house in Ridgewood there was a large, old, Victorian house, known as the Cameron estate, that sat back beyond a little cut-off road. The entrance drive led over a small bridge that crossed a brook. We and our next door neighbor, "Aunt" Winnie, would cut through the estate if we were walking over town, but no one else ever walked there — except Grandma Cole.

There was a caretaker/gardener, Alec. He was a disheveled, shaggy individual, missing a few teeth. He usually did not appear when others would pass through. He was not sociable, and lived alone in a room off the big kitchen. When I was with Grandma, it was different. He would approach us, all gappy smiles, and they would greet each other like old friends.

We would walk over to the well-kept garden, designed in the English style, with walks, lawns and flower beds surrounded by high hedges, and a long arbor that resembled a tunnel, so heavily overgrown with vines was it. The mismatched pair would sit on one of the benches around the perimeter and soon be deep in conversation. My grandmother was a passionate gardener herself, particularly known in Sandy Lake for her gladioli. There they would sit, their wizened heads bobbing with enthusiasm, lost in conversation about their common interest, while I played along the paths.

I entertained myself by running around the gravel walks, exploring here and there, and ending up in the arbor cave that reminded me of the stained glass window at church. Here there was another bench, and I would wait in the cool dimness for them to finish their discussion, so we could proceed to town.

On our way again, we would bear to the right along a dirt drive that ran into Oak Street, a quiet, residential road leading to town. While still on Cameron property, however, we had to pass a dilapidated, falling-down cabin situated not far from the railroad embankment. It had a dismal look on the sunniest day, and smelled damp and musty, even in dry weather. Grandma Cole said it had been a secret stop on the underground railroad in the slave days. Perhaps Alec had told her that. Now it was an impromptu shelter for hobos who sometimes jumped off the trains there to spend the night. I always felt better after we had passed it. At a future time, my sister and her playmate would come across one of them passed out on the ground there.

CHAPTER 7

Scenes from Childhood

Boats

My father always had a strong love of boats and, when I was little, we had one. It was a wooden sloop called *The Vagabond*. He already owned it when he and my mother met and married, and I recall sailing on it when I was very young. There were some short trips but I remember, when I was five, that we spent a week sailing up and back down the Hudson River. My sister was more than three years younger and was left behind with Mrs. Dench, a babysitter.

The Vagabond was kept at the Haverstraw boat basin, and I had been there before with my father. I'd played around the other boats and in the clubhouse, while he worked on his boat. When I was a little older, I helped scrape barnacles from the wooden hull.

To begin our voyage, we rowed out to the boat in a dinghy with all our supplies and suitcases. A section of the railing came away so we could climb aboard. The boat itself seemed huge to my five-year-old eyes, with its tall mast and broad aft deck. However, there were areas along the sides where even I had to squeeze to pass through. The railings of the boat came up knee-high if you were an adult, farther on me, so you could walk safely by the cabin to the prow. It, however, was a narrow passage.

I hated squeezing past the engine just inside the cabin, especially when it was running. It was very loud, and I preferred to avoid it when it was on. Beyond that, there was a galley with a makeshift table. There was also a toilet with a brackish odor. We slept in bunks at the back, in the heart of the cabin.

I remember more about the deck than the inside of the cabin as that's where most of my waking time was spent. I was out there at first light and only went in when necessary to use the toilet, or when ordered to take a nap after lunch. I was required to take a nap because the child-rearing book that my mother regularly consulted informed her that naps were important. The passing water, as we

Me and Mom on *The Vagabond*

cut through it, fascinated me. I spent time hanging over the edge, peering down into the depths, mesmerized, hoping to see beyond things floating, straining to see fish. But I saw nothing except moving liquid blackness.

Today's parents would cringe at the sight of the bottoms-up child leaning out over the rushing water, but, apparently, the book didn't mention this situation at all, its authors never even entertaining the possibility, and my parents took no note. I wore a life preserver so they felt that I was safe. Had I disappeared over the edge, I'm sure they would have stopped the boat and fished their bobbing, little, orange-jacketed child out of the water.

When not examining the depths, I looked out at the other boats we passed. Some pleasure boats like ours, some working boats, especially barges. If we were going in the same direction, it took forever to pass the latter; they were long and low, often loaded with coal. Sometimes the bargemen would wave at the small child hanging over the railing of the sailboat. I waved back.

Not too many years later, when I was in fourth grade — I remember because I had been at home with the measles or mumps, which I had developed within two weeks of each other — I was lying in bed on Sunday evening, enjoying the fact that I didn't have to go to school the next day, and would be allowed to lie awake and listen to one of my favorite programs, *Lux Radio Theatre*. Eugene O'Neill's *Anna Christie*, was on the schedule that night. At nine, I probably didn't understand the significance of the story, but I had a vivid memory of the barges I had seen on that boat trip, and that was the setting I imagined. I could hear the boat whistles and disconsolate fog horns. I could see the shore lights blinking like myopic owls at night. I placed myself in the story.

One morning, we went ashore for supplies. I'm not sure what town it was, but we rowed to a pier behind some stores, tied up, and walked up steps to the town. When the characters in *Anna Christie* went ashore, I saw them going up those steps and into those buildings. I could easily see Anna and her father on their barge. When I read the play many years later in college, it was still these images that were vivid in my mind.

After the experiences on my father's sloop, I wanted a boat when I grew up, but have not yet gotten one. The men in my life were never interested in boating as a sport. The irony is that my sister, who remained at home during that boat trip, was the one who had boats as an adult, sometimes at great financial sacrifice. It's still on my wish list; I'd be satisfied with a kayak.

Switchings

When I was between two and three years old, my mother began to understand that I was going to be less than the perfect child, and that I might actually cause her some embarrassing moments. She already had a leash and harness that she used when we went shopping. I suppose I was just having a case of terrible twos, but she took my behavior as a personal affront.

When I was three, my mother had a horrifying moment during a Sunday afternoon call from Mrs. Brown, the pastor's wife. I don't know what prompted me, but I managed to call this lady, who had done nothing to me, a pickle-puss. Perhaps that was how I interpreted her elderly face. She was a little taken aback, but regrouped and laughed. My mother was mortified. Fortunately, I wasn't yet old enough to have my legs switched, so got off with a scolding that time.

It was not long, however, before the switch appeared, broken from a branch of the apple tree that grew in the side yard. My mother stripped it of little twigs until it was smooth as a willow whip. There were many switches over the next years, a replacement provided when the current one wore out. I was not the only one who received its ministrations, as Nancy had her hell-raising moments as well.

My father never condoned these switchings but hesitated to cross my mother. She was the one reading the book, which didn't condone switching either, and making the child-rearing decisions. He would make himself scarce at such times, taking refuge in his ham radios, or finding something to do out in the yard. My mother was self-satisfied about them, justifying herself by the fact that my sister and I were never seriously damaged — physically. I, however, received more switchings than my sister. When I was ten or eleven, I developed nerve enough to climb up and remove the offending switch unobserved. My mother would go to look for it when she felt the occasion warranted its use. Finding it gone, she would have to take time to cut another one and strip it of its twigs. That gave me time to make my getaway and hide. Unfortunately, she often found me and administered the punishment anyway, her anger having increased in the process.

It was her firm intention that the neighbors (just which ones has never been clear) could not point their fingers at our family and find fault with our behavior. We had only three near neighbors: Aunt Winnie, next door, would not have had us beaten; the Demarests on the other side barely recognized our existence; and the Orrs, on the end, were busy going about their own business. There was no one on the other side of us. The Zabriskies were too far away down the hill and around the corner. But Mary Ann's pride still ruled my mother. You would have thought there were some neighbors hidden somewhere who had their sights continually trained on our house.

Nancy developed her own way of dealing with the switchings from Mom. Her ultimate escape had been to refuse to cry. She accomplished this at about the same time that I was destroying the switches. Nancy convinced herself that pain was just another sensation, albeit an unpleasant one. One day she slid down a tree and scraped a large area of skin off her left arm. Rather than tell Mom and have her yell at her for climbing the tree, and then treat the wound with iodine, Nancy decided to take care of it herself, including the iodine. It was a painful process but she learned that she could control it. The next time she was switched, she refused to cry. She also thought that it was her own efforts that had ended the switchings.

It is interesting to note what is being said of us in other households. I had always thought the switchings had come to an end because my sister and I, each in our own way, had stood up against them, or that we just got too old for them. In the course of writing this book, the true reason was discovered. Uncle Ned's oldest daughter, Snooky, told us what she had been told by her father. Dad had told him that he threatened to turn our mother in to the police if she didn't stop beating us. She must have been teaching in Hasbrouck Heights, New Jersey, at that time. His hope was that she would stop beating us rather than run the risk of having her peers at school find out that she had been arrested. As ever, "What will the neighbors think?" won out, this time to our advantage. I was twelve when the switchings stopped.

After I learned about what my father had done, I thought back to the only time I could remember my parents having a major fight. My mother was sitting on a chair in the dining room, sobbing that my father was leaving. He was, at that moment, rummaging around in their bedroom, presumably packing. In panic, I ran next door to Aunt Winnie's and pleaded with her to come and stop my father from leaving. Bewildered and uncertain, the poor lady followed me back to my house. I had been gone only a few minutes as the houses were close together, but in that time, the argument had been resolved, and my mother's tear-stained face was smiling. I was embarrassed, Aunt Winnie was embarrassed, and my parents were sheepish. There was some mild remonstrance about not dragging the neighbors in, but Mom and Dad were too relieved that the crisis had passed to be angry. The situation never occurred again that I know of. I wonder now if the issue of the switchings was the subject of the argument on that day. I was never told.

Dad

My cousin, Snooky, said that Uncle Ned thought my parents didn't know what to do with me and my sister once they had us. It was his opinion that they would have been happy to put a picture of us on the wall and point to their children, rather than have responsibility for our care. I corrected this assessment to apply to my mother only. This was not the case with my father. He tried to soften the rigidity of our family routines and cushion the discipline.

Dad had also come from a family that once had money from their coal and lumber business in Brooklyn. For different reasons, my father's branch lived close to the bone. My grandfather, Benjamin Frith, was the son of a second wife who was much younger than my great-grandfather Frith. When my great-grandfather died, his sons by his first wife were adults and pushed aside the second family, giving them little of the inheritance. My father, however, never developed the craving for wealth that my mother did. Different genes.

I remember making him really angry only twice; both occasions were when I was a teenager. Both were for being mean to my sister. One time, he just yelled. The other time, he hit me with an open hand, raining slaps on my hunched shoulders as I protected my head with my arms. I'm sure that this time I must have really deserved it, but even though he was so angry that he had no concern about hitting me above the knees, it did not hurt as much as the switch, and his blows left no mark at all. I got over it.

If Uncle Ned and Aunt Evelyn wondered how Nancy and I survived our childhood without a nurturing mother, they can look to Dad for the answer. As Nancy put it, "He adored us and liked to be around us. I never had any doubt about that. He always took an interest in what we were doing. He was the one who called all the time when I was at Drew. I seldom spoke to Mom. He was the one who helped with my homework all through high school. He was the one who worried about us until he died. Did you know that he encouraged me to move in with you in New York City so that he could have more of a connection to you? He worried about you all the time."

I remember sitting on my mother's lap only once when I was young. I don't remember what the occasion was — just that it was so unaccustomed that I soon slithered down. I remember my father often trying to hug me, and I would pull away. When I was much older, in college, and staying at Uncle Ned's, Aunt Evelyn spoke to me about observing this when we were visiting them. She said the look that would come over my father's face broke her heart.

Mom was an excellent reader of bedtime stories. She read with great expression and Nancy and I looked forward to the evening reading. We had one anthology of children's stories that I would have liked to have kept for my girls, but Nancy had children first, so she laid claim to it. I don't know what happened to it from there. It had a light green cover and it was thick. There was a wonderful story about Aiken Drum, the Brownie, and I haven't seen it in any other book. My very favorite was about Baba Yaga, a Russian witch who lived in the forest in a house on chicken legs.

There were some nights when Mom couldn't make the performance for whatever reason. Dad would try to fill her shoes, without much success. Maybe he just wanted a turn to try his hand. His efforts to inject feeling and emotion were too overdone, and we would soon complain that he didn't read like Mom. He seemed to take it in stride, but, looking back, I'm sure he was hurt by our criticism.

Politics

My mother, no doubt prompted by her concern for what the neighbors might think, also hid the fact that my parents voted the Democratic ticket. What shame if that was to become known by her Republican friends. While Franklin Delano Roosevelt was freely applauded at home, I was cautioned never to breathe a word of it at school or Sunday School. Ridgewood was a Republican town, and the Methodist church was a Republican stronghold, but my mother was a closet Democrat. It wasn't until years later when they moved to Katonah, in Westchester County, New York, that Mom and Dad came out of the closet for John F. Kennedy. I doubt that they would have been ostracized in Ridgewood, but my mother was taking no chances.

Misadventures

The summer before I started first grade, my mother sent me to the school playground for the activities program. It lasted all day, and gave her a break from having me underfoot. I met this really nice boy there, quiet and shy, and I invited him to come over to my house to play after the day's program was over. I lived a half-mile away, and I was walking home that day. He agreed to come with me, and we set out down the street.

After we had gone about half the distance, he started getting nervous about how far it was. I kept encouraging him that it was only a little farther. By the time we reached my hill, almost to the house, he dug in his heels and refused to go another step. I grabbed his wrist and started pulling him up the hill, yelling at him to stop being such a big baby and we were almost there. At that point, he started screaming and crying and pulling in the opposite direction. At last, he slipped from my grasp and fled, screaming in terror, back the way we had come.

I proceeded on home, thoroughly disgusted, and told my mother what had happened. She dropped what she was doing, got into the car, and went after the boy to see that he reached home safely. I did not go with her. He apparently had been taught the same lesson that I had, and refused to get into the car with her. She couldn't call his mother, because I didn't know his name at that time. He did reach home safely, however, because he was back at the playground the next day, staying on the opposite side from me.

Of course, I eventually did learn his name — it was Cliff Thompson. By junior high I had developed a crush on him because he turned out to be very good looking, and smart. He did not return the crush, and, in fact, still shunned girls in general. I've wondered if it was because of the traumatic experience I caused.

When I was in fourth grade, I developed a crush on Albert. I thought he was just the cutest thing. He was a friend of Cliff Thompson's, as they lived in the same neighborhood, and he treated me like poison. In fact, I think they actually called me that on occasion. That whole year, I suffered the agonies of the ignored, the rejected.

I got over Albert, and replaced my interest in him with interest in others over the next years. By ninth grade, he was short and round.

More Misadventures

Down the hill and around the corner from our home was a large Victorian house of the type that my mother adored. Three generations of Zabriskies lived there and the oldest grandchild, Rett, was my playmate. My mother had sent me, at age four, down on my own, through the intervening fields, to make his acquaintance when he was two. This was her way of creating an entree into their circle for herself. Their father was second generation nouveau riche, but their mother, a Wheelock, was old money.

One summer day when I was seven or eight, I enticed my playmate, Rett, his younger brother, Ricky, and my sister to go on an adventure exploring up the hill into upper Ridgewood. We were gone a little more than two hours with stops along the way when other children were in their yards. I had led my little band up one street and down another in order to see what we could see. I knew where we were at all times, having an excellent sense of direction. If we turned right, turned right again, and yet again, we would come back to Glen Avenue. The younger kids, however, didn't understand that logic, and by the time we came back under the railroad underpass into our neighborhood, they were whining and sniveling, and Nancy was outright bawling. The scene that awaited us gave me pause. My mother, Mrs. Zabriskie, and the police, were grouped together, watching the road.

After securing her children in her late model station wagon, Marian Zabriskie approached me. With her flaming red hair and platform shoes, she looked down her nose at me with a haughty stare, and, in her best Kathrine Hepburn tones, said, "Don't you ever set foot on our property again!" She was livid. She turned on her heel and slammed herself into the driver's seat of her car. The police, now that we were found, were amused. Unsuccessfully hiding their smiles, they got into their police car and left. My mother was red faced and almost speechless, and looked as though there was no hole big enough for her to hide in before the formidable Mrs. Zabriskie's anger. Mom saw her social aspirations going up in smoke as she grabbed my arm and pulled me along.

I was marched home and tied on the end of a rope, like a dog, to the apple tree in the side yard, on display for all who might glance that way while passing by on the road. There I remained for the afternoon until my father came home from work. He had been informed of my misbehavior because my parents communicated on the phone at 4:00 P.M. every day without fail. He released me from my leash and gave me a present he had brought. There was a twinkle in his eye.

Mom's Painting

Another of my mother's talents was painting and she returned to it several times throughout her life. I have several pieces of her work hanging in a guest room. One of her early works from college was a still life of three oranges on a blue plate. It hung for many years on Uncle Ned's kitchen wall, forlorn in a dime store frame. Uncle Ned loved it and wouldn't part with it. When I was at the house after his funeral, one of my cousins snatched it off the wall and thrust it into my hands. "Here. You might want this. Dad would never let us take it down and we all hated it."

The painting was certainly plain, but once I got it home, I took it to an expert framer and had it put into a beautiful wooden frame that picked up the gold-orange tone of the oranges. It looked like a credible primitive. The next time my cousins visited, they would not have recognized it if I hadn't called their attention to it.

Franklin Delano Roosevelt, and Other Political Observations

One year for Christmas, I received a new doll that was probably a precursor of the Barbie trend. It was a pretty, adult-shaped doll with beautiful thick, curly red hair. She came with a small wardrobe of pretty outfits and one of my passions at that time was making doll clothes. From an early age, I pieced together little items, the ones when I was quite young being very rough and frayed around the edges.

I sat on the floor for hours in front of our big, floor-model RCA radio, surrounded by my scraps of fabric and other sewing supplies, and whichever dolls or stuffed animals were due to have a new outfit. I listened to my favorite programs: *Captain Midnight,* and *Uncle Don,* before he got kicked off the air for saying, "That'll hold the little bastards for awhile," while the mike was still live.

It was during one of these sewing sessions in front of the radio when I was seven that I heard the announcement that Franklin Delano Roosevelt had died. Knowing how my parents revered him, I ran to find my mother, who was in the backyard, hanging wet clothes on the line. I felt very important being the one to break the news, but she didn't believe me at first. She dropped the clothes and ran into the house to hear it for herself on the radio. She began to weep. I didn't have much political savvy at that time but sensed that his death had been a great loss.

The next year, when I was far more mature with an expanded world view, my political astuteness soared. Whatever prompted my epiphany remains lost in the mists of time but I was riding in the car with my mother driving, and we were almost home. Realization hit me out of the blue, and I asked, "Do the Japs think we're bad and they're good?"

My Mother, the Girl Scout Leader

Included in my mother's image of the perfect mother, as outlined in her child-rearing book, was involvement in the child's activities. When I reached the appropriate age to become a Brownie, my mother volunteered to be the troop leader. Since that time I have seen other mothers take on that role, but without the singular devotion that Mom put into it. Once again, everything was organized to a tee from creative projects during meetings to cookouts and field trips. She had two or three co-leaders to assist her, but there was nothing co- about it. She was in charge. My mother did not stop when I became a Girl Scout, but "flew up" with me when I did.

One of the things Girl Scouts do is earn various badges reflecting an acquaintance with certain skills, deemed by Juliette Lowe, the scouting founder, to be suitable accomplishments for young women. In order to motivate the scouts to complete the required tasks, prizes were offered. I never won one of these coveted prizes, not even the sewing basket that was presented for the sewing badge, although I was sure my skirt was as well sewn as the winner's. And why was that? I could not be allowed to win a prize because that amorphous, disembodied group referred to by my mother as "people," might think she was showing favoritism. I think these "people" lived somewhere near those "neighbors" who were so concerned about our behavior.

One of my mother's talents was sewing, and she made dresses for me as a child. They had ruffles, sashes that tied in the back, and puffy sleeves. Sometimes they had lace with ribbon running through. She usually made our Halloween costumes, and she created my Princess Out-All-Night costume for a fourth-grade class play. I don't think I ever disliked anything she sewed for me. However, once I outgrew homemade clothing and was more interested in store-bought fashion, our tastes diverged. Her choices were deadly dull and ladylike while mine were more colorful and dramatic. This, of course, led to a frequent clash of wills. There were numerous items that she ordered for me from Sears, Roebuck or Montgomery Ward catalogs that were worn once, then hidden in the back of the closet, never to see daylight again. There were others that I chose that met the same fate, once I realized my error in judgment, but that was never confessed to my mother.

The Echo

All through elementary school, I was in scouting, and my mother continued to be the Girl Scout leader. When I was in the sixth grade, there was to be a competition with troops from other schools. Three one-act plays would ultimately be presented to the parents for an evening's entertainment. Each of several troops was given the scripts of all three to cast and rehearse. I was selected by my troop (my mother did not have the decision in this) to play the Echo in the play of the same name. Once our parts were learned and rehearsed, the divisional leader, Miss Davidson, or Davie, as she liked to be called, was to select who would perform the parts in the big evening production for the parents.

My mother was making the costumes for my play, *The Echo*. I watched as she made the cute, little, blue-flannel Echo suit with neatly bound holes for the arms and legs. The head was a hood of the same fabric with holes cut out for eyes, nose and mouth, then the features were embroidered around them, including long eyelashes. The Echo would wear *my* fuzzy, tan fleece slippers. I was eaten up alive inside with the desire to wear that costume in the production, but thought I had little hope of winning the competition. I assumed my mother would find a way to sabotage me as she gave no encouragement when I looked longingly at the progress of the Echo suit.

Judgment day came. My mother had no say in who won — it was all up to Davie, who selected me to play the Echo.

When Nancy was old enough to be a Brownie, Mom was teaching and didn't have time to become the leader of the troop. There were few other mothers willing to take on that job, so Nancy had a sketchy Brownie career, although she might have had a fair shot at winning prizes. When we moved to Katonah, New York, Nancy was in the sixth grade and she joined the Girl Scouts there. Again, our mother did not lead the troop, but still exercised her opinions about the activities.

The troop was taking a major trip to Washington, D.C., and Nancy wasn't allowed to go because she hadn't completed some requirement to qualify. It was actually something Mom was responsible for doing, some bit of paperwork, and she was furious that the leader would not let Nancy go. Our mother, of course, maintained that it was the leader's fault, not her own negligence of the issue that caused Nancy to miss the trip. Mom tried to reason with the leader, but Mom's idea of reasoning was to issue imperious edicts. Nancy stayed behind. Mom advised Nancy to quit the Girl Scouts, and could not understand when she refused. Mom felt that a great injustice had been done and she would have quit the troop in Nancy's place. Nancy did not quit. All her friends were in the troop.

Movies

When I was seven, I started going to the movies at the Warner Theatre in Ridgewood every Saturday afternoon with twelve-year-old Addie Orr from up the street. At first, Addie liked the company, but after a couple of years, she preferred her peers and considered me a hanger-on. She sometimes made me sit by myself, but I didn't care. I never informed my mother because I was happy just to be going. On Saturdays, the theatre was teeming with kids, but I shut them out and lost myself in the silver screen.

By the time I was ten, Addie was at an age where she was into boys, and I was very much in the way, so my mother sent me alone. My father chauffeured me in bad weather, and I called home when the movie let out. In nice weather, I walked home. In another year, my mother gave me an ultimatum: drag my sister along or stay home. I did not make Nancy sit alone. It was a delightfully long afternoon: a double feature, ten cartoons, a chapter of the serial, previews of coming attractions, and the MovieTone News. All for twenty-five cents. I loved it.

During the years with Addie, she took great delight in scaring me. When a frightening scene came on, I scrunched down in my seat, closed my eyes and held my ears with my arms tight against my head. During Alfred Hitchcock's *The Spiral Staircase*, with Dorothy Maguire as the heroine, the floozie, played by Rhonda Fleming, goes down to the dark cellar for something and George Brent, the psycho murderer, is hiding there (but you don't know yet that it's him). She has a candle. By now I was well tucked up into myself and not watching. Addie leaned over and said, "You can look now. It's over."

I looked up just in time to see Rhonda's elongated head. It was years before I could sleep with my closet door open. And, of course, I had to continue the tradition of terrorizing when I had my sister along.

The theatre itself had ornately painted walls with lights that dimmed just before the red velvet curtains opened, setting the mood for excitement, adventure, romance. The seats were also red velvet, and even the ladies' room was elegant, with a velvet-curtained entrance. The plush-carpeted lobby had a big counter where you could buy candy, soda and, in later years, popcorn. The balcony was always closed during the matinee to discourage kids from getting into mischief. The ushers had enough to do in the main theatre. The manager was Mr. Costa, a short, round, moustached, jovial fellow. I remember him as jovial because he laughed on the day I told him my plans to be a movie star.

When those red velvet curtains opened, there it was! Life in all its twists and turns. Much of what was shown in the Saturday afternoon matinees was family fare with comedies like *Cheaper by the Dozen*, or *Mr. Belvedere*, both with Clifton Webb, prevailing. There were musicals like *Easter Parade*, with Fred Astaire and Judy Garland, swashbucklers like *Captain Blood*, with Errol Flynn, and westerns with Alan Ladd or Randolph Scott. My fascination with Queen Elizabeth I was born at the movies when I saw *Young Bess*, starring Jean Simmons.

When the matinee program ended at 6:00, the ushers swept through with their flashlights, attempting to corral the kids and herd them toward the exits. My game was to elude them so I could stay to see the first showing of the evening feature. My father didn't come until I called home, so I was free to stay as long as I could succeed at evading the enemy.

It was then that I was introduced to the magnetism of stars like Bogart and Bacall in *Dark Passage* and *To Have and Have Not*. "Just put your lips together and blow." I absorbed Gene Tierney in *Laura*, with Clifton Webb in quite a different role from his comedy appearances, Jane Wyman and Lew Ayres in *Johnny Belinda*, and Olivia DeHaviland and Montgomery Clift in *The Heiress*. My big regret was that one Saturday the usher caught me and made me leave just as the plot of *Gilda*, with Rita Hayworth and Glenn Ford, was unfolding.

I had been to the movies before I started going with Addie. My father took me to see *Bambi*, one of the most traumatic children's movies ever made. One doesn't have to see Bambi's mother drop down dead, when the shot is heard, to know what her fate is. To my five-year-old mind, it was actually happening at that moment. I sobbed with grief and haven't been able to even think of killing an animal since. For years after seeing that movie, I took all my stuffed animals and animal-shaped toys — even wooden ones — to bed with me to keep them safe at night. It made for a very crowded bed and probably explains why, all these years later, I don't move much in my sleep.

My parents took me to other movies as well. When I was in fourth grade, my mother kept me out of school for an afternoon to take me to see *Bells of St. Mary's*. She believed Ingrid Bergman and Bing Crosby were good enough reasons to miss school, and perhaps they were. In her mind, the religious theme of the movie justified my truancy. When I was older, my father took me to see *Gentlemen's Agreement*, with Gregory Peck. My sense of injustice regarding antisemitism stemmed from this film, and other of my ethical views would also be influenced by movies that I saw as a child.

Discrimination against other races was not expressed at home, and derogatory labels were not used, although I eventually learned that my parents held some negative and discriminatory views. My sense of ethics was formed by films where, in those days, justice usually triumphed. True love and fair play won in the end.

As a child, I lived for those Saturdays. I was going to grow up and be like Cyd Charisse and dance around gracefully in a floating, flame-red dress. I would be Ginger Rogers dancing to paradise with

Fred Astaire or Dan Dailey. I would be Judy Garland in *Meet Me in St. Louis*, hanging off a trolley car as I sang. The heck with Captain Blood's love interest — I could play a pirate myself and learn to use a sword. I was sure I could ride a horse with the best cowboy hero.

On the occasions when I was able to evade the ushers, there were the black and whites — the "films noir." Robert Mitchum, Dana Andrews, James Cagney, Barbara Stanwyck, Bette Davis, Bogart and Bacall. All larger than life. And I would not just act in movies. I would travel to exotic places. I would have adventures. And the serials. Each chapter always ended with a cliff-hanger, and I couldn't wait to see what happened the following week. I saw almost all fifteen chapters of *The Mask of the Red Death* and *Wild Bill Hickok*. Movies were my reality, my life.

When I came home from the movies, my mother paid for her afternoon of freedom. My family could look forward (or not) to a blow-by-blow recap of the stories of both features — and the first showing of the evening feature as well, if it had been a lucky day, with intonations and gestures, every innuendo of plot, every facial expression and a description of the costumes and scenery. That was the Saturday night dinner table entertainment. My mother had all she could do to keep me in my seat as I demonstrated various scenes while my father smiled indulgently. We were a long time at the table.

One Sunday morning, not many years ago, I turned on the TV and was flipping through channels. A scene caught my eye and I stopped. A man in a hat and a trench coat was walking down a city street past some brownstones. His hat was pulled down over his eyes and it was raining. I said aloud to myself, "Laura." Just then, he walked up some steps to the doorway of a brownstone and rang the bell. Close-up of his face. Dana Andrews. Then the Laura theme began in the background.

How did I know from that little clip of action? There was nothing to indicate what it was — unless it was so ingrained in my brain that a moment could trigger recognition. I had seen that movie only once in the theatre and maybe once on TV. The degree to which I had internalized these movies became apparent in a moment of illumination. I can visualize in vivid detail the settings, music, costumes, facial expressions and scraps of dialogue with their inflections. Yet I can't remember a mathematical formula from one day to the next.

I never became a movie star although I did major in drama in college. I was supposed to major in English, but once away from parental control, I changed to follow my interest. When the moment of truth arrived, and I had my chance to follow the dream in the real world after college, and follow an acting career, I found that I liked eating more. I sold out for a steady paycheck. But now I have more than 400 DVDs, including *The Spiral Staircase*, and I can watch Rhonda Fleming's head elongate and never flinch.

CHAPTER 8

Misadventures, Friendships, and Dad

Graydon Pool

When I was a child, my mother saw to it that I had swimming lessons. Certainly, when we were sailing on *The Vagabond*, I already knew how to paddle around with confidence in the water and had no fear of it. In Ridgewood, we were fortunate to have the most elegant public swimming facility at Graydon Pool. I grew up thinking every town had such a place and was sorely disillusioned then we moved to Katonah some years later. Graydon Pool was only about a half-mile from our house, and we went there often in summer.

I remember that it was perfectly round and looked like a small lake within a landscaped park. It took up a whole block. All summer, you could see bathers sprawled out on blankets on the grass under the trees around the edges. The bottom was sandy, and, although deep in one area for the more advanced swimmers, it graduated to a beach-like edge with a low stone wall around the perimeter. There was an area blocked off for kayaks at one end, in the middle of which was a small, round, stone-edged island with grass, and one weeping willow tree in the center. The grass was always neatly mowed and, it occurs to me, they must have floated a mower out to it. There was a large area for younger children, with two rafts and a water slide, and a raft with a diving board for advanced swimmers, as well as a high-dive tower in the third section. You were really grown up if you could go to the third raft.

To reach the pool area, one crossed the Ho-Ho-Kus Brook via a picturesque, but sturdy, wooden footbridge from the parking lot. There was a low stone building off to the right, housing the office where you bought your season badge, as well as showers and toilets. I don't recall any snacks or drinks being available at first, but later this convenience was added. We frequently brought our lunch to the pool, then had to wait the obligatory hour for it to digest before jumping in. Wading on the edge in anticipation was torture.

There was a channel for a small tributary from the brook so water could enter the pool. When I was older, and more often in the third raft area, I discovered there was also an exit channel for the water, flowing out under a small bridge, back to the brook, to keep the level of the water in the pool from flooding. The entrance and exit channels were lined with cemented stone. The entrance channel also flowed under another small footbridge, some of the water being diverted to a heavily chlorinated wading pool at the side. Bathers were encouraged to wade here to clean their feet before entering the main pool. I don't recall if the water in the main pool was chlorinated as well. There were fountains in the boat area that frequently aerated the water and there was a constant flow in and out of the pool, so perhaps chlorinating was not necessary.

When I was little, of course, I went to the pool with my mother, and sometimes my father. The water slide was a big favorite, my father waiting to catch me at the bottom. It was very high, and I would let go, and slide down screaming with pleasure. There was always a long line of kids all the way up the steps, so it would be several minutes before I could repeat the slide. My mother preferred to sit in the shade and read.

As I grew older and became a more proficient swimmer, I was able to swim first to the first raft, where the water was not too deep, then to the second raft where it was a little deeper. At that point, I was in upper elementary school. By this age, I was often allowed to go with Addie Orr, my movie companion from up the street. My mother could convince herself that I was being well watched by Addie and the lifeguards. However, between Addie's preoccupation with her friends (and the lifeguards), and the lifeguards' preoccupation with the bevy of girls hovering around them, I may as well have been alone. I survived.

When I was in junior high school, I was allowed to walk to the pool unattended and sometimes made to take my sister. I now preferred to be in the grown-up area by the third raft. Fortunately, I had a fear of heights by then, and never chanced the high dive, but I swam to the raft, dove from its diving board, and flirted with the high school boys who were found there. My sister was somewhere around, hopefully not drowned. I gave her little thought. I, like my mother and Addie, assumed the lifeguards would watch out for her.

Jersey Shore

The summer when I was six, we began spending my father's weeks off at the Jersey shore, renting a cottage from various of my father's co-workers. Several people in his office owned one. At first, we stayed in Breton Woods on the Metedeconk River, two different summers at two different cottages. This very wide river had the advantage that you could wade far out before the bottom dropped off to deeper water. Breton Woods was a small shore-edge community with a clubhouse where activities were provided for the children, and I remember spending a rainy day making a hammered metal ashtray when no one at home smoked — except for my mother's semi-annual cigarette. I found these activities extremely boring, but when it rained, there was not much alternative. In the evenings, the clubhouse also provided some diversion for the adults, but my parents didn't participate. Other families brought teenage girls with them to babysit, but our sitters were usually elderly and didn't leave home.

The first cabin we stayed in was small and brown, and had an ice box rather than a refrigerator. In the morning, we waited for the ice man who delivered a large block of ice and placed it into the box with giant tongs. We were discouraged from opening the lid too frequently lest we melt the ice prematurely.

The second cabin was much larger, with two stories, and belonged to the Beveridge family. It had a cathedral ceiling in the center with a balcony all around, off of which were bedrooms. Some bedrooms, used by the owners, were closed off, but there was still plenty of room for us in the others. Nancy and I played tag along the balcony, to my parents' dismay. They were afraid we would manage to fall over the railing onto the floor below, or do some damage to the house. We didn't.

It turned out that the purpose of these vacations was to see how we liked the shore, then to give my parents the opportunity of finding their own cottage. They looked at many, but could not find one they liked. In order to get something suitable in their price range (*The Vagabond* had been sold to finance this project) they bought land on which to build. They found a waterfront property on Beaver Creek in the Midstreams development, on the other side of a peninsula that divided it from the Metedeconk River. Princeton Avenue ran down the center of the peninsula for several miles, with waterfront houses on either side. Both the river and the creek flowed into the same bay but Beaver Creek was narrower and shallower all along, and originated a little farther inland from Midstreams, in a marsh. There was a long, narrow island across the lagoon that fronted our property, and continued down along our neighbors' beach fronts. It was about thirty feet across to the island, which was only about fifteen feet wide at its broadest point, and in the hottest weather, it caused our protected lagoon to reach bathtub temperatures. The deal was struck, and work began on our house. A well was drilled, and an outside pump installed.

My father had bargained for the shell of the house, planning to finish it off himself over time. Some weekends he would go down alone to work on it, to not subject us any more than necessary to the discomforts of camping. My mother helped him as well as she could when we all went down there. He knew the limitations of her construction talents and called on her only for specific tasks, such as holding one end of something while he hammered.

As the building progressed, we made more frequent trips to the shore. There was no Garden State Parkway yet, and the Friday night traffic was bumper to bumper as it wound through towns and residential areas. The car was not air-conditioned, so hot air blew in through the open windows. Gerda, our Norwegian Elkhound, would make the trip with us, scrunched in at my mother's feet in the front, panting, while Nancy and I, in the back seat, fussed and listened to Lucille Ball in *My Favorite Wife*, on the radio. Sometimes our mother would drive for awhile. If she did, Gerda threw up. Gerda never threw up when my father drove. The highlight of the trip was the stop for dinner at Howard Johnson's, and selecting one of the twenty-eight flavors of ice cream for dessert.

Until our house was livable, we slept in the car, my father contriving various arrangements to make us more comfortable. One of the most claustrophobic was when he placed wide boards across the backs of the seats going from front to back. As they were taller, our parents slept on the top layer, while we, being shorter, slept crosswise on the front and back seats. We did this once, for one night. I don't know where poor Gerda spent that night. And, of course, there were mosquitoes.

My father traded in our green Buick for a blue Nash, which was one of the first cars to offer seats that folded down into a bed. Even with that, the night of the next trip to the shore was still spent in restless tossing and turning. We stopped at a gas station before arriving at our property to perform our evening ablutions, and ventured out early in the morning for the same purpose. Our toilet for emergencies was a hole dug behind some bushes off to the side of the yard. One of the first tasks on our arrival, before we even went into the house, was to prime the pump so we would have water. After sitting in the well shaft for a week or more, it ran rusty orange at first, then clear but with a brackish taste.

Goaded on by the discomforts we endured, my parents soon contrived a way for us to sleep in the house, there being enough floor laid down to fit some army cots. Soon after the flooring was completed, we arrived one Friday night, weary after our long, hot journey. We opened the car door and Gerda leapt out for a much-needed run. She would always return to us after relieving herself, and getting a little exercise, and come into the house for the night.

This particular night, however, she made a beeline for a yet unfilled window opening into the crawlspace under the house. We heard yelping and a commotion, and she emerged a few moments later, a skunk close behind. I'm not sure how their entanglement played out, but we were spared the smell of skunk spray in the crawlspace. Gerda was not so fortunate. At that late hour, my parents had to spend some time washing her down, with only a slight reduction of the odor. We had not had the foresight to bring tomato juice with us, the home remedy to counteract the smell of skunk. We got through the night, isolating Gerda in one unfinished room, and tomato juice was procured early the next day and applied. After several dousings, she was just bearable enough for us to endure the return trip home on Sunday with her in the car.

One of the first families that came to visit us at the shore was Uncle Ned's. Uncle Ned was the sort of man who had smile lines around his eyes. As I said before, my sister and I loved him. I remember that I acted hurtfully to him during that visit. Our country was involved in the Cold War with Russia at the time, and Stalin was in his heyday. Uncle Ned refused permission for my cousins to join us in some activity I had devised. I was at a brazen age, and in a fit of pique, I called him "Stalin's Brother." Instead of being angry, he was hurt and dismayed. Had he responded with anger, I could have smirked with self-satisfaction. As it was, I felt guilty and ashamed. As much as I had saddened him, however, he did not relent, and the issue was dropped for that evening.

Girls' Club

While the house continued toward completion at a tortoise pace, we were now able to enjoy it. There was a Finnish family building a house next door and they had a girl my age, Sylvia. We soon met Carol and Linda from elsewhere in Midstreams, and Sue from Princeton Avenue. Carol lived there year-round and Sylvia would, too, once her house was finished. The rest of us were summer people. Sue's house faced the river on the other side of the avenue, a fact that offered variety to our adventures. We became a little group, and we biked or walked from one house to another, dispersing to our homes for meals, then joining up again after lunch (and the inescapable nap in my case). It was during the time of polio, and the son of one of my mother's church friends had contracted it and was encased in an iron lung. She was determined that we would not become ill.

During those summers we spent hours swimming in the bathtub-warm water of the lagoon, crabbing with bits of bacon tied to the end of a string, then scooping them into a crab net. Sometimes the crabs managed to escape with the bacon. We would mess about in our rowboat to which an outboard motor was eventually added. If our father came out to call us in for a rest or a meal when we were swimming, I would ignore him for as long as possible by ducking under the water when I saw him approach, pretending that I didn't hear him. When my mother called us, we would come as quickly as we could because we knew she meant business.

As I grew older and taller, I could touch bottom all the way across the lagoon to the island, but neither I nor any of the other girls liked to. The bottom was slimy muck, and Sue informed us that sally-growlers lived in it. None of us really believed in sally-growlers, but we didn't want to take a chance. At worst, there were crabs that would grab our toes.

Sylvia's family had been living in a small, improvised shack while working on their house. When it was finished and they moved in, the shack was scheduled to be torn down. I saw them taking it apart in sections, and had an idea — it would be perfect as a clubhouse for us. The other girls jumped at the plan, but the problem was to find a place to reconstruct it. We canvassed the five sets of parents, most of whom vetoed the idea of having the ugly structure in their yards. Carol's house was on a double lot with the second one behind, continuing out to a back dirt road. Her parents offered the space behind their garage, where it would be out of sight from the front and not detract from their well-kept yard.

The problem now was that Carol lived a distance away from where the sections of the shack lay. Between us we could probably carry the sections a short distance, but not the half-mile down the road to the new location. River travel — or creek travel, in this case — was the obvious solution. I suggested that we carry the sections to the creek in front of Sylvia's house, and float them to a small beach not far from Carol's. We would have to traverse a short dirt track connecting the beach to the main road, then go just a few hundred yards to the site. The plan actually worked well; there was a little awkwardness when we steered the pieces through the water, as we swam alongside to guide them. It took a couple of days to get all of the shack down there, but finally the sections lay on the ground out behind Carol's garage. We were pleased with ourselves.

Now to get the shack reassembled. We looked at each other. We were pretty good at having ideas, especially me, but carpenter skills? We made some half-hearted suggestions and vague gestures about how we would tackle this next challenge. The long and the short of it was that Carol's father and younger brother reassembled the sections, and our clubhouse was finished. We used it for the remainder of that summer. By the next summer, we had reached a new stage of development, and the clubhouse sat forsaken. Carol's father eventually tore it down, and I think they burned the sections on their back lot.

Cats at the Shore and Other Misadventures

Carol had a gray tiger cat named Pepper. Having my beloved Angel torn from my arms at an early age no doubt led to my need for association with felines. I don't think I had a cat at home during my early years at the shore, but if I did, it did not come on vacation with us. Carol's cat was my substitute, and soon learned to run when he saw me coming. Her parents were amused at the way I cried out and lunged toward the poor animal whenever I saw him. Sometimes I actually caught the unfortunate beast, and it would be mauled and cuddled until he finally engineered an escape. Often he outran me and hid, and I would philosophically wait for the next opportunity to grab him.

The summer after the clubhouse adventure, we wandered farther afield through the still-undeveloped areas of Midstreams. The development is probably now a jungle of houses and paved roads, but at that time, even the water's edge was sparsely built up. We came across a small, old, beached boat wreck, curiously about a mile inland, derelict and full of holes, parts torn off and the whole, a weathered gray. That year's project was to reclaim it, make it seaworthy — or at least creek worthy — so that it could be our new clubhouse. Of course, this was again my idea. It didn't go very far, being an impossible and impractical task. We took a few licks at it with our non-existent carpentry skills, and deserted it.

Sue had a big sister Barbara, nicknamed Boo, who was in college at Colby. Boo had an old sailboat, a skiff, and she passed it down to Sue. We were delighted. Now we could sail. Of course, none of us knew how, my early experiences on *The Vagabond* not having prepared me to sail a skiff. We whacked ourselves in the head a few times with the boom, attempted to bail out the water that had collected in the bottom, and generally made feeble attempts to figure it out. Boo was rarely around and Sue's parents, who were always entertaining guests or preparing to do so, seemed to have no inclination to give us any pointers. Perhaps this was like my parents giving me skis, then providing no real opportunity to use them. The sailboat went the way of the skis, and ended up beached in front of Sue's house. She had two cats named Nit and Wit, but they were much better than Carol's cat, Pepper, at eluding me.

Movies Again

We never had a television at the shore, so on Saturday nights, our whole family would go to the movies after dinner. Mom continued her slavish devotion to routines, however, and the dinner dishes — sans dishwasher — had to be washed before we could leave. This job fell to Nancy and me, but hurry as we might, we usually arrived at the theatre after the feature had started. Nancy resented missing the beginning of the movie, but I managed to live with seeing the beginning at the end by staying to see what we had missed. It never occurred to our mother to serve dinner a little earlier on Saturday evenings. Nancy vowed never to allow routines to rule her life and make her late for the movies.

Flying Rocks

When I was in elementary school, children who lived within walking distance did not take the school bus. Walking distance was considered to be at least two miles. Today, children who live across the street from schools are bussed. I lived more than a half-mile from the school and had to cross a dangerous intersection to get home. However, it had a traffic light, so school officials presumed that I had the intelligence to wait for it to turn green.

Children who lived in Ho-Ho-Kus, on the side closer to Ridgewood, also went to my school and were within the walking radius. I often walked as far as my corner with Billy Schnitzer. He would then continue his solitary journey on to his home. Billy was an inoffensive individual, somewhat shy. At school, he was on the fringe. He and I got along fine, walking home, never discussing anything important; at worst, we did some sporadic arguing.

When we were in the fourth grade, we were still walking together occasionally, by chance — nothing planned. However, lines between boy things and girl things were starting to be drawn. One afternoon he ran on ahead and I thought nothing of it. When I approached the bridge across the Ho-Ho-Kus Brook, Billy darted out from under the abutment where he had been waiting, and I suddenly felt a sharp pain in my forehead. Blood flowed down my face. Through the red haze, I saw Billy running off up the road toward Ho-Ho-Kus, and no one else in sight. I never saw the rock.

I was close to home, and although sobbing and scared, I knew I could make it. I carefully waited for the light, still sobbing, then crossed the road. The only vehicle in sight now was a pick-up truck coming down the hill toward me. When the driver saw me, he slowed and called out the window. "Little girl! Are you okay? Can I give you a ride home?" He sounded very concerned and I must have presented quite a picture. Blood was everywhere.

Remembering what my mother had taught me about accepting rides from strangers, I replied as calmly and politely as possible, choking back sobs, "No, thank you. I live just up the hill."

"Are you sure?" He sounded doubtful, and, in hindsight, I truly believe he was acting out of concern.

Trying to appear in control of my situation, I continued to repress the sobs. "Yes, I'm fine."

With some reluctance, he drove away, glancing back in my direction with a worried look.

I had continued to walk during this exchange and had almost reached my driveway. I ran into the house, where I found my mother in the kitchen. She reacted with outrage once she had heard my tale. She marched me up to the bathroom and washed the greater part of the blood off my face and hands — I had used them to try to wipe some of it away myself. The wound was minuscule.

Mom then announced, "Billy Schnitzer should see just what he has done — and so should his mother! We're going to let his mother see just what her son has done."

I was horrified and embarrassed, but she left no room for argument, dragging me by my arm to the car. As we rode along, I hoped against hope that no one would be home when we arrived. But they were. Billy was an only child, his mother's darling. When my mother called her to the door to display my now clotted and all but invisible wound, Mrs. Schnitzer rose on her dignity, effectively dismissing my mother. She stated cooly that she would deal with her son. My mother marched me back to the car.

When my father came home and saw the small bandage that now covered the wound, and heard the story, he couldn't quite equate the unimpressive wound site with what he heard from my mother about the enormity of the event. He was, of course, sorry for me, but felt that my mother had over reacted, embarrassing me. It was her wounded pride — the idea that someone had attacked *her* daughter, that had prompted our flight to Ho-Ho-Kus, that did no good in the long run.

The next day, both Billy and I were called to Mr. Maggio's office where a peace conference was held. Mr. Maggio was the principal. It seems that the other boys had started teasing Billy about walking home with me, with taunts that I was his girlfriend. Of course, nothing was further from the truth, and I was indignant when I heard it. Billy and I agreed that we would let bygones be bygones, but between ourselves, we avowed we would not walk together again.

My Father Defends Me

Two years later, when I was in sixth grade, all the kids were out on the playground at lunchtime. Some were about to start on their walk home for their noon meal, while others waited for rides from parents. I don't remember how it started, but a group of boys had cornered me against a chain-link fence at the edge of the playground, and were tormenting me by throwing a basketball at my legs. My father, who was at home that day for some reason, was the one to pick me up, and he witnessed this scene. He sent me to the car while he attempted to use reason with the boys, ever the peacemaker. When he returned to the car, he told me not to worry, they would be my friends now. Like an idiot, I believed him. Dad was very innocent about many things, and the nature of boys on the playground was one of them. Intimidation was the only thing they would have understood, and my father was not one to do that.

Anyway, I was happy all through lunch and couldn't wait for the afternoon at school to begin with my new friends. When I got to the classroom, I boasted to my classmates about this turnaround. I was mortified when the boys laughed and told me they had only said what my father wanted to hear, and had no intention, then or ever, of being my friends. That was when I discovered that my father was only human, but I didn't view it so benignly at the time. My first reaction was a feeling of betrayal.

By the time I was in seventh grade, I had accepted my father's human limitations, so when I ran into a problem with my worst enemy, Richard, I didn't expect much more than sympathy from the well-intentioned man. Richard was a big boy, and I suppose some would say he was handsome. I never thought him so because he had a mean streak that, for some reason, was often directed at me. His eyes glittered and his mouth formed a cruel sneer. In high school, he somehow ended up in the popular group — at least for awhile — but to me he was just a big, nasty, bully.

On this particular day, I had worn a dressy dress and stockings to school because I was going somewhere afterwards. This was like waving a red flag in front of a bull because, ordinarily, Richard didn't get so obviously physical with his tormenting. Like most bullies, he was a coward at heart — a push here, a furtive pinch there, a nasty remark under his breath. In math class, he sat across the aisle and back one seat, but, with his long legs, he could reach my feet.

Whenever the teacher, Mr. Holt, looked away, there was Richard, kicking viciously at my stockinged ankles. I tried to keep my feet away from him but something blocked me on the other side. I must have made some noise, because Mr. Holt looked my way, pointedly stopping his explanation, and glared at me as if I were the wrong-doer. Out of the corner of my eye, I could see Richard smirking. I looked down at my stockings which by now were full of snags and runs. I would gladly have stepped on Richard's face.

I don't remember what was done about my appearance for whatever the event was that I had dressed for, but when my father heard about this incident, he was enraged. He seldom became enraged, so it was a noteworthy occurrence. Dad decided to call Richard's mother, who used some colorful language on the phone. My father had been civil to her, explaining what had happened calmly but firmly. I can only guess what she said, judging from my father's sputtering, and the alarming change in his color. I could hear her screaming. Dad was not given to profanity, and he finally slammed down the phone, not having been able to inject another word. I don't remember what he said to me other than that Richard's mother was a very rude woman, but I did understand that, through it all, his concern was more for me and the pain and humiliation I had endured from Richard, than for his own ego. This differed vastly from my mother's motivation.

I was gratified later in high school when Richard was smitten with one of the most popular girls, Susan. I had grown up with her, and, although we were never actually friends, she had never been unkind to me. They were an item for awhile, and then she dumped him. I figured she probably found out what a bully he was.

Agatha

I had another friend who lived in Ho-Ho-Kus besides Billy Schnitzer. In fact, she lived across the street from him. I don't remember her in kindergarten; perhaps she was in the afternoon group and I went in the morning. But Agatha sat across the aisle from me in first grade, in Miss Johnson's class. Agatha wore her sandy-colored hair in two pigtails pulled away from her round, freckled face. She was chubby and bossy. In first grade, she tried very hard to make me write with my right hand, making me feel that there was perhaps something wrong with being left-handed. Fortunately, Miss Johnson was young and modern in her outlook, and diligent about telling Agatha to mind her own business. In the end, Agatha had no influence about which hand I wrote with.

This friend did, however, exert another, more sinister influence on my life, one that has filtered down to haunt me even now. From an early age I was a firm believer in fairy tales and the honesty of others. Therefore, I believed Agatha when she told me that she was my only friend and that I was lucky to have her or I would have no one.

Nursery schools were not yet in vogue, and my preschool experiences had been limited to family, neighborhood and family trips. I learned to get around my parents, and then to dominate my sister. The year before starting school, I also dominated Rett, since he was younger. I was the alpha child, used to being in charge. Once I started school with children my own age, I soon learned that they did not take kindly to being ordered around. I began to have self-doubts and acquired an intense shyness when with my peers. Therefore, I was easy prey for Agatha's assertions regarding my alleged inferiority. I struggled against this for the rest of my life and continue to live with the aftereffects. It partially explains the solace I experienced from the world of films when I eventually began attending the Saturday matinees starting in second grade.

Throughout elementary school, Agatha was, indeed, my only friend. Looking back, I can see that her motive was to protect herself from being friendless, but at the time, it was a self-fulfilling prophecy. I became unsure at times, aggressive at times, and except for short intervals when other associations were attempted, Agatha was in fact my only friend at school.

My mother observed this phenomenon and tried to combat it, as she did not consider Agatha a suitable companion for me. Her family was not in the social sphere that my mother had targeted, and that was possibly valid under the circumstances. My friendship with Agatha was not constructive. She did not share my creative or adventurous interests. She was merely someone to be with.

There were two girls in my class, Joanne and Carolyn, who had been inseparable since starting school, and their mothers felt that introducing a third person into their friendship would reduce its intensity. My mother became a party to that plan, and I was to be the third person. The mothers arranged playdates, and I was invited to birthday parties. However, you cannot force children who do not have an affinity for each other, to develop friendship. It might have gone better if my mother had not made me privy to the reasons for being thrown together with these two girls, but that awareness made me constrained around them. In any case, it did not work out. I liked them, we got along. But no bond was forged, and the plan soon fizzled. Agatha was back in control.

It remained thus until junior high school, when there was a larger pool to draw from for friends. No one stands out above another, but I did have short periods of friendship with different girls. However, I still didn't know how to be part of the group, conforming to the group's norms. I expressed my ideas too openly, and those ideas by now were strongly influenced by the movies that I saw or books I read. I made my peers uncomfortable. I dreaded lunchtime in the large cafeteria at Benjamin Franklin Junior High School because once my tray was full, it was the moment to face the problem of finding someone to eat with and possible rejection. I was usually able to spot a friendly face, but the specter always loomed.

At home, throughout most of elementary school, I still had Rett when there was no one else available whom his mother deemed more suitable. Whenever one of her socialite friends was expected to bring her offspring to play, I was told in no uncertain terms, that my presence would not be welcome. However, she could not fill his every afternoon with playdates, and there were many times when I was it. I had my little band that included Rett, his brother, Ricky, and my sister. When the Demarais moved in across the street into the old Cameron place, Johnny was included as well. For the most part, we still followed my ideas, and when Rett tired of giving in to them, he would draw himself up, and borrowing his mother's imperious tone, order, "Get off my property!" I would leave, but return the next day, and we would continue on as before.

By the time I reached junior high, the groundwork was already laid in the world of school, and with the added havoc wreaked by puberty, I was a morass of insecurity and self-doubt. I was socially on the fringe, not knowing how to make friends, always uncomfortable in a crowd. The in-crowd rejected me, although most of the girls were not overtly cruel. One on one, some of them were even friendly toward me at times. I disdained those in the lower strata, the other fringe dwellers like myself, finally breaking away from Agatha. At home, when I had reached the upper elementary grades, Rett and I were on separate tracks according to our interests, and the two-year difference in our ages became more vast. By the end of sixth grade, we seldom saw each other. My world was the world of movies, books and theatre. As long as someone else wrote the script, I could act it out. I spent my time traveling between the heights of joy when someone befriended me, and the depths of despair when I was excluded.

Leeches

There were several other escapades that I engineered during my later elementary school years, my imagination ever active. One of my occasional friends was Joan Sawyer, who lived in Ho-Ho-Kus, in a pretty, old farmhouse, on the banks of the Ho-Ho-Kus Brook. Her father was some sort of New York executive, and she was a studious girl. I enjoyed spending time with her on the rare occasions when she wasn't studying. An invitation to her house was a treat. After offering our services as detectives to the local police one day, which they, to their credit, accepted straight faced and politely, I suggested to Joan that it would be great fun to float down the brook in inner tubes, the primary beach toy at that time, to the corner of my street by the bridge. My mother could then drive her back home. Joan agreed and we found two tubes in her family's collection in a shed. We had on old shorts and shirts so were ready to go.

The Ho-Ho-Kus Brook was not deep, but it was very rocky. There were no dangerous rapids, as the water was shallow, but in some places the water moved swiftly enough to make it a piece of work to steer ourselves around and over the rocks. We were exhausted once we reached our goal, and knew we would never attempt it again. It had not been as much fun as we thought. As we gratefully climbed out of the water by the bridge at my corner, we caught sight of each other's legs. Leeches! We both had several on our legs. We screamed, then tried pulling them off, but they were stuck tight. We ran, still screaming, up the hill. Fortunately, my mother had the solution. Salt! The beastly things loosened their grip and fell off. I don't remember that I was invited again to Joan's after that.

When I later saw *The African Queen*, I knew just what Humphrey Bogart was going through after he pulled the boat through the reeds.

Halloween and Other Holidays

Many of the traditions held in our little family had their roots in my mother's earlier life. Her experiences on the island, and the attitudes she breathed in with the air at her home there, directly affected my early years. Some were hallowed and carried on. Others were rebelled against and Nancy and I rode the countercurrent.

Halloween was one of my favorite holidays. I think I liked it even better than Christmas. It was an action holiday. There was something about running free through the dark in the crisp night that was exhilarating and scary at the same time. When I was little, my mother made our costumes, then she would take us around the neighborhood, after which my father would drive us farther afield to their other friends to show us off.

Among my parents' friends from church were the Emigs who lived by the cemetery. One Halloween, when I was still old enough to be gullible, we stopped at the Emigs' house. Norm Emig was something of a prankster, and thought Halloween was a perfect time to display his talents. He had his trick all ready for unwary kids. He called me into the kitchen where my father was having coffee with him and his wife, Dretta. I should have guessed something was up by the sly grin on his face.

"Do you want to see my World War II souvenir?" he asked, all innocence. He had been in the military.

"Sure." Why not.

He pulled out a small box of the size earrings would come in. "It's the thumb of a Jap." He removed the lid.

There, before my horrified eyes, in a nest of red-stained cotton, was a thumb. I shrank away, screaming, and ran back to the living room where I had left his daughter, Phyllis. She was laughing hysterically.

"You fell for it! He sure fooled you. That's his own thumb. He loves to pull that trick on people, especially at Halloween. He just put mercurochrome on the cotton to make it look like blood. He sticks his thumb in through a hole in the end of the box." I was red-faced at having been taken in, but had to agree it was a good trick. I never forgot it.

When I was in upper elementary school, we were allowed to go trick-or-treating by ourselves, and Rett and Ricky were allowed to go with us. Their mother had long since forgotten the episode of the exploration trip. I remember finding my way by the back path, in the dark with a flashlight, adrenaline flowing, down to Rett's house to pick him up along with his brother. Nancy trailed behind, complaining that I was going too fast down the path. We collected the boys, received instructions from their mother, then set off up their back driveway and over to the path that ran behind the four houses on my street.

We had to run; the night invited it. We ran like the wind, our feet flying over the ground in the dark on a trail well-known to us. Joy welled up in us and spilled over into conspiratorial laughter. From house to house we went, collecting our loot, running in between. There was a Halloween moon, and one could imagine bats and witches flying across its bright face. Once we had exhausted every house we knew — and some we didn't — in our area, we returned to our home, dropping Rett and Ricky off on the way. Dad then took up his duty of driving us farther afield.

I remember bits and pieces of Halloweens, but what I remember most is the feeling of invincibility and exhilaration we felt on that particular night, that particular Halloween, racing through the dark, over the lawns, down the paths.

At Easter we colored eggs and got new clothes — including hats. We wore little white gloves. Easter morning there were baskets of candy waiting, and some years there were other presents as well. It depended on my mother's mood. The colored eggs were supposedly hidden by the Easter Bunny, and we hunted for them while our mother prepared breakfast. Then came Sunday School where we had no doubt rehearsed some special presentation for our parents.

Thanksgiving was a turkey feast. We often had our Frith grandparents join us for dinner, and sometimes other relatives as well. One Thanksgiving Aunt Gladys and Uncle Arthur were there. Donny, their youngest son, was with them, but I don't remember that the other cousins were. They were older and were probably either away at school or out on their own.

Fantasia was playing at the Warner Theatre, and, after dinner, we were allowed to go, in Donny's care, to see it. It was the only time I didn't tell the whole story of the movie on my return, possibly because my mother didn't want her sister's family to realize how familiar I was with going to the movies and re-enacting the stories.

Christmas

Grandma Cole always sent us money for our Christmas tree. That was our family present from her. She never sent individual gifts. It was a tradition that my mother carried on as well, although she did give gifts to her grandchildren when they were small. In later years, that was all we received from her, although she could have well afforded more.

Nancy and I went with Dad to pick out the tree several days before it was to be put up, so we would have it before the supply was picked over. Dad put up the tree like an engineer, fastening it with wires from the top on two sides to window frames so it would not fall over. He would then string the lights and put the star on top. As we got a little older, it was then up to Nancy and me to finish the rest.

There would just be a light supper Christmas Eve, nothing special. I remember only once or twice going to the candlelight service at church that ended at midnight, and that was when I was in high school. Nancy and I were encouraged to go to bed early to give Santa Claus the chance to get all his work done. Once she and I were past the age of believing, we would help bring the presents out (they had diminished in number by that time) and place our own along with those from my parents and other family members who had sent gifts.

When I was young, I tried to stay awake as long as possible to see Santa Claus, and spent my time in the dark peering at every shadow, trying to see him lurking. Every squeak and whisper had its possibilities. What a time my parents must have had trying to get their job done of setting out the presents, knowing I was lying awake, listening. They would know that if I heard them, I would come flying down the stairs to catch them in the act.

Eventually, I would fall asleep only to awaken before dawn. The rule was that we had to wake our parents and get permission to collect our stockings. I, being the elder sister, claimed that privilege, running down the stairs in the dusky dark, darting my eyes covertly around the living room as I passed by on the way to my parents'

Nancy – age 5

room at the back of the house. I took note of outlines in the dark, of the gifts arranged around the room. Hearing my knock on their door, they would groan and glance at the clock. If it was reasonably close to sunrise, one of them would mumble the okay to take the stockings. Otherwise, I was gruffly directed back to bed. If the hour was approved, Dad would get up to come out and light the tree, and put the last-minute touches on the arrangement of the gifts. By the time he emerged from his room, Nancy and I would already have stumbled our way to the fireplace mantle to retrieve the stockings, and scurried back to my room to examine the contents.

Finally, the call would come that all was ready, and we could come down. My parents stood there with anticipatory grins on their faces, camera poised. Down we came, awed by the array below. When we were very young, we tore into our gifts like wild heathens. As we got older, we were more sedate, taking turns opening our gifts. Once all the packages were open and we were busy examining our loot in depth, my mother slipped away into the kitchen to prepare the Christmas breakfast. It was difficult to tear ourselves away from our gifts, but anticipation of the traditional popovers, loaded with butter and jam, drew us into the kitchen. Bacon and eggs were the other component of the meal.

Nancy and I would then amuse ourselves with the gifts until it was time to do our share to help with dinner. Mom always tried to provide the kind of Christmas dinner that she remembered from the farm, with turkey and homemade cranberry sauce. Pies were a must. Sometimes we went to Haverstraw to visit the Frith relatives, in which case, we would all have dinner at Aunt Goldie's. She had a talent for feeding large groups and doing it well. On those occasions, there would be some of Uncle Fritz's relatives there, too. The atmosphere at Aunt Goldie's was always relaxed and informal.

During my middle childhood years, there was a very special Christmas treat that we anticipated with eagerness. The next town down the line from Ridgewood was Glen Rock. It got its name from a large, glacial rock that was located in the middle of a residential area. It sat in a small, fenced-in park with a rotary around it, and various streets leading away from it like wheel spokes.

One corner was completely taken up by a large property — not quite an estate — owned by an architect, according to my mother. It was surrounded by a high, wrought-iron fence. Standing on the sidewalk, one looked down into the yard, then up to the house. A brook ran through the property and under the road. The topography of the yard was varied, whether by nature or by design, with craggy outcroppings of rock forming nooks and grottoes. There were groupings of bushes and trees, ravines and eventually a slope up to the house beyond. Every year, this park-like yard was transformed into a magical place with story-book scenes and Christmas tableaus, crowned by Santa Claus's sleigh, with reindeer flying across the roof of the house.

Mom said that this architect had a staff of people who worked all year on these scenes and the result was elegant. These weren't just a few cut-outs thrown up on the lawn. Each character was beautifully made and three-dimensional. There was movement — the characters moved smoothly, almost humanly, and there was interaction within the scenes themselves. A small train ran throughout. The reindeer legs that pulled the roof Santa moved as though running on air, and Santa waved.

There was music. The topography was such that, as the viewers on the sidewalk above walked along from where the property began, to other locations around the corner to the far end, the sound of the music from one scene was projected out to that area of the sidewalk. Yet the music would be contained by the topography and technology, and not spill over into the next section. As you moved along, the music from one area would fade, and the music for the next would drift in. At no time was there a cacophony of mixed sounds. The lighting was in a state of constant change, as the action within each grouping depicted the content of the scene. The viewer's eye was continually drawn from one scene to another.

Year after year, we made our pilgrimage to Glen Rock to fill our eyes with this vision and see what was new, for it was never the same. The people on the sidewalk would stand three and four deep to see this wonder, jostling for position, then moving on to the next vantage point. They came from everywhere, and every year the crowd was bigger.

Unfortunately, as time went on and the crowds grew, the architect's neighbors did not share his enthusiasm for the event, as the viewers trampled their yards and blocked their driveways. The lights and music disturbed their sleep. The town received complaints, and an injunction was served to prevent the display. It seems to me that, rather than lose an artistic treasure, the town could have sent police to keep order and prevent damage. However, that was not the case, and it ended. Yet, the memory of that magical production lives on and is the unmatched benchmark for any Christmas displays I have seen since. I have tried to describe it to my children, but no words can give an accurate picture of the awe and wonder that we were privileged to experience during those years. There was no admission fee — all people had to do was come and look. It was there for everybody, and they trampled it under their feet.

CHAPTER 9

Mom: Daughter of Neville Island

Mom's Friends

Mom was a social climber, who tried to be accepted into circles above our modest means. She was, after all, a Cole of Neville Island. However, she had many friends, some from childhood, some from our church and later from her teaching associates, who were talented, interesting people. She did not have to seek outside this pool for intellectual stimulation and good conversation.

My mother's closest friend was a woman we called Aunt Louise, but hers was an honorary title. She had been my mother's friend since high school, when Louise's family moved to Sandy Lake. Aunt Louise followed my mother to Houghton, appearing at the door of her dorm room as a surprise just before the term started. Aunt Louise was colorful, a bit flamboyant, and had a penchant for chunky jewelry that was flashy but appropriate on her large frame. She was tall and big boned, with thick, dark hair, always done up in a sophisticated style, and her dark eyes could dance with pleasure or snap with anger. She was not beautiful, but she had attitude and a forceful personality that made you pay attention. She was also a chain-smoker, which accounted for

Mom

her gravelly voice. Those characteristics (except for maybe the chain-smoking) certainly enhanced her success as a teacher of high school English in Bay Shore, Long Island. Nancy and I looked forward to her visits. I remember standing at the window for hours, alternately sitting on the arm of a stuffed chair, or squirming restlessly, watching the street, anticipating her arrival.

One of the reasons for our anticipation was the little presents she brought for Nancy and me — until the day we killed the goose that laid the golden egg. As she was unpacking, we hovered close by and finally became impatient and asked where our presents were. Actually, I was the one who asked. She let us know exactly what she thought of rude little girls, and she never brought us another gift. With Aunt Louise, justice was swift and final.

Sometimes, in honor of her visit, my mother would buy theatre tickets for a New York show, and the three of them, Aunt Louise and my parents, would set out for a night on the town, dressed in their finery. My mother loved to emulate Aunt Louise's style for those occasions and managed to make herself elegant. She also favored the chunky jewelry but did not have the large frame to carry it off as well as Louise. Nancy and I were left behind with a babysitter.

Social Climbing and Dr. Attila

My mother continued to reach above herself on the social ladder, but remained on the periphery of the elite group. In a way, she was like the *Little Match Girl*, in the story of the same name by Hans Christian Andersen, looking in at the window of the merry party, trying to warm herself in the light. My mother was well thought of, and admired for her accomplishments. She was an energetic, well-organized, and intelligent woman, who had put herself through college and graduate school when it wasn't the norm for women to do so. But she was never part of the inner circle that she thought was her rightful place.

Frequently, this ambition spilled over to involve me. Our family doctor, who had the bedside manner of Attila the Hun, my nickname for him, was highly respected in the community for his medical knowledge. My mother worshiped him. To give him credit, he was always pursuing further knowledge, on the cutting edge of the latest advances in his profession. He spent his days off taking courses in New York City.

I found myself accompanying my mother on some routine visit, and while sitting in the waiting room, she insisted that I knock at the door of the doctor's residence, as the office was in one wing of his house. She instructed me to ask to play with his son, Louis, a boy my age. I did not know Louis, and was shy about invading the doctor's private quarters, but my mother pushed and I had no choice but to comply. Red faced and stammering, I presented myself at the door, and was admitted by Mrs. Attila. She smiled sympathetically and led me to where the boy was playing. We exchanged some cursory greetings, I hung around for a few minutes, said good-bye, and left. I had followed my mother's orders. On the way home she said, "wouldn't it be wonderful if you and Louis became good friends, grew up and got married!" I was appalled. I was only in elementary school. I diligently avoided accompanying her on any future visits to the doctor.

When I was a sophomore in high school, shortly before we moved to Westchester County in New York state, I found myself in French class with Louis. He was a nice-looking boy, a brilliant student and the teacher was deferential toward him. His seat was on the other side of the room, and he had no idea who I was. I did not tell him.

It is interesting to note that Dr. Attila, and thereby his son, Louis, were Jewish. My mother, her Methodist background notwithstanding, was free of prejudice when it came to making a good marriage. Her stated view was, "Jewish men make good husbands." This was in the 1940s at the time of *Gentlemen's Agreement* in an environment where strong prejudice against the Jewish people still flourished.

Perfect Mother — Schedules and Routines, and the Facts of Life

Mom approached motherhood with all the zeal that she had put into becoming the perfect student and the perfect teacher. She also intended to be the perfect wife and mother. Teaching had been temporarily abandoned when I was born. Our house ran like clockwork, with little deviation from the pattern she established. Meals were at set times and followed the recommended food groups. From my job of setting the table, I knew that it was of utmost importance that a plate of bread be placed on the table at dinner. The table was not complete without it. If I inadvertently overlooked the bread, it caused my mother intense consternation, and everything would stop while I went back to the kitchen to fetch it. No one ever ate it.

Washing, ironing, cleaning and grocery shopping all had their special days of the week and all were set in stone. Monday was washing, Tuesday was ironing. When I got older, my job was to iron the towels. Wednesday was major grocery shopping day, as my father received his paycheck on Tuesday. Wednesday was also piano lesson day, as the trip to town could be combined with grocery shopping. Miss Hudgins's apartment was not far from the A & P, and I could walk there to help my mother with the packages afterward. I'm not sure what Thursday was — miscellaneous errands or bridge club, etc. June Cleaver could have been patterned after my mother except that Mom didn't wear pearls or high heels while vacuuming. At one point, she hired someone else to do that chore.

When my children were little, I used to bake oatmeal raisin cookies from my mother's handwritten recipe, and I thought it was one that was handed down. One day while waiting for a batch to bake, my glance fell on the Quaker Old-Fashioned Oats box, and found myself reading the same recipe off the box.

When I was ten or eleven and started asking the usual questions about sex, my mother handed me a book, *The Stork Didn't Bring You.* I'm grateful that she chose that method for my instruction, because if she had tried to explain the facts of life to me in person, I'm sure I would have been put off sex forever.

Money

Having descended from a line of frugal people, and having survived the Great Depression, my mother was parsimonious. Add to this my grandfather's inability to hold on to his fortune, and the result was a woman who liked her comforts, but cut budgetary corners and bought cheap. The only real jewelry my mother owned was her wedding and engagement rings. Everything else came from Woolworth's or the department store. Her dress clothes were bought from the better stores, but at home she wore slacks and tops from the bargain basement or from the Sears, Roebuck catalog. Our clothing was the same — she either made it or ordered from the catalogs.

Our house was comfortable and well made, but inexpensively furnished in a traditional style. We were the last family in our neighborhood to own a television, and the first one we had was built by my father from a Heath Kit. We saw *Howdy Doody* in blue. After many complaints from my sister and me (we saw television in black and white at Rett's, whose family was the first to own one), my father bought one. We owned a green Buick that my father bought at the end-of-the-year sale, and he also had a little jalopy that he drove to the train station on the occasions when my mother couldn't drop him off. I remember the man who came to buy that jalopy because he could blow smoke rings. I thought this was a great talent.

Bought new, our house was in a nice neighborhood, but was something of a bargain. It was built for Rett's parents, his father being the younger son of the wealthy family around the corner, but they opted instead to create an apartment on the second floor of the big house, the grandmother and Great-Aunt Nell occupying the floor below. Thus, they wanted to sell the little house quickly, and my father snapped it up. Our house was small but cozy. It had three bedrooms, one and one-half baths, a fireplace and a separate dining room. The kitchen had a double window over the sink that made the room very cheerful. There was a small walk-in attic behind the little second-floor bedroom. When we sold it fifteen years later, it wasn't on the market more than a few weeks before it was bought. My father was the one who actually made the real estate decisions, and he chose wisely. Mom knew enough to agree.

Mom gave generously to the church — more than my father liked — and to her alma mater, Houghton College — again, much more than my father liked. He gladly paid for various lessons for Nancy and me, as well as cultural pursuits. We went to New York City to shows at Radio City Music Hall, and to the Barnum and Bailey Circus at Madison Square Garden, then had lunch at Horn and Hardardt. We went on other vacations than to the farm or the shore — although not as much after we built the shore house. I have vague memories, before Nancy, of Canada and Maine. Ridgewood was rich with local cultural events for children, such as professional children's theatre troupes. When we were older, we were taken to summer stock plays in other towns, and once to Stratford, Connecticut for the Shakespeare festival. Adequate money was spent on food, but not the best cuts of meat. That was very wise, as it only would have ended up fit for shoe leather after my mother was finished cooking it.

Although my mother eventually had the higher-paying job, she remained deferential to my father in money matters, handing over her paycheck to him. When we lived in Katonah during my teen years, she bought new andirons for the fireplace. She worried that my father would be angry at the expenditure. As far as I know, he took it in stride. He was not against having our home look nice, and they did add to the look of the living room. He actually gave my mother free rein when it came to interior decoration, but left her with the illusion that he was watching every penny. This kept her happy, but prevented her from going overboard.

Skiing

According to my mother's manual, it was important to encourage the child's interests. This Mom did whenever those interests coincided with her plans. If, however, they did not, she would eventually attempt to short-circuit them, denying us opportunities for full development. There was a childhood rhyme, "Mother, may I go out to play, out to play, out to play. Mother may I go out to play?" "Yes, my darling daughter. Yes, you may go out to play, out to play, out to play. Yes, you may go out to play, but don't go near the water." One Christmas I desperately wanted skis. I don't know why, probably from a movie I had seen where the stars skied — maybe *Spellbound* with Ingrid Bergman and Gregory Peck. The skis appeared under the Christmas tree, but my mother allowed me to ski only down the meager slope in our backyard. I never saw an actual ski slope until I was an adult.

Mom never took me to a ski center for lessons or experience after giving in to my request for the skis. However, she did not want my gift to be totally wasted on the backyard hill, and she had me bring the skis with me when we went to visit her friends, the Emigs. They lived near a large graveyard, and their daughter, Phyllis, who was only a year older than I, had also received skis for Christmas. Grandma Cole was with us at the time and was along on the visit.

Phyllis and I took our skis to the graveyard to find any slopes we could among the graves. Nancy remembers being with us with her sled. There was a row of little mausoleums with low walls between, built into the side of a bank. I had the bright idea of ski jumping off one of the walls. Looking back, I note that Phyllis did not offer to try it, but encouraged me. It looked quite easy — just ski down the short, gentle slope above, and sail off the wall. I did. I made a one-point landing on my thumb.

My thumb hurt like hell. Somehow, between me, Phyllis and Nancy, we managed to get ourselves and our skis and the sled back to Phyllis's house just as the visit between our mothers and my grandmother was winding up. Mom, as usual, minimized my injury, being annoyed with me for sustaining it. When we arrived home, it was Grandma who examined my thumb, which was swollen and purple by then, and announced that I had "stoved" my thumb. That sounded terrible to me, but it was not broken. She pulled on it and massaged it, and after a few days, it looked more like its old self, and was once again usable. I was very glad she was there; otherwise I would have been in for another visit to Dr. Attila.

Dr. Attila Again

As I've said before, my mother worshiped Dr. Attila. I dreaded him. One of Dr. Attila's virtues was that he made house calls. Of course, in those days, most doctors did that, so it was not as much of a virtue as it would be today. When I was very young, I was sick in bed with some bug or other, nothing life threatening. Anyway, my mother escorted him to my bedroom, then left for some reason.

I was scared, whimpering and crying, terrified by his forbidding sternness. The image remains of how he fixed me with a cold stare, pulled an extremely long needle out of his black doctor bag, then told me in blood-chilling tones that would have given John Houseman pause, "If you don't stop crying, I'll stick this needle in your heel." My crying changed to gulping whimpers, and the examination was duly performed.

A year or two later, when I was in second grade, Dr. Attila announced to Mom that it would be necessary for me to have my tonsils out. I was taken to the same hospital in Hackensack where my sister was born. Of course, I was again terrified, not having the slightest idea of what to expect. If there was such a specialty as pediatric nursing at that time, it hadn't yet reached Hackensack Hospital (which today is a world-class facility).

Nobody told me anything. My reaction to frightening situations is to retreat into myself, rigid with fear, and hope it will go away. I do not yell and scream when truly afraid. This is what I did then. I was taken from my room to the operating room and placed on the table. In came Dr. Attila. In his calm, icy voice, he said something about putting me to sleep, placed some sort of cone over my nose and face, and the last thing I remember was a minty smell, and everything turned cold, watery green. I was drowning.

I woke up in my hospital bed, and my throat hurt. There was a dish of ice cream on the bedside table. I would let it melt and eat it later to soothe my sore throat. I saw my mother sitting near the foot of my bed, reading. I went back to sleep for just a few more minutes. When I woke up, the ice cream dish was empty, just the spoon and a smear of vanilla remaining. My mother was licking her lips.

Laissez-faire Child Raising

As an adult, my sister has been very concerned about the amount of freedom we had as children, and put great effort into protecting her own from the evils and dangers of the world as she saw them. I, on the other hand, carried over more of the laissez-faire aspects of my mother's child-raising techniques. That had no ill effect on my children except that, when building a tree house, Julia accidentally dropped a hammer on Sarah's head. They had been delivered from school before I returned from work, so Julia wiped away the blood from her sister's face and hoped that her hair would hide the lump that had formed. Sarah, however, wasn't one to keep quiet about an injury to herself. When I returned home, just as the last blood was cleaned away, she provided the full account. I didn't punish Julia for the accident, but advised her to check with our friend and neighbor, Lynne Simms, who was a nurse, should any more traumas occur in my absence.

The same laissez-faire approach that I experienced growing up was even more pronounced in Nancy's case. It's as if Mom expended whatever little inclination she had to supervise us in her efforts with me, and the supply was spent by the time my sister reached school age. When Nancy was still in elementary school, she would go home with friends after classes and stay until they were ready to sit down to their dinners. When she arrived home shortly before our meal, Mom made no inquiries about where she had been.

Growing up on the farm, Mom had often been left to her own devices as long as she was home at mealtime, or known to be visiting a friend. That mind-set carried over to her own children, even in instances where some parents might have been a little more cautious. History has revealed that our generation had a lot more personal freedom as children, giving us the opportunity to pursue our interests and develop our creativity. Our mother was not alone in that practice.

Nancy said, "When I had children, I was horrified when I realized how much freedom we'd had at such an early age, especially since we played around water, deep wells and railroad tracks, putting pennies on them to be crushed by oncoming trains." And, of course, we actually lived to tell the tale. Having three boys was a challenge to Nancy's maintaining their safety, and there were a number of occasions where they came close to disaster. Jimmy, her youngest, disappeared from their yard when he was three and was found by the police on the other side of a busy highway near a train station. A few years later, she rescued the same child from hanging when she looked out the window and found a friend of one of the older boys placing a noose around Jimmy's neck, after having thrown the other end over a branch.

Visits to the local emergency room for various injuries sustained by the boys were numerous, and she was particularly watchful when she took them swimming in a nearby lake. She claims that, when we were children, I had occasionally held her under the water until she was sure she was doomed to drown. I suppose she felt that the boys might indulge in the same entertainment with each other. If I did "duck" her, as we used to call it, she did not drown, no CPR was ever needed. Apparently, my judgment was astute enough to release her before her lungs reached their capacity to hold air.

One of Nancy's biggest fears was the possibility of kidnapping. When Jimmy, her youngest, was in school, one of his classmates was kidnapped, not far from Nancy's house, taken out of state, then sodomized before he managed to escape. She had memories of two narrow escapes herself as a child, one of them being very frightening. She would not elaborate on the details. However, I remember when her eldest was an infant and I was with her and some other people, whether friends of hers or cousins I don't remember, and we stopped at a local family restaurant for an afternoon snack. One of the waitresses was taken with infant Sean who had red hair, and asked to hold him while we relaxed. Nancy could not enjoy herself for constantly craning to see where the girl was with her child, for fear she would make off with him.

My own childhood experience gave me only a fleeting scare. I was seven or eight, and was on my way to school. I was late for some reason. No other kids were on the sidewalk. A car, going in the same direction, slowed down to a crawl, keeping pace with my steps. A man called to me from the window, "Little girl, would you like a ride?"

Remembering my mother's admonitions, I responded negatively and kept walking, increasing my speed, meanwhile mentally measuring the distance from the sidewalk to the nearest house. The man closed his window, sped up, and moved on. No further incident occurred. At no time did I feel that I was losing control of the situation, and while it has remained as a memory, it did not make me overly concerned for my own children's ability to handle similar situations. They were, of course, given the usual warnings, and we had a secret code word in case someone tried to pick them up, saying I had sent them. If that person couldn't provide the correct word, the girls were to run screaming.

Illness — Leave It Alone and It Will Go Away

I was seldom sick as a child, aside from the usual chicken pox, regular measles and mumps, but when Nancy was in third grade, she was at home, sick, for three weeks. The first week, Mom stayed home with her. The second week, she had a nurse, and the third week, she was on her own. She managed to survive; we both had good immune systems. Actually, Nancy was probably lucky to have had the nurse for a week. This was during the first year of Mom's return to teaching. She probably didn't dare call out from work to take care of a sick child for any length of time because she was intimidated by Dr. Mohair, her principal.

When we lived in Katonah, and she was in high school, Nancy was sent home with the Asian flu. She remembers being extremely sick, light-headed and feverish. She was left home alone, even though she recalls that she was so sick that she thinks she must have been incoherent from the high fever. Fortunately, Nancy survived this illness as well. Whether she was actually incoherent, or only thought she was, I doubt that our mother would have recognized it, the tendency in our family being to minimize physical illness.

Growing up on a farm, a touch of flu for a teenager would not have been cause for much concern for Mom. If there was no blood or broken bones, and the victim was conscious, minimal nursing would be forthcoming. Dad tended to be more concerned, especially since Nancy had suffered two bouts of pneumonia when she was little. Worrying less about illness, Mom might have believed that Nancy was capable of calling her at school, if necessary. Of course, I had desensitized our mother by staying home sick many times when in junior high school and high school, and after a day in bed, I always made an excellent recovery for my return to school the following day. It never seemed to occur to her that I had become an expert at faking minor illness.

Swimming with Snakes

I have read in a number of sources that our generation, without the protective laws and safety restrictions, and so-called advantages and entertainment inventions currently available, produced the greatest number of risk takers, problem solvers and inventors ever. Perhaps unfortunately, some of the problems they solved and the inventions they made have reduced the opportunities for today's children to have the same mind-opening experiences.

Some of these folks looked at the dangers we faced (along with the freedom and challenges) and, like my sister, were appalled. They proceeded to pass laws to reduce all childhood risks, eliminate problems that might befuddle childish minds, then invented childproof lids on aspirin bottles that can be opened by most children but not by adults, designed brightly colored helmets that must be worn at all times when biking or skating, and announced that everything we had always enjoyed eating was horribly bad for us. Others invented video games to keep children safely indoors, content and imprisoned. With the advent of cell phones and the internet, children soon found these to be fascinating distractions as well, and many hardly venture out at all anymore. I wonder what breakthroughs this generation will heap upon us.

An example of this hypervigilant thinking comes to mind. When my daughter, Julia, was a child, I taught piano lessons at home. One of my students was a very bright boy, a bit on the hyperactive side, whose mother, also bright, fostered his freedom of expression. She, herself, was an artist. We became friendly, as we held many views in common. One day, she invited me to bring Julia and accompany her and her son to a local swimming hole. It was just that — a pond on some land where the owners didn't mind people swimming. There were a number of other mothers with small children there as well that day.

My friend and I, with our children, were over to one side, away from the others. We saw a small garden snake slide into the water. We did not live in an area where water moccasins and other poisonous water snakes abounded. I knew enough about human nature that my first reaction on seeing the little snake, was to say nothing in order to protect it from any violence from the crowd. My companion, the innocent, being a free spirit and thinking the best of everyone, immediately thought the others would like to see it as an interesting phenomenon of nature, and called their attention to it. Another mother, an Amazon of a woman, who I later learned was a nurse, quickly stepped up to the plate and took charge of evacuating all the children from the pond to save them from this supposedly dangerous reptile, thus exposing her own ignorance about poisonous snakes. She then attempted to hunt down the poor creature who, fortunately, eluded her.

The children's afternoon at the swimming hole was cut short because a little garden snake decided to go for a swim. My friend and I looked at each other and just shook our heads.

Children of a bygone era frequently played outside until dark, returning to the house, unscathed, at mealtime. They swam in ponds with garden snakes. That's the way it was on Neville Island when my mother was young. Life was hard by our standards, but easier going in many ways. The children had a few chores, but came and went pretty much at will. The Cole family viewed life as good until the government made other plans.

10

Developing Aspirations

Actress, Writer

When I was almost a teenager, and more inclined to think and behave independently, I brazenly told my Wesleyan Methodist Grandma Cole my future theatrical plans. She looked sad for a moment, then smiled gently, her eyes hard. She said she hoped I wouldn't enter into that wicked life, a life that would lead directly to hellfire. I tried to explain that making people laugh, or entertaining them with a good story, would help them. What could be more godly than that? We were sitting in the back seat of the car on the way to our shore house. My mother glared at me from the front. My father, who was driving, was trying not to smile.

I don't know if Grandma's words had anything to do with my getting stage fright at auditions when I tried to break into theatre after graduating from college, but I did decide early on that I preferred a steady paycheck and eating. A few years later, I became an elementary school teacher, where I found a creative outlet, and I think Grandma would have been satisfied.

Once I had started going to movies, and taken part in a few elementary school productions, my life was focused on stage and screen. When I was in the fifth grade, I adapted a story into a play that I planned to present in my basement. I was amazed when my mother allowed me to carry out this production. She didn't throw up the usual roadblocks. It may have been because I told her I had cast several of the popular girls from school in the roles. Their mothers were planning to come to see the production, and Mom viewed that as a social opportunity.

I drafted my sister and Rett to round out the cast. I made the scenery, planned the costumes, and directed. Some of the mothers made costumes, and I made the rest. The short story was about the witch's surprise, with all the forest creatures trying to guess what it was — it turned out to be a baby — innocuous and cute. The mothers who came to see it gave due praise, and Mom served refreshments. I thought my career as an impressario was off to a successful start.

I immediately embarked on finding another play to adapt to the limitations of my basement. I found a much more ambitious one about wicked trolls and was busily rewriting it when I eagerly mentioned my plan to my mother. Absolutely not. One was enough. There had been no subsequent invitations from the girls or their mothers. I hadn't expected any, but Mom was disappointed. I had better look around for some other project as there would be no more plays in the basement. She offered no reason for her refusal, and there was to be no argument. She turned away, humming softly, tunelessly. It was her way of indicating that the last word had been said.

When I was in junior high school in Ridgewood, I started to become serious about writing, in addition to theatre. I wrote several short stories that I found to be quite humorous when I recently rediscovered them in a carton. They had not been meant to be funny when written — especially the one that took place in seventeenth-century London where the heroine, a young damsel who had grown up in the lap of luxury, decided she wanted to become a pirate queen. She goes out, with her maid to protect her, and buys a "seaworthy ship" — she knew it was seaworthy just by looking at it — rounds up a crew of questionable characters, repairs and outfits this ship — all out of what she had saved from her "generous allowance." The tears streamed down my face as I read this and my sides ached from laughing.

Another effort was several chapters long and titled, *The Jade Temple*. This one was full of derring-do. I had either been watching a lot of Tarzan movies at the time or reading *Sheena, Queen of the Jungle* comic books. It was action and romance packed into a few short chapters. After I had written it, I proudly presented it to my mother, and innocently awaited her praise.

The following week, I found myself sitting in a psychiatrist's office at Columbia Presbyterian Medical Center where our family doctor, Dr. Attila, had suggested that my mother take me — whether to evaluate my sanity or my genius potential was never made clear. My mother would have been quite elated to have produced a genius, so I think that was the direction in which her hopes leaned. The psychiatrist and I sat in his large office, high up, overlooking the Hudson River, studying each other in silence over his immense desk. He began by asking me a few questions about how I felt about growing up and was I comfortable with the changes in my body, to which I replied, straight-faced, that I was handling it just fine. He smiled a little smile and dismissed me. The pronouncement was that I was a normal teenage girl. To be pronounced "normal" was the highest insult of all. I would have preferred a pronouncement of insanity. My self-image was badly dented, and I suspended my writing career.

A few years before my writing efforts blossomed, my mother went through a phase of trying to be a writer. She worked feverishly on a mystery novel during the hours that Nancy and I were in school. In those days we came home for lunch, and while we ate our sandwiches, we were the captive audience for what she had written that morning. Neither of us really understood much of the story, but it helped Mom to hear the rough areas as she read her work aloud to us.

I dabbled in writing from time to time, but Nancy was inspired, possibly by the sheer bulk of what Mom had written, and started writing short articles. When she was older, she wrote a weekly column called "The Young Learner" for a local newspaper. She was proud of this, as Mom had never been published. But Mom took very little interest in my sister's success at writing. She wasn't interested in the achievements of others in areas where she had failed, especially her daughters. Dad was the one who liked to read Nancy's column. After Mom's death, Nancy came across the yellowed manuscript of my mother's novel. It was her opinion that our mother gave up too soon on her writing hopes.

Unfortunately, I did not keep a copy of the most major literary work of my junior high school period, although my father probably squirreled one away somewhere; he saved most of my creations. We were assigned a research project for our ninth grade social studies class, based on American history. I was, of course, rebelling against the strict guidelines that had been laid out for this task. With few exceptions, the Ridgewood school system, at that time, boasted some very progressive teachers, and Miss Snyder was one of them. After a conference with her, she allowed me the leeway to write a historical novella, but I was admonished to be accurate in my research. Having just read a teenage novel about the Civil War from the southern viewpoint, I was eager to take on this challenge. I researched a deciding battle of that war that took place at Manassas, Virginia, and the subsequent surrender of General Lee to General Grant at Appomattox, and wrote the story through a Confederate soldier's eyes. I received an A. I have learned that two of my great-grandfathers, Augustus Cole and Harvey Henderson, were in the Civil War, but, of course, on the Union side. Neither was at Manassas.

Nancy observed, "I think Mom had a hard time sharing the spotlight with us, especially with you. I think there was a greater clash between you and her, since you possessed the talents she wanted. I was less of a threat to her stardom. I was her audience. But, when I did accomplish something she never had, the column, she ignored it. In her much later years, however, she finally seemed interested in my writing. She had a difficult time with failure. She gave up her writing ambitions way too easily."

Nancy and I and Mother-Daughter Relationships

Nancy had her own views on our mother and the relationship between our parents. While we always felt that Mom was the dominant one in their relationship, Nancy observed from her experience that it was because our father allowed her to be. She said, "Whenever I did things to upset Mom, Dad was there to make me feel guilty about it." Nancy believed that our mother always received a diluted account of her escapades from Dad in his efforts to keep Mom's feathers smoothed.

Neither of us ever felt close to our mother, who was incapable of such a relationship with her daughters. In her later years, she lamented about this to Nancy, saying that it was one of her disappointments in life that she was unable to establish closeness with us. During crises in our lives, her response was to advise, "Pray about it," or to launch into a long, ecstatic monologue about some tea held in some wealthy person's mansion. Neither was very useful to us.

When she married, Nancy was able to establish a close relationship with her mother-in-law, and she felt at first that this was an unusual thing. She later found, as her experiences with other women expanded, that many of her teaching associates also were in close mother-daughter relationships, and that it was her own experience that was unique.

When I married, my mother-in-law lived in Italy and didn't speak much English. But she was a warm and kind person and I enjoyed our visits there, and hers to us. My father-in-law was more like my husband, Ugo — reserved. Mama Boggio, however, always liked to hover close, especially when my girls were babies. This tended to bring out my pulling-away reaction that my father, sadly, often experienced from me. I attribute this to my mother's inability to show me affection during my childhood. Although Dad saw my reaction in full bloom, I tried to mask it where my mother-in-law was concerned in order to spare her feelings. I think she might have been aware of it anyway, and been hurt, not understanding that she was not at fault.

Nancy and Her Relationship With Me

Nancy remembers the time when we were children, and I regaled the family with the blow-by-blow of the most recently seen movies at dinnertime. Nancy enjoyed those performances. She was a good listener. She listened intently when our mother talked with her friends, picking up tidbits of useful information. She might have done well in a career as a spy, but settled for teaching history.

I was the one who directed our playtime, writing and producing the plays we performed in our basement, and organizing our various games and adventures. Nancy insists that when we played croquet, I created the rules as we went along, especially those that gave me the advantage just as she was on the point of winning.

As we grew older and no longer required a babysitter, Nancy claims that I often tortured her in the way that siblings do. She eventually refused to stay alone with me. She was tired of being locked in a dark closet while I made ghost noises outside the door. She received permission to go, instead, to a friend's house down the street, as long as she called ahead and got the okay from her friend's mother. On one occasion, the telephone operators were on strike, and male supervisors were putting through the calls. One of them told her that she could call only if it were a matter of life and death. As she was convinced that I would scare her to death, she had no reservations about saying that it was, indeed, a life and death matter. Nancy put on a convincing performance, and the supervisor put the call through.

Nancy and Grandma Cole

Nancy attended the years of Sunday School as I did, but she did not "fall away" from religion. However, an argument with Grandma Cole about religion stands out in her mind. "She argued that even people in India who never heard of Jesus would go to hell if they didn't believe. Grandma strongly disapproved of my Roman Catholic friends — particularly the one whose father owned a liquor store."

The summer following our move to Katonah our mother had Grandma and Grandpa Cole come to keep house for us and our father while she attended French language classes at Middlebury College. We had just moved into the new house at the end of the school term, and we were still surrounded by unpacked boxes until Mom's return. I managed to be out of the house much of the day, but Nancy was more often at home with Grandma and Grandpa,. who were then elderly. By their standards, we were out of control. We didn't like the food Grandma cooked — she had slipped from her earlier prowess and had resorted to cans and jars — and we would not obey her. When Nancy didn't wash the dishes in what Grandma considered a timely way, Grandpa held her down while Grandma wielded the switch. Nancy was twelve, and we were no longer being whipped by our mother.

Dad had to step in and reason with us about our behavior to prevent Grandma from taking a switch to us again, although we were teenagers. He was not going to confront her, so it was up to us to cooperate. Dad relied on Grandma to feed us and keep our clothes clean, and we were old enough to understand the situation. My grandparents were threatening to leave, and Dad couldn't allow that to happen. He didn't want to have to explain any friction when my mother returned home. We exercised more caution for the rest of their stay, although we never did acquire a liking for the food.

Singing

One thing that our mother did provide to her daughters were advantages after having been deprived herself. She made sure that Nancy received the same allotment of lessons that I did. Nancy had eight years of piano, clarinet, dancing, and even a few singing lessons. I had everything except the clarinet lessons, but I had far more extensive singing lessons. Nancy states that she didn't have much interest in these cultural pursuits and preferred to be out climbing trees and playing with the boys in the neighborhood. She would have liked horseback riding lessons but didn't get them. I got them only because I joined the riding club in junior high school and the lessons were discounted. Also, I probably clamored more loudly for them than Nancy did, as I was in an adolescent horse phase at the time.

When I was a sophomore in high school, my father was transferred out of New York City to a new AT&T office in White Plains, New York. We moved from sophisticated, suburban New Jersey to Katonah, New York, in farm country. The high school was much smaller than the one in Ridgewood and didn't offer the quantity of theatrical opportunities that I had enjoyed. As a senior, I obtained a very minor role in the senior play.

My drama experiences may have dwindled, but my singing opportunity expanded. I tried out for the Glee Club out of desperation. I was put off by the title, which evoked an image of people with silly smiles skipping across meadows. What I found was a new experience and revelation.

Mr. Finlayson was the talented director and he was a perfectionist. As well as modern, bouncy numbers, we performed classics such as *Jesu, Joy of Man's Desiring*, and Negro spirituals like *Sometimes I Feel Like a Motherless Child*. He taught us to produce crisp enunciation, to sing pianissimo, and to pour forth joyfully according to the direction of the music. Mr. Finlayson soon discovered my contralto voice, and I was assigned some short solos. When spring came, I was one of the few selected to represent the school in a statewide concert. I didn't have any solos in that, but the experience expanded my appreciation for choral music.

When I lived in Ridgewood, I had a year and a half of private voice lessons, from Irene (Rusty) Richards, an attractive, auburn-haired young mother married to a New York advertising executive. She had once been in a Broadway musical, and was the soprano soloist in our church choir.

Rusty was also my surrogate mother — the one to whom I brought all my teenage problems. My lesson time was half singing and half advice, and, as I had the last lesson of the day, it often ran over the hour. It was during my lesson that she encouraged me to follow through on my wish to ask this good-looking boy named Billy to the upcoming Sadie Hawkins Dance (in which the girls ask the boys).

She prepared me for the phone call, teaching me to say, "May I please speak with Billy?" instead of "Is Billy there?" She told me just what to say and stood by while I dialed. Maybe he was impressed by my polite, well-spoken manner, but he said, "Yes!" My knees were shaking.

I went to the dance with Billy and he was polite and attentive. We did a lot of talking and I hoped to see more of him, but he lived in Glen Rock and I lived halfway to Ho-Ho-Kus — too much distance for people without cars.

French

When I was in high school I wanted to take Spanish. My father spoke Spanish as well as French, and I thought it would be a much more interesting and useful language. By that time, my mother was teaching French and Latin in a town two counties away. What would people think if her daughter did not take French! It was bad enough that I refused to take Latin. I took French.

I was assigned to the French I class with Madame Cru, a native French woman. I found it difficult to understand her and hated every minute, watching the clock until the bell signaled release. I did not do well in that class, failing the second marking period. My mother was almost apoplectic. "The shame! What will people think? How can I hold my head up? What if someone from Hasbrouck Heights finds out?" I was too old for the switch. As it was, I was grounded, and worse — my mother undertook serious oversight of my French studies for the rest of the year. You can lead the horse to water…but I squeaked through the year.

French II the following year wasn't much better. Fortunately, in the middle of that year we moved to Katonah, in upper Westchester County, New York, when my father was transferred to White Plains. I dropped French toute suite. After a semester's break, I retook it the following year, as a junior, starting back with French I. I got straight "A"s. The same with French II my senior year. I was redeemed, but the whole French experience strengthened my mother's mantra for the rest of my academic career: "I was valedictorian of my high school class (of six) and salutatorian of my college class. What happened to you?"

English

I was fortunate during my high school years to have had two outstanding English teachers. The first was during my sophomore year in Ridgewood, and sadly, that exposure was short. Mr. McCutcheon introduced me to Dickens when we read *David Copperfield*. This teacher was formerly a newspaper reporter and had a crusty view of the world. I was caught up in his enthusiasm for literature, and it was then that I became a serious reader. Part way into the first semester,

147

his small daughter was seriously injured in a tragic fire, and he was out of school until just before we moved to Katonah. His substitute was unmemorable.

When I was a high school senior in Katonah, I had the second great English teacher for the whole year. Mrs. Schechner and her husband had been college professors. After his death, she turned to high school teaching to the benefit of all of us who were destined to go on to higher education. She knew the ins and outs of requirements for college term papers and passed her knowledge on to us through the experience of writing college-level assignments.

Mrs. Schechner was tall, thin and beaky, looking much like a large bird, wearing her glasses on the end of her nose. By now I had a best friend, Ann, and, although we were not in any group, we were friendly with individuals in all the cliques. Ann and I shared many creative interests, and she was as odd in some of her thinking as I was. Mrs. Schechner led us into a renewed interest in short story writing, and we diligently produced piece after piece, which our teacher kindly critiqued for us. She stressed brevity. We constantly heard about a student named Paul whom she had taught the year before us, who could write in one sentence what most people took a paragraph or more to present.

The culmination of the year was writing a research paper, using the rules of style as put forth by Strunk and White in their book. My paper was a comparison and critique of seven French authors, including Colette, Zola and Balzac, among others. I read at least one book by each, and read both *Nana* and *Germinal* by Zola, being fascinated by the seamy side of life that was painted in those novels. My mother, from her French studies, had a copy of *Nana* in her library, but I had no idea that it was such an interesting book until I wrote the research paper. It was about the rise and fall of a French courtesan. I received an A.

When I got to Allegheny College, I found that one of the required freshman courses, called broadly, "Communications," encompassed what I had already learned with Mrs. Schechner. Most of my classmates had not had the benefit of such a teacher in their high school classes. Our Communications teacher was uninspired, and we had little latitude in choosing a topic. I could not work up much enthusiasm for the project and received a C. I don't even remember what the paper was about.

Mrs. Schechner's influence remained with me, however, and if a topic inspired me, and sometimes even if it didn't, I was often able to put together an A-worthy paper in future classes. While others were slogging through the mysteries of footnotes, I was able to breeze through the process of creating them. The admonishment to brevity echoed in my mind, although I didn't always honor it. When, in my senior year, I had to write an eighty-page comparison of three plays about one historical figure, I mentally thanked Mrs. Schechner for the jump-start she gave me in high school.

Math

When my mother taught in Tompkins Cove all those years ago, she was required to teach a course in math — a subject in which she was less than proficient. She had a major struggle to succeed with that class and, according to Nancy, if it weren't for help from my father, an engineer, our mother would have failed at it. At the time we moved to Katonah, she and Nancy went up a few weeks ahead of Dad and me, in order to start her new teaching job. My father and I remained behind in New Jersey, trying to sell our house. Dad was the one who usually helped with homework as my mother had no patience with it. But now he was not there to help Nancy with her sixth grade math. It was up to her mother. She was a very poor substitute, and Nancy was shocked that Mom had once taught the subject on a high school level. I'm gratified to know that I come by my math deficiency honestly.

Mom, the Language Teacher

The teaching position that my mother obtained was in Somers, a small town on the Westchester/Putnam County line, and fortunately, she did not have to teach any math. Somers was the town where P. T. Barnum introduced the first circus elephant on this continent, and the elephant was the school symbol. My mother was in her element. She eventually became head of the language department, and threw herself into building the French and Latin Clubs and their associated after-school activities.

Both groups performed plays in French or Latin and went on various appropriate field trips. The Latin group put on banquets wearing togas and reclining on couches. The French group also presented a French dinner. Thinking back, I hope my mother did not prepare it, given her cooking record. The French and Latin cultures were explored in depth and most of her students went on to college. Her greatest joy was when any one of them majored in French once there.

Comparison

Mom was never one to hide her light under a bushel, as the Bible says. Nancy and I were always aware of her many talents and accomplishments. I think I was always in competition with her, playing a game of bob and weave, trying to excel in areas that she didn't. I was a little dark cloud child — few pictures show me smiling. I am usually wearing a sullen little frown — probably plotting my next move in the contest of wills.

Nancy was the sunny one — at least on the surface. Where I felt challenged, her reaction was a feeling that it would be futile to try. Mom occasionally tried to force Nancy to succeed where she felt she had failed with me. I refused to take Latin, so Nancy had to. She suffered through two years before being allowed to drop it. She took three years of French in high school and excelled. I had to take it twice to get it right.

Nancy was more interested in having fun with her friends than she was in succeeding in school, although she did well enough. One area where she could establish her individuality was in physical prowess. Mom had been good at tennis until a knee injury intervened, and had done well at other college sports. I had no talent at all for team sports and didn't have much opportunity to develop proficiency in individual sports. Nancy found her niche, however, in being a tomboy, challenging a schoolyard bully and winning while the other boys cheered her on.

When she was a little older, Nancy sought her friendships among the other girls. She was not a scholar, but she was smart and chose her closest friends from among the very bright. One of them became the valedictorian of her class. This tendency continued throughout her life as she found that most bright women were interesting as well. She had watched Mom surround herself with bright and educated people, and Nancy perpetuated that habit.

Allegheny

Through most of high school I had determined not to follow my parents' wishes about going to college. I was in a hurry to go to New York City and start my acting career. At the start of senior year, my parents and the guidance counselor, Mr. Faveraux, redoubled their efforts to change my mind. The old caution thing kicked in, and I did an about face.

The problem was that I had been haphazard about my grades, and although I did well in the English portion of the SATs, my math scores were abominable. I applied to Simmons College in Boston, where I did not get accepted. I also applied to Syracuse University, in New York, where I was accepted. After all, I had two cousins who went there and succeeded, Marian and Robert Bernhoft.

Mr. Faveraux had another school for me to consider — a small highly-rated liberal arts college in western Pennsylvania. It had excellent English and drama departments, and it required no math once you were there. To me, that was an unbeatable combination and I applied. When I met with the school's representative, he said that my acceptance would depend on how the reviewing committee members had enjoyed their breakfasts that morning, and it would be in spite of my math scores, not because of them. I was accepted.

During my senior spring, I went to the special weekend that the college offered for those who had been accepted for the following fall. It was a long train ride on the Erie from my old hometown of Ridgewood, and there were several other potential classmates traveling as well. The fraternities and sororities went all out to sell us on the school, and we went from one party to another. No alcohol, of course — the legal age in Pennsylvania was twenty-one, and even then, Allegheny forbade it. It was somewhere during that round of parties that we were informed that Allegheny was famous for having expelled future president,

William McKinley for taking a cow up into the bell tower and tying the bell rope to its horns. The cow had to be butchered to get it down. I never did learn whether this story was true or not.

Me and Gerda

CHAPTER 11

Gladys's Story

Aunt Gladys was not Everson and Helen's first-born but was the first child to survive, baby Frank having succumbed to diphtheria. She was my mother's older sister, much loved and admired by her, but Mom harbored a tinge of jealousy for her sister's perfections of face and character. My mother often spoke about Gladys, and my sister and I were familiar with our aunt through Mom's stories.

Gladys had a big influence on Mom, and therefore on me. My aunt was portrayed as the beautiful one, the accomplished one, the perfect one. This was a reflection of my grandmother's attitude about her two daughters, and my great-grandmother's special treatment of Gladys. By extension, Gladys's children were held up to Nancy and me as examples of perfect behavior and demeanor, even the boys who gave their parents more than a few headaches along the way.

I was always in awe of my eldest cousin, Marian. If she was the benchmark — and she was — I could never succeed. I barely knew Marilyn, the second eldest, as she moved south when she reached adulthood. I knew Robert briefly, but he married and was gone from

Grandma and Grandpa Cole with Gladys (center)

home when I was in my early teens. Donny was my favorite, five years my senior, mischievous and fun. I was comfortable with him.

Aunt Gladys resented her father's profligacy at losing the family fortune and her inheritance along with it, although her grandmother, Mary Ann Cole, had paved the way for her education. My aunt no longer had status by fortune, but she had other means of gaining recognition. She acquired religious expertise, and this gave her emotional capital.

During her teen years, Gladys was seldom at the farm in Sandy Lake, having been sent to live with relatives. After high school, she went off to Houghton College in New York State, and to her destiny. She preferred the small Wesleyan Methodist school in the Genesee Valley over the large, impersonal environment of Margaret Morrison College, where her grandmother first sent her. At Houghton, Gladys became a Greek scholar in the seminary division, and an expert on the Bible. Although she completed the seminary program, she did not continue on to obtain her degree. That lost its importance when she met and married her classmate, Arthur Bernhoft.

The young couple lived in the village where Houghton College was located, until Arthur completed his studies. After Arthur's graduation, they moved to Tompkins Cove, New York, where Arthur took a position as principal of Tompkins Cove High School. At the local Methodist church, Aunt Gladys taught the adult Bible class and honed her missionary skills.

Being so much younger, my memories of them in Tompkins Cove are very vague. My recollections really began once Gladys's family moved to Fayetteville, near Syracuse, New York, after Uncle Arthur accepted an invitation from his cousin to work for him selling dairy equipment. Nancy and I looked forward to summer trips to visit our cousins. My focus was on my cousin, Donny.

Both my mother and my Uncle Ned often aired their views within their homes that Gladys had a controlling nature and brought maternal pressure to bear on her children's life choices, just as Mary Ann Cole had done with her. My cousins now deny this, protesting that they had made their own choices, but my mother influenced my view.

Marilyn, the second daughter, caused her mother some sleepless nights. She got out from under her mother's thumb when she met and married a southerner. I met Jim Carlisle briefly on one of our summer trips to Fayetteville. From Marilyn, I learned later that he and their small son, Paul, had come to the Syracuse area so he could find work, but he did not see eye to eye with his in-laws. Jim and his son subsequently boarded a plane to head south, back to Marilyn.

There was a terrible storm that night, resulting in at least one plane crash. When Marilyn spoke with her mother on the phone to assure her that Jim and Paul had arrived safely, Gladys expressed her anger at the failed outcome of his visit to her, and an argument followed. Whatever was actually said led to a rift between mother and daughter. Tempers flared, and Marilyn's version of what Gladys said was, "She told me she prayed Jim's plane would crash!"

When Marilyn told me this, years later, I was shocked that my aunt would say such a cruel thing as she had never been anything but kind to me. However, the tension I had felt as a child between her and Jim on that earlier visit remained in my memory.

My mother, in her comments at home, was critical of Gladys's ambitions for her children. However, Mom herself was guilty of the same fault, all in the tradition of their grandmother, who had deemed the little seamstress from Sandy Lake to be unworthy of her son. Gladys and my mother shared several of the Cole traits of stubbornness, pride, religious zeal, and the drive to control their children and grandchildren. Gladys was more direct in exercising these controls than was Mom.

A mainstay of her church, Aunt Gladys wielded her influence, backed up by extensive Biblical knowledge. She was tireless in her efforts on behalf of less-fortunate church members, and was the person to whom the pastors looked for advice. Her grandmother, Mary Ann Cole, had performed that role on Neville Island for the community. Although Marilyn had remarked to me that she felt that more of her mother's attentions should have been devoted to her own family, Gladys was regarded as a near saint by her church and community.

In her later years, Aunt Gladys became a practical nurse, doing home care with terminal cancer patients. When Uncle Arthur was diagnosed with cancer, she gave up her other patients and cared for him at home. I visited for a day or two a few months before he died. I could not think of what to say to him. He had been so vital a person, smiling, joking. I remembered his many kindnesses to me and his love of teasing his nieces, more than I remembered my relationship with my aunt. Now his body was wasted, and there was pain in his eyes. The smell of Ben-Gay permeated his sickroom. At night I could hear his muffled screams. In 1966, he died, in pain, at home in the sunny bedroom overlooking their backyard.

Morphine was available at that time for relief of cancer pain, but some doctors were hesitant to prescribe it, and some people hesitated to use it, considering it an evil drug that would drag you down into the hell of addiction. To many, it seemed somehow immoral to cheat the pain of dying, and causes of addiction were misunderstood. For whatever reason, Ben-Gay was Arthur's ineffective pain relief.

The previous September, Grandpa Cole had also died, tragically, at Gladys's home. He and Arthur had been close, and Arthur's screams of pain had unnerved him.

Not long after losing her father and Arthur, Aunt Gladys decided to move my grandmother and herself to Florida to be near her brother, my Uncle Ned, and his wife, Evelyn. They were wintering there by then. Grandma still spent time at Ned and Evelyn's on McCalmont Street in Franklin, to give Gladys a break.

Aunt Gladys developed breast cancer but, with dogged determination that would have impressed even Mary Ann Cole, she continued with her church work and caring for her mother. She lived on in Florida for awhile. In time, my parents retired there, and I remember seeing my aunt on a trip to visit them when my first daughter, Julia, was a baby. Gladys was so small and shriveled that she sat on the phone book to reach the table at lunch. It was a shock to see her so withered and near death. Yet she remained stubborn and drove her car, sitting on cushions to see the road.

When she could no longer care for herself, Aunt Gladys agreed to sell her Florida home and travel north to live with her daughter, Marian, in Poughkeepsie, New York. Marian and her husband had a beautiful new sunroom on the back of their house with a large window into Gladys's bedroom. From there, she could lie in her bed and look out beyond to distant hills. She saw no steamboats passing by on the horizon, but her death was like Mary Ann's, with family gathered around. Gladys had been a strong influence on her children's lives.

All her life, Gladys harbored resentment against her father for losing her birthright. There was other resentment as well. He could not be blamed for the loss of the Neville Island farm — what individual could fight Carnegie Steel and win? — but he lost the rest of the family fortune, including the Sandy Lake farm, by his knack for imprudent investments and misplaced trust. Gladys had grown up in comfort on Neville Island, favored granddaughter of the matriarch, Mary Ann, groomed by her to expect the best. It was certainly Mary Ann's influence that prompted Gladys's focus on successful alliances and prestigious careers for her children. They were successful, but not by following the paths that Gladys set for them.

Aunt Gladys's Children

Marian maintained her religious beliefs and spent time at the farm in the company of Grandma Cole. She remembers once when they were together in the apple orchard down the road from the house. A cloud passed over the sun, creating a shadow. Grandma turned to her and said, with a kind smile, "That's how your sins get taken away." That thought remained with Marian throughout her life, softening the religious hard line of her childhood.

In the barn, the horses were stabled on the left side, the cows on the right. If Uncle Bob was there milking when Marian and her sister wandered in, he would squirt some of the warm milk into their open mouths. They would giggle and wait for more. This was a good memory. Later, Marian's little cousin, Darlene, would remember similar experiences with distaste.

It was shortly before I visited Marian many years later with my girls that Marian and Bob went to Pittsburgh and visited the Carnegie-Mellon Library and other historical sources, as well as Neville Island itself. Uncles Ned and Bob joined them, and Marian interviewed them about their memories. They stood on the paved spot where the farm used to be. The research, encompassing newspaper and other documentary accounts, as well as transcripts of the interviews, was compiled into a booklet along with photos, then distributed to family members. I have used my copy extensively as a resource in writing this book more than twenty years later.

Although I saw Marian frequently throughout my childhood, I did not see her sister, Marilyn, until many years later in 1985 when I attended a special sewing seminar in Huntsville, Alabama. It was a long while after Gladys's death and shortly before Ugo and I divorced. Marilyn now lived near Huntsville in Guntersville. The afternoon I arrived, we met at a coffee shop next to my hotel. We hadn't seen each other since her brother Robert's wedding when I was a teenager, but we recognized each other on sight and for the same reason; we both looked like our grandmother, Helen Cole. We chatted and laughed, and arranged that I would stay a night with her before returning home to New Jersey.

When the seminar was over, I headed to Marilyn's home. She lived in a neat double-wide in a peacefully pretty, wooded setting on the banks of the Tennessee River. Jim was not there, so we had the house to ourselves. That evening, after dinner, our conversation turned serious as we washed dishes. That was when she told me more about Jim's long-ago trip to Syracuse and how it had ended. Her old wounds reopened.

Marilyn talked on late into the night and I had difficulty reconciling her version of my aunt with the woman I had known. I remembered my mother saying that Gladys tried to control the lives of her children, and I could see the truth in what Marilyn was telling me.

Robert Bernhoft's first wife, Marilyn (not to be confused with his sister), was a willing ally to Aunt Gladys. This Marilyn once told my sister that she was crazy about Robert. Aunt Gladys had strongly encouraged, if not engineered, the relationship.

Nancy said, "I remember Marilyn telling me that once at a football game where he taught, she was tickled to overhear some female students oohing and aahing over his good looks and then telling them he was her husband." Robert tried hard to keep it together, but, after five children, it ended in divorce.

Robert was a psychologist when he and his second wife, Sherry, moved to a horse farm in Ohio. After seventeen years, this marriage, too, ended in divorce.

Betty was his third wife, and she did the choosing. This one took. When Robert was making the rounds, and visiting the homes of his Aunt Corinne and Uncle Ned to introduce his girlfriend, he took the matter of the bedrooms well in hand. In each case, he asked where the guest room was, picked up both their suitcases and installed them there. He just smiled at his nonplussed relatives.

When I saw him recently, I was struck by how much Robert now resembles Uncle Ned, as I remember him, with the same slim frame, bandy legs, and twinkling eyes. He and his wife had a new kitten, who had taken over their household. Robert's eyes glowed with pride when talking about him and his little accomplishments, his silky black fur and little white bow tie. That was the way Uncle Ned was about his dog, Candy, who was buried in the backyard on McCalmont Street, with an engraved tombstone. Grandpa Cole was also fond of animals.

Donald is five years older than I, but the youngest in his family. When he was a boy, he was often in a pickle due to his mischievous nature. Once, when he was visiting our home in New Jersey with his parents, I, at the precocious age of ten, discovered him smoking in the woods behind our house. He was fifteen. Smart aleck that I was, I turned informer and told his parents. I expected him to get a talking to or maybe a mild switching, which is what I would have received from my own parents by that time. I was mortified when he was beaten with a belt, and I was heartily sorry for my treachery.

Many years later, after his wife's death, I visited Marian with my daughter, Sarah. By then, the surviving Bernhoft siblings all lived near each other, Marilyn having died some years before, and we skied with them again. This time I was able to participate on more challenging slopes, but on the day I spent with Don, after patiently doing the intermediate trails with me, I sensed he was itching to fly down the advanced courses where he excelled, even in his late sixties.

That evening, we visited Don's house. Talking with him alone in the kitchen, I tried to apologize for ratting on him for the smoking incident when we were children, but he had forgotten about it. "There were so many," he said with a smile.

CHAPTER 12

Getting Ready for Life

Mom's Next Trips

When I was in college and Nancy in high school, Mom spent another summer in France with my father in tow. I was left home so I could carry on with my summer job, and Nancy was shipped off to Aunt Gladys's in upstate New York, where Grandma and Grandpa were also living at the time.

Mom made one more trip on her own when Nancy and I were young adults. Leaving my father at home, my mother tried to persuade Nancy to go and stay with him, keeping house while she was gone. We all feared he would exist on soup and cereal without my mother there to provide his meals. However, Nancy was just starting out on her own with a new apartment and a new job, so Dad had to fend for himself. He survived. I did invite him to my apartment in New York for a weekend, so he at least got a few good meals and avoided starvation.

Grandma Frith

When I was home from college one summer, my mother and I went to visit my Grandmother Frith. She and my grandfather were living in an apartment near my father's sister, Aunt Goldie, who bore the brunt of caring for the aged couple. Perhaps my mother had felt some pressure to shoulder a belated share of that responsibility. I know my parents contributed financially.

We were on our way home in the car, and my mother seemed upset. I had a good visit with my grandmother, who was always my champion and expected great things of me. She loved my music and my theatre aspirations. Unlike Grandma Cole, she had always encouraged me, trying her best to bolster my frail ego. I don't remember what led up to it, but my mother came out with, "Grandma Frith never liked me."

I was taken aback, because I had never before given any thought to their relationship. They had always conversed quietly on our monthly visits with my father along. My grandmother would talk about the trivia of the week, and my father would interject an appropriate reply where indicated. My mother seldom spoke much during these visits, sitting nearby. The conversation was seldom, if ever, animated. I had never noted any strong animosity between the two women, nor had I in fact noted any actual affection. How fortunate my mother was that her mother-in-law, unlike her mother and grandmother, always remained civil. Of course, they didn't have to share a house.

Looking back, the reason was obvious. Grandma Frith was very plain speaking and down-to-earth. She was a good woman who had enjoyed life before she had to live with pain after a bus ran over her and left her crippled with two broken legs and a broken hip. She always took unreserved pleasure in her grandchildren, accepting them for who and what they were. She was not impressed by my mother's airs and pretensions. She and my grandfather seemed to live their lives without dwelling on what might have been and trying to recapture it.

I was an anomaly to my paternal relatives, but they loved me anyway.

Thou Shalt Always Encourage Your Child's Interests

When I was in my last years of high school, and again in college, my mother once again dangled the carrot, encouraging my interest in theatre. After all, Aunt Gladys had dabbled in theatricals and so had my mother. By then, my involvement with theatre had grown consuming. I was taken to live performances, both in New York and in summer stock. I remember seeing Helen Hayes and her daughter, Mary MacArthur, who was to die tragically of an illness at a young age, in a summer production of *Alice Sit by the Fire*. Of course, Mom enjoyed these productions as well as I did.

In those days, the way to break into theatre for a career on the stage was to obtain an Actor's Equity membership card. About the only way to do that was to work in summer stock with an equity company, albeit as a slave. Had an equity company offered pay, my mother might have allowed me to go. However, there was either no pay or it involved a question of paying the company. At best I would have to pay for my living expenses. I was not allowed to go, and was informed that I would have to find a paying summer job at AT&T and put away some money for college. "Of course, you can act in plays. Teach English in a high school like Aunt Louise and there will be opportunities to perform."

College Drama Major

After high school, I deserted my dream of being either a movie star or a Broadway actress, and went to Allegheny College in Meadville, Pennsylvania, not far from Uncle Ned's in Franklin and the farm at Sandy Lake. I was accepted as an English major, but in my sophomore year, I took the year-long acting course as an elective. I had to get permission from Mr. Tillinghast, the professor, and made the mistake of telling him, "It's going to be my fun course." He glowered at me with outraged dignity and replied, "Well, it's not mine!" I had to do some fast backpedaling to assure him that I would take the course seriously and put every effort into it. By the end of the year I had switched my major to drama.

Jack Tillinghast was a graduate of Yale Drama School, as were several other members of the Allegheny drama faculty. One of the

Me – college senior

newest movie stars to hit the silver screen was Paul Newman. Every coed drooled over him. He had been Jack Tillinghast's roommate. This gave Jack a particular aura by proxy in our eyes. He didn't speak at length about his former roommate, and I sensed a case of sour grapes, but he did mention Paul's new wife, Joanne Woodward, who was also beginning her film career. Mr. Newman had been married to someone else in his prefame days at Yale, and Jack seemed to see Ms. Woodward as an interloper. One of Joanne's early movies was coming to downtown Meadville, and Jack recommended that we see it because he grudgingly admitted that she was a good actress.

The movie was *No Down Payment*, and after the unmemorable stars, she was billed as "introducing Joanne Woodward." I sat through the movie, a black and white, and was rather bored by the performance of the two main characters. I had arrived after the movie started and thought the wife was being played by Joanne, probably due to influence of her husband. But who, I wondered, was the talented actress playing the trollopy, white trash wife of the next door neighbor? It was a much meatier role and was played to perfection by the blonde with the southern accent. I saw my error when the final credits came up. I was impressed.

Ann

Ann is not her real name, but my friend deserves mention here as her illness affected choices I made later in life. When I came home for spring break my sophomore year, and called my high school friend for a get together, I was informed by her mother that she was in a state psychiatric hospital. I had considered her a little flighty, but this was unacceptable. I couldn't get my mind around this news. Ann's mother did not know what to say to me and directed me to Ann's aunt, a social worker.

I called the aunt who invited me to her house so she could explain the situation to me in person. She was laid up in bed with a broken leg, so couldn't meet me elsewhere. I went, feeling awkward in her bedroom, but she was gracious and tried to make things clear to me, and validate the fact of Ann's illness. There had apparently been some bizarre behavior and she had been hospitalized for her own protection. She was subsequently placed in the state facility for in-depth therapy.

The next time the family visited Ann, they were kind enough to take me along. The state hospital complex, north of Poughkeepsie was impressive but drab. The red brick buildings were sprawled over a large acreage. We found the appropriate entrance and went in. We were allowed to meet with Ann in a large, supervised visiting room filled with plain chairs. Ann's parents, her two brothers and her sister were with me.

After a few moments of awkwardness, Ann and I began to speak more freely to each other. She told me about the insulin shock treatments she was receiving — a new modality. Because of them, she had gained weight and her thin frame looked puffy. She complained to me that other patients stole the few belongings she was allowed, and asked if I could bring her a lockable box on my next visit.

I replied, not thinking, "What do they have here — a bunch of kleptomaniacs?" Ann and I looked at each other and laughed. Then we noticed the faces of her scandalized family. I had done the unthinkable and alluded to people who were mentally unwell. They were verbally tiptoeing around Ann and would never have dared to say anything remotely connected to mental illness. The existence of mental illness had to be denied, especially to the one who was mentally ill.

Ann and I looked back at each other and understanding passed between us. She knew the truth, and needed support from those who were willing to recognize that truth. She knew then that, so far, I was the only one who would be giving that support. In the long run, I was inadequate to the task. I was ill-prepared to take it on due to my own lack of experience and maturity. Her family and I met with her psychiatrist, who gave us a surface explanation of Ann's problem. None of us truly comprehended it at the time.

I went back on my own when I was home for summer vacation, and this time Ann was allowed out on the grounds with me. She was finishing her insulin treatments that had made her quite heavy. She was to have a long course of counseling and group therapy before being discharged.

I didn't see her again that summer; the facility was several hours away and my days were full, or at least I made them so. I returned to school in the fall for my junior year and didn't think much about Ann, although we wrote. Then she was out. There had been no counseling and therapy; funding had dried up, and there was a mass exodus from mental facilities. Ready or not, here we come. Ann was not ready.

I didn't have much contact with her again until after graduation from college, when I was invited to her wedding. I attended the ceremony but did not go to the reception. I avoided her family. About a year later, I was invited to her apartment for dinner one evening when I was home visiting my parents for the weekend, working in the city. Her husband was not there.

Ann ultimately had a daughter, and I saw her again several years later when the child was around five. Ann was then divorced. She and her daughter came to spend a weekend with me in New York. She flushed her medication down the toilet while there. When we were walking down the street, I noted that the little girl acted more like the parent, cautioning her mother who was cavorting on the sidewalk like a bizarre child.

A few years later, I saw her once more when I was living on the Upper East Side in New York, next door to a psychiatric nurse, Carolyn. Ann showed up at the door, carrying her shoes, accompanied by a young man. Her behavior was, again, bizarre, more so than I had previously seen it. She had walked in her stocking feet all the way from Grand Central Station, some 40 blocks. She was manic and out of touch with reality.

I called my neighbor to stop over and advise me. After observing her, she told me to get her out of there — there was nothing I could do. I had learned that the young man was not an old friend, but someone she had met on the train. He was apparently looking for an evening's entertainment. I encouraged them to leave, and they did. I called my mother and told her what had happened. The next morning she called Ann's parents' home to make sure she had returned safely. Mom spoke with her brother, John, who informed her with a degree of coolness, that she had. That was the last I heard of her.

In hindsight, I think that I should have disregarded my neighbor's advice, although she was supposedly the expert. Now that I am a psychiatric nurse, I think I should have dismissed the gentleman, called her family myself, and perhaps gotten her to a crisis center. I don't think I could have done more than that. I lived too far away from her to be of daily support. But not stepping in on that last occasion was surely a sin of omission.

First Roles

Returning to lighter topics, junior year was not a theatrically brilliant one for me, but I did play a minor role in a major production — the wife in Moliere's *The Imaginary Invalid* — and had good parts in several children's theatre productions. I particularly enjoyed my role as the witch in *Rapunzel*. "Rapunzel, Rapunzel! Let down your hair." Mimi Bates played the title role with a little droll humor. The prop people fixed her up with what was supposed to be very long hair, and we had a lovely tower at center stage. Mimi climbed up a ladder hidden in the back and perched at the window at the top. The "hair" was attached to a hook to secure it for when the prince or I climbed up on it. I was able to emote a full range of comic evilness in this role and loved every minute of it — this was the life for me.

The children's plays were such fun that I was thinking about having my own children's theatre. We were required to take courses both in theatre management and children's theatre, so I had some idea of what was involved. It's a direction that perhaps I should have pursued, but the old practical streak intervened — lack of money and a need for stability. My parents, products of the Depression and the loss of fortune, had fed me from the cradle on the importance of security. They made it quite clear that their help with my education and future career ideas would end with graduation from Allegheny. Of course, they did help me, several times, in fact. Looking back from a more mature vantage point, I think the theatre project could have succeeded, but as George Bernard Shaw said, "Youth is wasted on the young." I was afraid to take that step out into thin air, and I didn't do it.

Better Roles and Some Misbehavior

By senior year I was one of the big frogs in the little pond and finally landed some juicy lead roles in adult plays. I played the wife in *Witness for the Prosecution*, and had to learn German and Cockney accents — Marlene Dietrich had played the movie role. My roommate at the time had a father who was born in Germany. Her family lived near town, and her father was kind enough to spend an afternoon helping me to acquire the correct intonations, softening the accent a bit to make it more Viennese for the character. I picked up the Cockney on my own.

The next production that year was Thornton Wilder's *The Matchmaker*. My friend, Peri Grinnell, was to play the lead. I was assigned to be the stage manager, as all drama majors were expected to perform that function somewhere along the line. I had avoided it so far. Mr. Hampton was the director. He and his wife were new on the faculty that year, and he was also my advisor for my senior research project comparing the various dramatizations of the Joan of Arc story. He was an affable young fellow and much liked by the students. I muddled through my job as stage manager with a lot of help from my peers, most of whom were more knowledgeable about the stage manager role. When it was over, and we were rehashing, I asked Mr. Hampton if I had been the worst stage manager that ever was, hoping to garner at least some claim to fame.

His reply was, "well…not the VERY worst." Everyone laughed.

Christmas Vacation in New York

Peri lived in New Jersey, and I lived in upper Westchester County, New York. We decided to meet over Christmas vacation to see a play in New York. We didn't know which one, simply whatever play we could get last-minute tickets for. We met in the theatre district and had lunch, then headed for the box offices. Immediately, we spied the marquee advertising *The Miracle Worker*, with Anne Bancroft. She was one of our idols, so we decided to try for tickets.

Standing room only was all that was available. Our feet were cold and wet, as we had foolishly not prepared for the slushy city streets in our flimsy heels. Without a moment's hesitation we said yes to the tickets. I will not dwell on the performance, which was superb. We finally got seats for the second half, when the usher allowed us to sit where someone had not shown up.

When the play was over, we decided to go backstage and try to see Ms. Bancroft. We envisioned standing at the back of a crowd of well-wishers, catching a glimpse of her between the heads. We found our way to the stage door and told the man in charge that we wanted to see Miss Bancroft.

"Right this way. Just stand over there, next to the door."

We did as we were told, and watched as first Patricia Neal, then Patty Duke passed by on the way to their dressing rooms. We could hardly breathe. We kept looking for the crowds of well-wishers waiting to see Miss Bancroft. They had not yet arrived.

After a few minutes, the dressing room door opened and a smiling maid said, "Miss Bancroft will see you now."

Peri and I looked at each other. We looked down the hall for the crowd of well-wishers. There were none in sight. We looked at the maid, who was still smiling, and holding the door for us. We went in.

Anne Bancroft was sitting at her dressing table, smiling at us. Peri and I found ourselves in a struggle trying to hide behind each other. Anne laughed and said, "well, which one of ya's gonna talk first?"

We finally stammered out something about being acting students in college. Anne was absolutely gracious, inquired briefly about our aspirations, then excused herself. The audience was over. We almost fell out of the room. In a daze, in our sloshy shoes, we made our way back to the street.

The Next Role

After returning to Allegheny at the end of Christmas vacation, I prepared to snag the plum role of Joan in *The Lark* — Julie Harris's Broadway role. I succeeded and we worked on this one over the winter vacation in February, while most of the other students were away. The dorms were closed. My children's theatre professor, Ann Vliet, was a Texan, and she and her playwright husband were taking their little girl, Brook, home to visit family over the holiday. Peri and I could do them a favor and stay in their large apartment in an old Victorian house on the edge of town, and feed their neighbors' pets.

We accepted this deal gladly. The downstairs consisted of a very large, high-ceilinged living room with built-in bookcases lining the walls, and a fireplace — which we were not allowed to use. Behind that was a small dining room, then an unremarkable kitchen that had been created when the house was made into apartments. Up a back staircase were the bedrooms and Brook's "closet." Ann maintained that her preschool daughter slept in a closet and we expected to see some dark hole of a room. It was indeed the size of a large closet, but it had a window and was a cozy little nook.

On the second floor there was a door to a staircase bringing us into the third floor of the other side of the house where we were to feed the animals — they were mice, or something. Peri got the master bedroom and I slept on a cot somewhere in a large hall. Our exact locations have faded into history, but Brook's "closet" stands out.

Of course, we had class assignments to work on over the break, lines to learn and rehearsals to attend. But noting that Ann wasn't much of a housekeeper though she was an excellent teacher — I found time to give her kitchen a thorough cleaning in repayment for our stay. It was a little unnerving when I opened the back door to put some trash on the porch, to find a large rat staring back at me. I shrieked and slammed the door. I hoped it wasn't one of the pets we were to feed. We used the front entrance from then on.

One evening we had a visit from two of our fellow players, Rod Anderson and Dale Arnink, both of whom were staying with the head of the drama department, Mr. Hulbert. Apparently, it was his responsibility to oversee our morals for the week. Rod was playing the Dauphin and Dale was playing a priest — excellent casting, as he was actually a lay preacher for a small church. Peri and Rod weren't dating, but they did have an attraction for each other. Dale and I indulged in some mild flirtation in the small dining room, but the living room, where Peri and Rod were, was quite dark. It was late and Dale and I had run out of conversation. The phone rang in the living room, and I barged in to answer it. It was Mr. Hulbert, looking for Rod and Dale, who weren't supposed to be there. In a world-weary voice, he said, "May I please speak with Rodney or Dale?"

I replied, in a squeaky voice, suddenly terrified, "They aren't here."

A deep sigh poured through the phone line, followed by a pause. Then, "Well, just tell them it's time to come home."

"Yes, sir," I answered in a small voice.

Peri and Rod were rearranging themselves and Dale scurried for coats. He was the one with the car. They made a hasty exit while Peri and I looked at each other for a long moment. Then we burst out in nervous laughter. We were feeling apprehensive about what punishment might be in store for us. Mr. Hulbert struck fear into the hearts of his students, especially females who he felt had no place on this earth, and certainly not in serious theatre courses. We were sure we would be cast as the Jezebels who had lured the boys to our den.

The next day, Peri was picked up in a car to go to the Playshop early to work on costumes. That was her function in this production. I was due there later for rehearsal. There had been a thaw, the roads were slushy, and the air was cold. No one was coming to pick me up, so I bundled up as best I could and trudged off for the two-mile walk, up the hill to the college. It began snowing again. After awhile, I could hardly see where I was going, but "the show must go on." I dragged myself in the door of the Playshop. Mr. Hulbert was there but said not a word about the previous night. There was also no word of appreciation for the ordeal of cold and wet that I had endured to get to the rehearsal. The only acknowledgment was a grunt in my direction. This was to let me know that, even though I was playing the main character in the production — the star of the show — my position was very low in the grand scheme of things. Nothing was ever mentioned about the incident with the boys.

Performance Stories

Eventually the students returned from their break, the rehearsals were over, and performance time had arrived for *The Lark*. There was a dress rehearsal with an audience on Thursday, then three performances over the weekend. During one performance, I suddenly developed a dry cough and could not speak until I had cleared it. There was nothing for it but to cough it out, then pick up as if nothing had occurred. Fortunately, my partner in the scene was one of the professors, and he was professional enough to freeze the scene until I could resume. The audience waited with no whispers or laughter. I wiped away the tears that the coughing had produced, then closed my eyes for a moment, getting my character back. I was Joan again, and the play continued.

During another performance of that play, my attention wandered while I was backstage waiting for my cue. When I refocused, it occurred to me that I had not heard that particular dialogue before. I began listening very hard for my cue, and became more and more bewildered until finally, with a tone of desperation, the actor ended his sentence, with exaggerated enunciation, "ON THE OUTSIDE COMING IN! I suddenly realized that I had missed my cue and he had been adlibbing for some time, hoping that I would appear. I rushed in and picked up the thread of the scene. After grateful and relieved looks, we carried on as though it was all part of the play. The audience never knew.

The other on-stage situation that occurred in that production was due to the great variation in height between the two student actors playing the guards who were to tie me to the stake, then carry me offstage to be burned. The setting for the play was a stark one, similar to the one in the Broadway production. All the action took place on the stage floor and a series of levels, different scenes being defined by area, level and lighting. The fire was depicted by a light wheel offstage with turning colors throwing the impression of flames onto the back curtain. When I was carried off, my exit would be followed by the rising of the flames with crackling sound effects. We were not to exit at stage level but had to drop off from a level about two feet above the stage floor. Because one guard was extremely tall and the other extremely short, I was carried at a precarious angle. They never did drop me but I dreaded that exit every evening. I was supposed to be praying as I was carried off — and I was.

I actually was dropped when I played Stella in Tennessee Williams's *A Streetcar Named Desire*. During rehearsal, Stanley, played by Dale, my cohort from the winter break episode, was carrying me up the winding staircase outside the apartment house when his balance shifted. He lost his grip on me, and I went rolling down the steps. Fortunately, the result was no more than a scrape on my wrist where my watchband dug into me.

Streetcar was the big spring production, and a former graduate, then attending Yale Drama School, returned to direct it as his graduate project. His professional actress wife played Blanche. I was ordered to become a blonde for the part, to contrast with her. I proceeded to bleach my dark brown hair on my own with some drugstore product. It came out the color of a bright new copper penny. My friends in the dorm advised me to throw a scarf over my head while they rounded up a car, and we made a mad dash to the drugstore in town, to get something to tone it down. The next day I splurged on a professional dye-job at a beauty salon. My roots were beginning to show by the last performance, and the day after closing I was back at the salon to be returned to my natural dark color.

The other notable event connected with *Streetcar* was that, after it closed, at the cast party at Bill Seybold's house, after consuming numerous Salty Dogs — vodka and grapefruit juice — I became drunk for the first time in my life.

Uncle Ned and Aunt Evelyn, my staunch supporters, faithfully came to see me in all the plays. My parents came when they could, but it was still a long trip even though the two-lane highways had been replaced by huge interstates. I sang in the talent shows and for Friday night dances at the Student Union. I wrote a short children's play based on the fairy tale *The Nightingale* and presented it in my basement at home over Christmas vacation, with a neighbor child playing the lead.

My Pal

Tucker never lost his boyish devilishness. I remember one occasion when I was visiting on McCalmont Street during my college years. I was a sophomore, and Tucker was a high school senior. One evening Aunt Evelyn took us to the movies. I don't remember what was playing, but I remember that there were several cartoons first. Tucker and I would look at each other and go into gales of laughter at each turn of the cartoon story. It was so bad that Aunt Evelyn got up and moved several rows away from us, not wanting to be seen with us. We laughed even harder until our sides ached.

I saw less of Tucker when he went off to college; our weekends at Uncle Ned's didn't always coincide. When he brought Carol home to meet the family, I was happy for him, but felt some pangs of jealousy because I was losing my pal.

Vets

Senior year was also the year of big romance. I discovered the Korean vets. Of course, I already knew of their existence, but now I was thrown into their circle. Several of them were English majors and were friendly with Al Kern, the professor who taught the modern novel. Peri and I heard that he defended his friends at a faculty meeting when another professor was complaining that at all times one could find alcohol and women in the vets' apartments. Professor Kern stated, "No, you won't always find women in the apartments."

Their friendships overlapped into the drama department, and Peri was being pursued by one of them. Riding on her coattails, I was invited to their parties. At one of them, I was noticed by Jim Riley, an attractive, round-faced fellow of Irish descent, who had a love for alcohol. He was angry, romantic and morose. It never would have worked in the long run because he had an unreasoning hatred for cats, horrifying me with tales of shooting them on sight at his upstate New York home. I knew a little about him already as one of my former friends, who had graduated the previous year, had an unrequited interest in him. He had often been the topic of her conversation.

My relationship with Jim was up and down for awhile, and, during a down phase, I was fixed up on a blind date with Tony Arthur, another vet. He turned out to be a tall, good-looking, serious young man, more focused on his goal than most of the others in that group, and less involved with alcohol and partying. Of course, I found him totally dull — at first. However, his quiet steadiness, and his silent disapproval of my relationship with Jim, eventually caught my attention.

This all began in the fall, and made for a stormy year, emotionally. I could not settle on one or the other. I was attracted by the outrageous Jim, and drawn to the quiet Tony. When I was with one, I was angry at the other, and the other would pursue more strongly. I would switch, and the pattern would reverse. At the end of the year, after some waffling back and forth, I went to the final formal dance with Jim who was staying on at college for summer school to make up one more course for graduation. I was headed for New York City. Jim did come to New York after he finished his course, but I had moved on to other things. I lent him some money to get home, and that was the last I saw of him or the money.

I exchanged some sparse letters with Tony over the next years, but ours was not a steady correspondence. He was busy earning advanced degrees and building his career. He ended up in California, and I was surprised when I received a letter inviting me to come to see him there. I often think I should have done that. He was a nice guy, smart, and good looking. The same fear of risk taking that by then had prevented me from taking a real gamble on a career in acting, kept me from taking that trip. By this time, Tony had earned his Ph.D. and was teaching at a branch of the University of California. As far as I know, he was the only one of the veteran group who did well. I didn't go. Had I gone, I wouldn't have Julia and Sarah.

Rett Revisited

During the spring break, I returned to Ridgewood with my mother. She was going to visit a friend and I planned to stop in and see Rett. We had not seen each other for years but I hadn't called ahead — I would surprise him. If he wasn't home, nothing was lost; I could go to meet my mother at her friend's.

I walked up the long driveway and front steps. Rett's family now lived on the first floor, the elder Zabriskies having passed on. Marian Zabriski answered the door. She was still wearing platform shoes, and her hair was still auburn. She still looked down her nose at me with hauteur. But I was taller!

Rett was not at home, but Marian invited me in for tea and a chat about my acting plans. She finally found something about me that was interesting, and actually seemed impressed. I lost touch with Rett after that. I heard that he married a minister's daughter and became a minister himself — he who always enjoyed playing the bad guy in our childhood games. His family disowned him over it at the time, but there was probably an eventual reconciliation.

Many years later, our paths almost crossed again when my parents moved back to New Jersey for retirement, to the village of Lebanon. Rett had lived in the town they moved to, but was leaving to take up another post. He heard of their arrival and wrote them a note to let them know he was sorry to have missed them. My mother misplaced the note, and the link was broken. When my parents subsequently decided to moved to Florida, they sold the New Jersey house to my husband and me. In the course of things, I met a woman at church whose mother had been friendly with Rett during his stay in Lebanon, and I approached the mother to ask if she could contact him and give him my address and phone number. She acted quite strangely about it, asking why I wanted to contact him. I explained that I had grown up with him and he had been my childhood playmate, but she seemed to suspect some ulterior motive. There was none, but she never did pass on the message.

Meanwhile, after graduation, I moved to New York City to begin my acting career. Just how I was going to do that was still a mystery.

CHAPTER 13

Robert's Story

Christmas, Easter, Thanksgiving and Halloween were always antici-pated and enjoyed with pleasure at the homes of Aunt Gladys, Uncle Ned and our family. Our celebrations were the most secular, but theirs were memorable as well. This was not the case at Uncle Bob's. His strict adherence to all that was rigid in the Wesleyan church prevented an outward show of holiday spirit. Halloween was not celebrated at all. It was considered sinful and immoral — the devil's holiday.

If Ned was her darling, Robert was my mother's hero. He was the one who had rescued her cat from the perils of the swirling waters of the Ohio River. He was the one who stayed on the farm with her father and grandmother to fight the invaders. Once all was lost on the island, he came north to Sandy Lake and helped his father build the farm business there. He was my grandfather's right-hand man. For years he devoted himself to that work, and attended the small Sandy Lake Wesleyan Methodist Church on Sundays whose congregational beliefs allowed little leeway for pleasure.

I also liked my Uncle Bob when I was little. On visits to the farm, I demanded his attention, and he would sometimes stop work long enough to play a game with me or tell a story. He was a big man, not handsome. His nose still retained the evidence of an earlier school-yard fight. He had the Cole brown hair and blue eyes.

I remember threshing time one year. I came down with a summer cold and was reclining like Cleopatra on the sofa in the dining room, where the threshers would eat their noon dinner. I wanted Uncle Bob to entertain me. He would not. He tried to explain gently that he had to work with the threshers, but I would have none of it. I flounced upstairs to my room and sulked. I was three or four.

Later, Uncle Bob called me to come outside. He wanted me to see something, and his urgent tone piqued my curiosity. I roused myself from my sulky state and came down the stairs and outside to see what was so important. He yelled with sadistic glee, "there's a chicken without its head!" Indeed there was. Grandma, whose chickens they were, had massacred one with her axe and it was running headless through her garden, leaving a bloody trail. It began to flop, dropped to the ground, and died. I did not eat chicken for dinner that day.

I think my uncle always had a mean streak. He was in his late teens when he left Neville Island, and had considered himself the heir apparent of the farm. He was often put in charge of the younger children — my mother and Ned — and enjoyed lording it over them. Losing that farm hit him the hardest of all the children. His resentment grew and festered.

Eventually, Uncle Bob married a placid and innocent country girl named Jeanne Tenney, and brought her to live at the farm. She was nineteen, and he was thirty-seven. My mother later said that he thought he was getting a workhorse, but her health was not up to the expectation. Uncle Bob and Aunt Jeanne had five children: Norine, Marsha, Roberta, Helen and Keith. These children had a hard time with their father's interpretation of his Wesleyan Methodist religion, which circumscribed their lives so tightly, and kept them isolated from the mainstream of life.

His two oldest daughters grew up witnessing the cruelty their mother suffered, not only at Bob's hands, but from my grandmother as well. If Bob paused to show his wife a scrap of affection on his way out the door, his mother would quickly intervene with sharp words. "That's enough of that. Get on to work." She, too, had become embittered.

Those scraps of affection were few and far between, and Jeanne was expected to sit up until everyone else went to bed in case they should want anything of her, and to be up early in the morning to serve them. Her eldest daughter, Norine, told me of a particular instance that was fixed in her mind's eye. Her mother's parents had come for a rare visit, and Jeanne took a few minutes to sit and talk with them. Uncle Bob happened upon this scene and hurried to fetch a broom. Thrusting it at his wife, he said, "Let's go. There's work to be done."

Jeanne immediately jumped to do Bob's bidding. Her shocked parents did not return again to the farm. Jeanne was a timid soul and afraid to fight back against the treatment she received at the hands of her husband and his mother.

When Aunt Jeanne came to live at the farm, she had little knowledge of cooking the way her mother-in-law wanted it done. It was up to Grandma, who was an excellent cook, to teach her. Grandma did this with a sneering condescension that did nothing to increase the young bride's confidence. Throughout her life, Jeanne's cooking was demeaned by her husband and his mother.

During threshing season, and again at apple harvest, Aunt Evelyn, Ned's wife, came to the farm to help with the cooking. She soon became aware of what was going on and took every opportunity to relieve her sister-in-law of her burdens. Evelyn would tell Jeanne that her work was done, and to take time to relax with her children. Evelyn would then inform my grandmother that she had taken over the kitchen, that Jeanne had finished her work, so there would be no reprisals against Jeanne.

From my mother's comments at home, it was apparent that she also witnessed and disapproved of Bob and Grandma's treatment of Jeanne, but she was not there often enough to effect much improvement in the situation. She contented herself with informing our family of her observations after we returned home to New Jersey.

When my cousin, Snooky, was a small child, she and her parents, Ned and Evelyn, lived at the farm for a short time just before Bob married Jeanne. For some reason, the little girl, with a child's keen sensitivity, developed a strong hatred for her Uncle Bob, perceiving his underlying tendency toward cruelty. She delighted in playing mean, childish tricks such as pouring talcum powder into his underwear drawer. When she grew older, away from the farm, she was not made aware of the depth of his meanness toward his wife and children, and she developed guilt feelings about her hatred of him. When, in her later years, she learned from Norine the extent of his cruelty, she felt vindicated.

Uncle Bob arrived at the hospital after Jeanne had borne his third daughter, and found that she had already named the baby. He was beginning to despair of having a son and wanted a namesake. Without consulting her, he took it upon himself to change the name to Roberta, incorporating his first name, Robert, and his middle initial, A, for Augustus.

After Aunt Jeanne produced her fourth child, another girl, my mother commented at home that Bob seemed bent on killing his wife in order to get a son, and that Jeanne had been told by the doctor to stop having babies after the birth of her second. But Uncle Bob was determined to produce a son and heir, and his submissive wife finally fulfilled his wish. The last child was a strapping boy that Bob named Keith, after his old friend, Keith Louden, from Neville Island.

Norine and Marsha lived under the harsh religious dictates of their father and grandmother. I and some of my other cousins were turned away from the church as a result of religion as practiced by our parents. But Norine and Roberta maintained the religious convictions that almost destroyed their lives, taking from their mother a belief in God's love, rather than hellfire and damnation. They have clung to this aspect during times of adversity. Jeanne had been loving to them, and kept up her own faith in spite of the nightmare of her life. Her children did not hesitate to confide their miseries and their problems to her, although her powerlessness to help them in any material way must have frustrated her beyond what she already endured.

The girls were not allowed to participate in school activities; the classroom, church and farm comprised their world. Most certainly, they could not aspire to cheerleading like their cousin, Darlene — the skimpy, short skirts ruling out any consideration of that sport. Grandma refused to shorten Darlene's skirts, but Darlene soon figured out how to do it herself. Bob's girls had their school clothing ordered from catalogs, and were always far behind the fashion, dressed more like little old women than like young girls. Cheerleading was out of the question.

When our family visited the farm, we brought bags of outgrown clothes in good condition for the girls. I thought they might resent the hand-me-downs, although they were nice, but when I met them as adults, they assured me that they had looked forward to these as gifts. Their father, of course, went through them first lest some devil's wear slip through.

One year, my mother noticed some of these items being used as cleaning rags — probably clothing that had been culled out by Bob. My mother refused to take them clothing again, not understanding the hardship that would wreak on the children. Grandma made dresses for the girls from feed bags. In earlier days, that was a common and accepted practice. In one episode of *Little House on the Prairie*, Laura Ingalls was anticipating a new feedbag dress. But my cousins later were embarrassed at school as this was no longer an accepted practice, and their classmates in the farming community recognized the source of the cloth.

When Darlene, Uncle Ned's daughter, attended her freshman orientation at Slippery Rock College in 1961, two students approached her, the girl saying that Darlene couldn't be, but the boy wanted to ask anyway. They had graduated from the high school in Sandy Lake and knew the Cole children there. They asked Darlene if she was related. When she said yes, they acted surprised. The Cole children they knew were never allowed to wear clothing that was in style, or knew any social graces. Darlene, by contrast, was a confident, well-groomed and fashionable young lady.

At Christmas at Uncle Bob's there were either no gifts, or gifts shared by all. One Christmas, Roberta asked for a horse, which was not an unreasonable request, as they had the means to house one in the barn, and work horses were already kept. Uncle Bob went to an auction and purchased a used, stuffed, threadbare zebra. This was her only Christmas present that year.

The one area where Bob did not stint his family was food. He liked to eat, as his expanding girth attested, although he constantly demeaned Jeanne's cooking. He did all the food shopping, as Jeanne wasn't physically able to do it. She gave him her list, but he would buy what he chose from it, and she would have to prepare the meals from what he brought home. For instance, if she had mastered some chicken recipes, she might be forced to confront a pot roast.

As his parents aged, Uncle Bob became anxious to receive his inheritance as the eldest son. My mother, along with other family members, was under the impression that he coerced my grandfather into signing the farm over to him with the threat of leaving the old couple to run the farm alone in their old age.

It could have been in Bob's nature to do that, but Norine, who was there, told a different story. Grandpa, the inveterate gambler, had put up the farm as collateral to finance one of his stock market deals. The deal fell through, and the farm was forfeit. Bob and Grandma went to the bank, took out a joint loan and recovered the farm. Grandma would not allow the farm to slip from her favorite son's grasp. Uncle Bob then went to work off the farm to earn the money to buy out his mother's half. Uncle Ned no longer had a vested interest in the farm and left the problem to Bob and his mother.

Aunt Jeanne did not have the strength to do her assigned household chores and help tend Grandma Cole's prize gardens. My cousins perceived that the gardens suffered neglect and the house fell into disrepair. As systems broke, they were not fixed. The elder Coles could not bear the decline and were no longer able to do the work themselves. Grandma grew embittered and constantly needled Bob about his failures. She began to make lengthy visits to my Aunt Gladys, in Syracuse. Grandpa stayed, but when his fights with Bob became more than he could bear, he would take the bus to Franklin to stay at Ned's for a week before returning to the fray.

Mom informed us that Grandma and Grandpa finally felt that their only recourse was to accept the invitations of Gladys and Ned to alternate staying at their homes throughout the year. The green

Victorian horsehair furniture, as well as their bedroom furniture, went with them to Uncle Ned's, a half-hour away. They made a short annual visit of a month to our house, and I remember Grandma complaining about conditions at the farm.

Uncle Bob took his pleasures in town, reportedly at the Stoneboro Hotel. There he consorted with the local women of the night, and drank. Grandma never knew of this behavior, and he would deny it if confronted. Uncle Ned, however, had some friends, Coonie and Lucy Counselman, who lived next door to the hotel, and they would report Uncle Bob's carousing to him. Uncle Ned had also done some drinking in his time, but was never deceitful about it, accepting censure as it was earned. Uncle Bob ignored any admonishments from his brother.

Jeanne had developed diabetes and was seriously overweight. It was not many years before Uncle Ned arrived at the house one day to find no one around. This was odd, because Aunt Jeanne was never away from home. Cautiously, he looked through the rooms, going upstairs to check the bedrooms. He found Jeanne lying dead on the bed in the little downstairs bedroom.

Ned was about to call the funeral director when he saw Bob's car pull up, and Bob emerge with two large bags of groceries. Ned ran from the house to inform his brother of the tragedy. Bob replied, "I know. There will be lots of people coming and I had to have food for them." He was calm.

Ned was aghast and asked him, "Did you call anyone? The coroner?"

Bob had not yet called anyone. Ned rushed to the phone and called the funeral director in Shakleyville. He uncharacteristically lied, telling him that his brother had returned home from the store to find his wife dead. Ned was too horrified at his brother's callousness to tell the man the truth.

As my sister and I grew older, and my parents became busier with their own lives, our visits to the farm became less frequent. My mother was incensed during one visit when Uncle Bob refused to let Norine come east with us for a visit, for fear that we would corrupt her with our heathen ways. We were not Wesleyan Methodist. Perhaps he sensed that my mother was itching to get her hands on the child and introduce a little affection and culture into her life, and show her other possibilities besides her existence on the farm.

Uncle Bob was no longer the hero, no longer the jovial uncle, no longer a very admirable person. The ever-hovering bitterness had taken over. He seldom smiled, and on those rare occasions when he did, it was a bitter smile. I don't recall staying the night there once my grandparents had moved out.

When I attended Allegheny College in Meadville — only a half-hour away from Sandy Lake — I visited Uncle Ned's whenever I could. I refused to visit Uncle Bob, although he and Aunt Jeanne, who was still alive, invited me. I was under the impression that he had driven Grandma and Grandpa from the farm. Aunt Jeanne was always in the background during our earlier visits, and I never came to know her well. I had no idea at the time what a nightmare her life had become. I could have done nothing to help her break away because she had nowhere to go. But a little understanding and affection might have gone a long way.

After Jeanne's death, Uncle Bob lived on at the farm. All of his five children left home soon after their grandparents had gone. The eldest, Norine, had been put to work in the fields at age nine, and she married at age seventeen, before finishing high school. Uncle Bob's eldest children were cut off from the outside world. They did not know what a normal family was, with affection shown between spouses. Their role model of a married couple was an apparently loveless mating.

Norine's father approved of her choice of husband — a thirty-five-year-old man who worked for him on the farm. Bob saw him as a steady workhorse. That was the most important attribute in a husband, as he himself had owned it. This man took Norine to his small cabin, not far from the farm, and made her a virtual prisoner. There was no indoor plumbing in the cabin, but there was an outhouse out back. Many years later, Norine described it, with little humor, as "three rooms and a path." However, she was not allowed to avail herself of even that small convenience, as she was locked in the house with only a slop jar to relieve herself, when her husband went to the farm to work. After a fierce beating, she finally managed to escape from the cabin. When she ran back, through woods and across fields, to the family farm, her father gave her a grudging welcome. One workhorse was as good as another.

Roberta was younger, and Bob's favorite in that she was his namesake. She had been allowed more freedom growing up, and was allowed to visit the homes of her friends. She realized that her family was not normal.

Uncle Bob was generous with physical punishment, doling out frequent beatings to his children. He once chased Norine around the outside of the house with a frying pan, attempting to hit her on the head with it. The younger daughters, Roberta and Helen, were spared some degree of punishment. Although Keith's birth was long hoped for by Bob, he was mercilessly strict with Keith once he had arrived, and he, too, endured beatings. Eventually, the harshness of his life drove him away from home to build a new life in Texas, returning for his father's funeral.

Darlene told me of an incident at the farm when she was an adult, visiting there with her dad. She and Uncle Ned noticed Grandma's old copper pot, which she had used to make jam, lying neglected near or in the barn. Darlene thought it would be nice to have it, and her father asked Uncle Bob for it. Uncle Bob replied that Darlene could have it for $500. This angered Darlene and she walked away. A few days later, Uncle Ned came home with the pot and presented it to his daughter. How he came by it is a mystery.

In time, the farm was sold, and ultimately passed to Fred Tenney, one of Aunt Jeanne's relatives. As the fates, in a jocular mood, would have it, Bob met and married a lady named Marie who was a force to be reckoned with. She was an energetic and pleasant woman, and tolerated no nonsense from him. Aunt Evelyn was her ally, advising her to stand up to Bob, after telling her about the unfortunate Jeanne. Marie whipped him into shape. He became almost amiable in his last years, his fear of approaching death giving him pause to reconsider his treatment of his family.

I saw Uncle Bob and Marie with my mother and father when we were on a family visit to Uncle Ned. Uncle Ned told us that Uncle Bob wanted to take us all to lunch. This was at odds with what I remembered as his tight-fisted nature. I was hesitant about seeing him, as

I still harbored ill will. Uncle Ned convinced me to let bygones be bygones for the day, at least, and I agreed to go.

Uncle Bob was expansive and seemed truly glad to have us as his guests at a little country restaurant. Marie was not with him, giving him time alone to make amends with his family. After lunch, he invited us all to his house where she was waiting, hoping to meet us. Uncle Ned had told us how she had effected a change in Bob, and after seeing his new persona, I was curious to meet her. She was, indeed, a pleasant, outgoing woman with a firm handshake — the opposite of the diffident Jeanne. I could see how Marie had taken him in hand.

After the introductions were over, Uncle Bob invited me for a tour of his gardens. When we reached his asparagus patch, he gave me earnest instructions on the proper cultivation techniques that had produced the family livelihood for so many years. I felt that he was passing on the secrets to the next generation. Perhaps I was the last hope. I, at least, had a garden at home. That was the last time I saw Uncle Bob.

Uncle Bob with second wife, Marie

Shortly before his death, Bob called Ned who was spending the winter in Florida and asked him to come home as he was not well. Uncle Ned told his daughter, Darlene, that Bob wanted to make amends, and they forgave each other. This enabled Ned, as well as Bob, to make peace after the lifetime of struggle and animosity between them. Uncle Bob died soon after from complications of diabetes.

During his eulogy, the minister said that Bob had recently asked God for forgiveness, and added that he thought Bob would be going to heaven. Family members had their serious doubts about that.

It's possible that Uncle Bob clung to such an extreme view of his religion because it helped him justify his inability to make something more of the farm and of his life. As long as he could blame everything on God's will, he could reconcile himself to that. Once the farm was sold, and he was out from under the heavy burden, his metamorphosis began. He still followed his religion, but with a kinder eye.

I saw Norine along with her sister Roberta, when I was researching this book. They were now mature women. Norine was a forceful figure — tall, well groomed and self-assured. Roberta had the sweet, gentle face of her mother, more diffident than her sister. I recognized them as soon as they drove up, although Darlene and Snooky were with me in case I didn't know them. The two women hugged us all, clearly pleased to see us again.

We met at a restaurant, the same restaurant where Bob had taken us so many years before, and I was afraid the noisy atmosphere would not be conducive to confidences. I was hesitant about asking questions that were too probing, as I sensed some reserve in Norine. Darlene was not so reluctant, however, and soon brought up the topic that was key to our meeting. She sensed their hesitation and told the women that all of us had bad experiences in the family, and that they were not alone. She asked them directly how they felt about their father. She asked if they hated him. As expected, Norine paused and her first response was noncommittal. Unexpectedly, Roberta broke the ice.

"We had an unhappy home life."

This was all it took. Both she and Norine poured out the story of their lives with their father as I have told above.

CHAPTER 14

Starting Careers and Other Calamities

Mom, the Matchmaker

When I finished college and moved to New York, I had to do it on my own with no help from home. In that way, my mother hoped to discourage me from pursuing a theatrical career. She figured I would eventually give up and go to work for AT&T like my father, find a nice boy — she had one in mind — and settle down. My father just wanted me at home. He didn't care what I worked at. He would tease and say I could just live at home and take care of him and that would be fine.

During that first summer, Mom pushed me at the son of one of her church friends, ever mindful of trying to keep my eyes on the ball that she was placing in front of me. Harold was a nice boy who had been in my class at school. In fact, he had been the valedictorian of my class. He wasn't malformed or anything, but I just wasn't attracted to him. He tended to be nervous and shy, pursuing his own interests rather than socializing. He had completed a pre-med course in college. My mother obtained tickets for a summer stock play and nagged until I called and invited him to go with me. We spent a pleasant evening but no sparks were ignited. He reciprocated politely by inviting me bowling. Again, we were amiable, but any thought my mother may have entertained of engineering a romance was doomed to failure. Neither one of us had the inclination, so we shook hands and parted forever.

New York at Last — Johnny

After graduating somewhere in the middle of my class, with only my acting achievements and a knowledge of shorthand and typing to recommend me, I headed for New York City. I landed a dismal office job at a charity organization and found a room in a dingy boarding hotel that I was sure was filled with all sorts of Runyonesque characters and out-of-work actors. By the end of the week I had learned that they were loud, arguing drunks, ladies of the night and others too colorful for my sheltered, suburban upbringing to appreciate. I found a sedate hotel on the edge of Greenwich Village, albeit more expensive. It had no air conditioning, however, and it was July.

One evening I could stand it no longer. I had no friends in the city at this point. Peri and I had spoken about finding an apartment together, but she had decided to go to graduate school in the Midwest, and I was on my own. The people I worked with at the charity organization lived in the suburbs of Brooklyn and Queens, and I didn't have anything in common with them. My dreams of New York adventures inspired by the movie, *My Friend Irma*, when I was in high school, were fast fading. I decided to go out alone to see what I could see. To make a long story short, this was my entrance to the world of the Beatnik subculture.

When I think back now, I realize what a risk I took and how it could have ended in disaster. I was standing on the street looking into a shop window when I was approached by a benign-looking fellow, not very prepossessing, who attempted to start a conversation with me. I ignored him at first, but something he said made me laugh, so when he offered to show me around the Village, I accepted. His name was Stanley.

This was one phase of my life where early influences came in handy. I was ever cautious in this new situation and played the observer. I wanted to see what would happen next, but was ready to retreat if things started to look dicey. My good sense of direction was my ally; I could always find my way back to the hotel. I accompanied Stanley to several clubs that evening and to a party at someone's apartment. I saw him frequently after that, but not as a boyfriend. He was simply my guide to this interesting world that came to include Johnny Walker. Johnny was not my boyfriend either, but I would have liked him to be.

Stanley lived with Johnny and another fellow named Steve Comacho. Stanley was the hanger-on — there by the forbearance of the other two. Steve was dark skinned, with some Spanish blood. Johnny was blond and blue eyed, with a slow smile, and handsome in an endearing James Dean way. He had migrated to the Big Apple from Rochester, New York. I never knew too much about Steve except that he was a musician and was always kind and polite to me, but I learned quite a bit about Johnny.

He came to New York to distance himself from his father. Johnny was a cellist and had lost part of a finger in a machine accident. It had healed, but had been a set-back to his music plans and he needed to retrain. I never knew just what the problem was between him and his father, except that it had something to do with Johnny's musical interests, and not wanting to follow the more practical career his father had chosen. Between the loss of his finger and problems with his father, Johnny was into the Beatnik "pot" scene, as were his roommates. However, unlike Stanley who lived by his wits on the street, both Steve and Johnny worked at steady jobs. Part of Johnny's philosophy was, "If you have more than you can carry in one suitcase, you have too much."

The hotel was expensive, and after paying for food, there wasn't much left of my paycheck. When Johnny and Steve invited me to move into the apartment, I didn't hesitate. Stanley had a small room behind the kitchen that looked out on an airshaft. He was far behind on his share of the rent, and was asked to leave. I felt bad for Stanley, but he would cadge a room from other acquaintances. He gathered his few belongings and was gone. The furniture consisted of a mattress on the floor, but the price was right.

Looking back, it strikes me as odd that I spent those summer months in the scene but not part of it. I remained an observer, and that earned me special treatment from both Steve and Johnny, especially Johnny. I didn't smoke pot with them, although I did smoke cigarettes — a vice learned in college. They looked up to me in a way, and it became Johnny's mission to preserve my innocence, maintaining my difference. I worked at a white-collar job, and was not a disillusioned drop-out from "the system." I had definite goals and ambitions, yet they saw that I was sympathetic to their lifestyle and their reasons for it. They did, however, find it amusing to try to get me "contact high," blowing smoke in my direction. This was acceptable to them as long as I never actually touched a joint. My own complicity in this strange abstinence was due more to my reluctance to take a chance than to any religious scruples.

The boys lived in a third-floor walk-up on the lower east side of Manhattan near Avenue C — quite different from anything I had known in my life. The neighborhood was a mixture of Beatniks, drunks, hard-core drug addicts and the remnants of ethnic groups that had originally settled there. The Henry Street Settlement was not far, and was well-known for its work with this diverse population.

In anticipation of the arrival of his girlfriend from out of town, Johnny arranged that I should sublet an apartment from a friend of his who had moved in with her boyfriend, but was stuck in the lease for this place near Avenue A. It was on the second floor and it was a wreck. It was also cheap, so I scrubbed dried dog shit off the linoleum floors — she had left her dog alone for long periods of time before relocating him to her new home — and cleaned it up as best I could. It was only a few blocks from where the boys lived, and I often saw them in the evenings and on weekends. When there were gatherings at the boys' apartment I was there, but I was seldom taken along when they went to parties where there was the possibility of more hard-core drug use. I was happy just to be around Johnny.

I was there when the girlfriend showed up. She was enrolled in college somewhere, and was from some high-class society background. I awaited her arrival with a mixture of curiosity and hatred. I don't remember her name, but she took command of the place when she arrived. I suppose she was attractive enough, but she had a very forceful, domineering personality. She tried to influence Johnny to get himself together and get on with his musical career, which was a positive thing. She also smoked pot heavily. Instead of mellowing her, it only made her more controlling. I thought that he might go along with her plans, but I couldn't understand how her personality could mesh with his. She had money and could help him. After observing the interplay between them for a while, I slipped out, retreating to my own place.

After the girlfriend had gone, Johnny seemed morose. At first, I thought he missed her. As it turned out, it was due more to the pressure of the relationship. One evening we were alone in the apartment, talking and listening to music. Johnny was smoking pot, and I suppose I was getting a little contact high. I wanted to lift him out of his black mood, and did that the best way I could.

If I had stayed, perhaps things would have gone differently. I knew Johnny liked me, but I wasn't comfortable with the lifestyle. In the fall, I moved to the Upper West Side to share a room with a girl from my class at the American Theatre Wing where I had been accepted as an acting student. Johnny said we would still see each other, but when I made the trip downtown after a couple of weeks, it was a different world. I was now an uptown girl and he was from the Village. It was over.

American Theatre Wing

I had gone home to my parents' house for a weekend to sort out my future plans. I had done nothing about my acting career, having gotten sidetracked on the Lower East Side. It had been a learning experience, but I couldn't stagnate there. The big problem was that I didn't know where to begin. I was still pretty naïve in the ways of the big city, and although this recent sojourn had been educational, it had done nothing to advance my goals. I had decided to apply to, and was accepted with a scholarship at, the American Theatre Wing. This school was strictly for acting and provided a thorough grounding. It was owned and run by Helen Mencken, daughter of H. L. Mencken, the famous author and journalist. The next hurdle was to get my parents to pay for my room and board. After some hassling, with tears and pleading involved, they capitulated. Or rather, my father did.

There were two groups in the one-year program. I soon made friends with those in my class, and solved the most pressing problem — that of housing. Ceci Carone was a vivacious little dancer — under five feet tall — from Toledo, Ohio, and lived in a women's rooming hotel a few blocks from the school. Her parents had her on a short financial leash, and she offered to share a room with me. I had to apply at the hotel, and have my character approved, but that was done and I moved in with Ceci. We had a small refrigerator and a hot plate in our room to prepare simple meals. Life was good.

The year was great fun, immersed in theatre with friends who were equally enraptured. Our modern acting teacher was a fiery-tempered Jewish man named Max Fischer. He was our guru and father figure. He yelled. The more he yelled, the more we knew he loved us and the more we knew we had talent. There were one or two in the class whom he hardly ever yelled at. We pitied them. One day we emerged from our classroom for our break to find the other class already in the hallway, smoking. They looked at us with concern and asked, "What did you do?" They had heard Max yelling. We all just looked at each other and smiled.

Our Shakespeare acting teacher, Mr. Cottrell, had been Marlon Brando's coach when he played Marc Antony in the movie *Julius Caesar.* To us, as serious acting students, Marlon Brando was an even bigger icon than Paul Newman. Mr. Cottrell was aloof, a marked contrast to the volatile Max, but he knew his stuff. We studied fencing, mime with Tony Montenaro, body movement and make-up. I had had some of this in college but not with such intensity. I loved it.

One of our perks was the occasional free pass to a Broadway show. I saw Tammy Grimes in *The Unsinkable Molly Brown,* and remember being impressed by her professionalism. She was in the middle of a dance number with another actor, when the spaghetti strap broke on her evening gown. A lesser actress might have become flustered and broken character. Ms. Grimes paused momentarily, picked up the long train of her gown, flung it over her shoulder, and proceeded on with the dance. The audience clapped and cheered. It was a wonderful theatre moment.

Acting school ended with the Tony Awards. Our school was one of the sponsors, so we were to wear identical outfits and were measured for them. By the time the outfits arrived at the school, classes were over.

A few weeks earlier, Ceci and I had moved into a spacious apartment in a real apartment house, with our neighbor from the hotel. She was an older, maiden lady in her thirties named Shirley, and she was somewhat neurotic. Once in the apartment, she became overtly possessive of Ceci, unnaturally so, I thought. Obsessive-compulsive behavior became apparent, and I became the object of an unwarranted vile jealousy. I had started a part-time job in the evenings as a key-punch operator — Shirley accused me of actually being out on the town with "men of the evening" — and I met another aspiring actress who was looking for a roommate for her ground-floor brownstone apartment.

By the time the Tony Awards came around, I had moved out of the apartment I shared with Ceci and Shirley. When I got off the elevator with my last load of belongings, Shirley was coming on. A gentleman entered the elevator when I did, and there were other passengers as well. He was a stranger. A fellow student, Bob Peters, who was friendly with Ceci and me, later told me that an indignant and fuming Shirley had arrived at the apartment and told Ceci that she had just seen me getting off the elevator with my "gentleman of the evening." I actually had no dates and no boyfriends during the time I lived with them.

Ceci was to pick up my outfit from school for me. She had brought the dress home, but when I stopped by to pick it up, Shirley, in an act of vengeful spite, refused to let me have it. She held my dress hostage and I missed the awards.

Lower East Side Children's Theatre Group

I chewed over missing the Tony Awards for awhile, but it was time to move on again, and start going to auditions. My knees shook, and due to their rattling, I couldn't even hear the piano accompaniment when I sang. I had no Actor's Equity union card so had no choice but to attend open auditions, referred to as cattle calls. There were hundreds of hopefuls who came for a handful of bit parts, which were probably already allotted to union members. I became discouraged. It didn't help matters any that my new roommate, Pat, was a very intelligent and talented girl who had graduated from New York City's prestigious High School of Performing Arts. She, too, was at a standstill with her career. If she was having trouble, what hope did I have?

Finally, I auditioned for a very far off-Broadway children's theatre play, a musical version of *Hansel and Gretel*. Only the desperate would attend such an audition — those like me who needed a credit — any credit — for their resume. The music was Humperdinck's, and some in the theatre group were actually talented. The costume designer had a particularly creative imagination. I was to play the witch, Rosina, wearing a fetching black hat tied under the chin with a huge yellow bow. A yellow rose decorated the brim. I was to play her as a very ugly

Me – the actress

witch with a very glamorous self-image. Unfortunately, the group was vastly under funded, and the production ran one weekend in the morning and early afternoon, during the downtime of a dinner theatre on the lower east side of Manhattan. It folded. The cast was supposed to receive a share of the profits as pay. There were no profits.

Undaunted, the group's founder and director, Lenny, proceeded to plan other productions. He and most of the others had known each other from their days as students at Emerson College, near Boston. He decided the group needed its own home where it could rehearse and give performances. I was now included in this group but was not part of the inner core. There were several good-looking guys, yet try as I might, none showed any interest in me other than friendship.

We proceeded to find a loft — again on the Lower East Side, not far from Katz's Delicatessen — where the rent was cheap and we had space to actualize Lenny's plans. We spent work time cleaning, painting and rehearsing. Lenny announced that another person would be joining the group, another old friend from Emerson — Kim. Up to this time, I had been the only girl, since the one who had played Gretel did not continue with us after the demise of the show. I looked forward to Kim's arrival.

She did, in due course, arrive. Lenny's big hope was that she would bring money with her. It seemed that her father was a very wealthy manufacturer of condoms so Lenny's hopes were well founded. However, when she arrived, it was with the news that her family did not support her theatre aspirations, and other than paying for her room in a posh Upper East Side hotel and providing her with some spending money, there would be no other funds. At about this time, my friend, Bob Peters, popped up again. I had told him about the theatre group and he was curious to see it. I brought him to the loft where he was welcomed by Lenny and the other guys.

Later that day, I had an opportunity to speak with Bob alone. I mentioned the fact to him that none of the guys seemed to have any interest in me although I was not a bad-looking girl, and had not previously experienced such massive romantic rejection. Bob explained it to me in no uncertain terms. "They're all gay! They've been coming on to me!" He thought it hilarious, and went on to elucidate further.

"One reason they brought Kim in was for you." I had told him previously that I thought Kim looked at me oddly now and then, but had not thought much about it. Now it was all clear. Bob decided he had no interest in the guys but would stick around and see if he could "reform" Kim. Bob was a bit of an oddball himself, awkward and outspoken in social situations. He had been trying to decide what his own sexual preference was, but as far as I know, he never allied himself with any of the fellows in the group, nor did he have any success with Kim.

Potage

My academic advisor at Allegheny, with great foresight, had insisted that I prepare for some sort of gainful employment, just in case. I had taken shorthand. In order to live, I became a Kelly Girl somewhere in the midst of this East Side children's theatre project. I knew I should leave some days free for making rounds and auditioning. But the paycheck! I liked it. Two of the guys in the theatre group — roommates, lovers — had friends who were straight. I'm not sure why they had been in New York, but they were leaving to accept better jobs elsewhere. The wife had a job at a TV advertising representative firm, and suggested I apply for her position. I interviewed and was hired. That, in essence, was the end of my acting career. Sold for a mess of potage.

A Visit to Marian

At about this time, I traveled by train to spend a weekend with Marian. I talked while she prepared dinner. I admired and envied her independent lifestyle in the apartment, which took up the second floor of a country farmhouse. There was a bittersweet note when I commented on her table settings, and she replied that she was now using the dishes and other items from her hope chest when she entertained guests, otherwise they might never be used. However, that would not be the case, because, in her early forties, she married Bob Morse, a man she had met briefly several years earlier through mutual friends while skiing at Gore Mountain in New York.

Enter Gordon

Gordon was a sociable young man who worked two doors down the hall from the office I shared with a girl named Gerry. Gordon is not his real name. Gerry was very pleasant, and we became good friends. The dividing walls of the offices were glass, and I noticed Gordon frequently watching me. He soon started asking me out, but this could not be known among the other employees as it was a small company. Of course, I told Gerry.

No one in the office really knew much about Gordon, but he was well liked. It turned out that he was Puerto Rican. He was bigger than the stereotype, being a muscular ex-Marine, and had a face that could have fit any number of ethnic models. At that time, the Puerto Ricans were the newest immigrant group in New York City and were engaged in the usual ethnic struggle for acceptance. Gordon's goal was to keep his ethnicity secret. Everyone at the office thought he was Jewish, and he fed into that belief by taking off the Jewish holidays.

In the course of things, he eventually had to let me in on the truth. He had a volatile personality, and the relationship was on-again, off-again for the next couple of years, but we finally married in a small ceremony at an Upper West Side Methodist church. He moved into my semifurnished apartment on the first floor of an old brownstone on West 76th Street.

Children's Theatre

I had become involved with a young adult group at the Methodist church, and noted that there was a large auditorium in the basement with an unused stage. This was the opportunity I sought to do something with my theatre interest. I had long ago left H-R TV Reps and had moved around in the TV and advertising fields, using my office skills. Nothing had caught my fancy for a career job. At least I could have something interesting to work at on the side, although there would be no pay. I suggested to the church group that we might try a children's theatre as a non-profit enterprise. The others were enthusiastic about the idea, and I became the first director. There was another young couple in the group who considered themselves professional actors and they participated for awhile and we were rivals for leadership. However, as there was no money involved, they soon tired of the power struggle and withdrew.

Over the next two years, we mounted several successful productions, running a couple of weekends each. I was very involved and enjoyed it, but Gordon, who helped now and then if only to see something of me, started doing little things to derail it. He was not doing well with his career, disdaining offers of help from older colleagues who recognized his abilities. He had a false sense of pride, insisting that he had to do it on his own with help from no one. He resented the fact that I had a pursuit that I enjoyed.

The Dark Side

There was another side to Gordon that had surfaced soon after our vows were said and I was trapped. He started by verbally belittling me and my theatre group, then proceeded to actual physical abuse. I have since learned that abusive men like to make their victim think it's her fault and that she deserves the beating. This didn't make sense to me at the time, but somehow, he succeeded in doing that. I was afraid not to believe it, backed up as it was by fists and feet. I finally appeared at a theatre meeting with bruised face and arms, and the young minister's wife took me aside and encouraged me to tell her what had happened. I was prepared to make a break.

Of course, as they do, Gordon was apologetic when I got home, promising — as he had many times before — that it would not happen again. The marriage limped on. A short time later, we moved to the Upper East Side, distancing ourselves from my friends at the church.

Nancy Gets Married, Has Kids, Returns to School

Meanwhile, my sister had gone off to college in New Jersey to Drew University. One evening she and some friends went to a small club where a jazz group was playing, and there she met Don Gallagher, a jazz pianist and clarinetist. One thing led to another, and when I was living in New York, before I married Gordon, I was summoned to New Jersey to be maid of honor at their wedding.

They proceeded to have three boys. Nancy did little jobs to supplement their income, but looking ahead, she realized that something more would be necessary. Not only would they need more income than Don's job provided, but she needed more intellectual fulfillment. With the inspiration of our mother behind her, and the encouragement of her mother-in-law, she returned to school, this time selecting Newark State, now Kean College. She finished a degree with honors in education with a minor in social studies, and obtained her teaching credentials. One more into the family footsteps.

Teacher

My neighbor on East 88th Street was a nurse at a city hospital, and she told me there were civil service jobs as teachers available with the newly formed New York State Narcotics Addiction Control Commission. It wasn't necessary to be certified as a teacher, you simply had to have a Bachelor's degree in anything and sufficient credits in the subject of choice. I met the qualifications in English, having taken many electives in that field as well as several required drama literature courses that came under the heading of English. I breezed through the civil service exam.

I was hired and reported for work in September. I had little idea of what I was expected to do with these incarcerated drug addicts from the streets of New York, but I would soon find out. The faculty consisted of me for English; Rita Ragosta, who was blind, for math; Ofra Holtz, a pretty young Israeli artist for art; and a shy gentleman for music. Mr. Salkin was our principal. We were assigned to the Edgecombe Center in Upper Manhattan but spent the first few days attending orientation classes at another facility. This orientation was given by social workers, psychologists, guards and other personnel, none of whom were involved with teaching. The focus was to prepare us for dealing with a dangerously manipulative student population, and to indoctrinate us about the types of scams they might pull on us to get drugs or favors. We felt daunted, but ready to begin, nonetheless.

The next phase of orientation was with the principal at our job location. I think he was as innocent as we were of what to expect from these pupils, having come from an academic setting. We were given some rudimentary guidelines and sent home to prepare lessons for our first week of classes. We were provided with a few textbooks and teacher copies of GED workbooks to guide us, but not much else.

I was very nervous, as we all were, about meeting our classes for the first time. Eventually, we would have an education wing with a library, but for the first few weeks we were crowded into small rooms in the basement. The students filed in. In spite of my worst fears, they were polite and quiet. Things went well, and I followed my lesson plan. I was congratulating myself on having survived the first class without incident when one student arrived late and took his seat. Most of the students were African-Americans, but this one was Caucasian. He sat quietly until the class ended. When the others filed out, he remained behind, turning on me with a diatribe about how dare I presume to teach English to him. How could I know anything about him or what his life was like or any of the others I was presuming to teach.

I was taken aback as some of what he said was true. He did not have much formal education, yet he was well spoken and had been doing some writing on his own. According to him, he also didn't belong in that program. He had never taken hard drugs, he only drank cough medicine with alcoholic content. I remembered what we had been taught in orientation and accepted what he said with a grain of salt. I told him that what he said had a lot of merit, but that I would do my best to overcome the handicap. Calmed, he left when the next class began to arrive. The rest of the day was uneventful, and the faculty met for a recap, and to regroup for the next day.

As the week wore on, additional students began to appear who had been on the roster but had not shown up. The classes were not mandatory, but were encouraged, and would look good on their record when they became eligible for consideration for release. One young man with very dark skin and a heavy mustache was one of these latecomers. I remembered seeing him when I came for my interview with the director of the facility, but hadn't thought anything particular about him except that he was big.

His name was Al, and he had a warm, kind smile. He recalled that first incident differently, saying that I had looked terrified of him. If I looked terrified, it was no doubt nervousness about the impending interview, not because of him. In any case, Al was always pleasant to me, and we had many good philosophical conversations about life during the ensuing months. He had a son he adored, and I hope things went well for him after his release.

There was a very young boy who had been in a youth facility for some time before ending up at Edgecombe, and his baby face belied his history. He had been involved with hard-core drugs, which he financed by prostitution. In many ways he was still a child, but his life was scarred by his experiences. There were hints that favors were expected of him here at night.

There was another gentlemen, a large man with a dignified demeanor, very quiet and polite, who did not attend classes at all, but he was often in the education wing at the library where he helped out. He read constantly. The other residents held him in respect, but whispered to me that he had killed many times in his quest for drugs. I did not doubt that this was true, but here, in this place, he did not invoke fear. He looked like an elderly professor, serious and intelligent.

Rita

Outside of the facility, I spent time with Rita, the math teacher, and we became good friends. She was an amazing woman, the daughter of a doctor from upstate New York. Having gone blind as a child, she still had memories of images and colors, and was able to draw on those in her life and work. She had a large German Shepherd dog named Kyna that guarded her religiously, guiding her mistress through the hazardous streets and subways of Manhattan. No one attempted to harm Rita when Kyna was on duty. She lived alone in a walk-up apartment, shopping for, and cooking, her own food, and washing and ironing her clothes.

She had ways of coding everything. She had a stock boy help her at the supermarket that was close by her apartment, then he or another would accompany her home and wait to tell her what the frozen boxes were so she could mark them with her Braille punch. Her clothing was arranged in the closet and bureau drawers by color.

From the feel of the style she knew what the garment was, and thus its color, and she never appeared at school uncoordinated. Her scarves and sweaters always matched her outfits. She rode to school on the subway and never took the wrong train. She once heard some street urchins discussing among themselves the possibility of robbing her, but one of the group spoke up and said they must never take advantage of a blind person. Kyna's presence probably also influenced their decision to pass her by.

Many of the residents of the facility were there by their own choice, sincerely trying to break their drug habit, or to stay out of the clutches of the law. Others were ordered there by the court. They were all treated the same. The big carrot was the extensive aftercare program that was supposedly being developed to ensure successful rehabilitation. The year wore on and aftercare seemed further away. No one was released except those few who were able to fight their incarceration in court. I recall one Caucasian fellow who was an excellent jazz pianist with a lot of talent and a lot to live for. He was out for a very short time when word came back that he had overdosed and died.

Rita Intervenes

Shortly after the school term began, I invited Rita to my apartment for dinner. Her eyes were blind but her other senses were sharp. It wasn't long after that that Gordon attacked me again with his fists for some imagined transgression, and I told Rita about it the next day that I worked with her. She felt the swollen lumps on my face and told me she had judged Gordon's character the evening she met him. She laid it on the line and told me in no uncertain terms that I had to get away from him before he killed me. I also had a dog to think of, which I had acquired several years before when living with Ceci. He was a friendly Golden Retriever mix, and cowered in a corner with fear when he saw me being attacked.

Rita invited me to stay with her, and bring Sebastian, my dog. She stood with me while I called the police, who met me at my apartment and kept Gordon at bay while I gathered a few things and the dog. My bruises were still evident, so they could see that this was a serious business. However, they diplomatically joked with him until I was ready to leave. They didn't allow me much time to be thorough.

I had spoken with my father to let him know the situation. He offered to come to the city the next day, pack up the rest of my things, and bring them to me at Rita's. Gordon, realizing he had finally gone too far, was contrite and offered no resistance to Dad. He had gathered my clothes and some other possessions together for him. However, in a fit of spite, Gordon hid many of my books and records.

The following day, I called out from work and located an attorney on recommendation from the Bar Association — they give you three names when you ask. My plan was to obtain a quick Mexican divorce as one of my friends had done, but the attorney vetoed that idea. As there were no children, he suggested that the split would be much more solid if I could obtain an annulment. A New York State annulment could never be questioned. The grounds would be fraud, alleging that I had wanted children and that Gordon had agreed to that before the marriage. It would be necessary to have two witnesses to attest to hearing him state that he had never really had any intention of having children.

Things happened so quickly that Gordon was in a stunned state of denial. He refused to retain a lawyer for himself, believing this would blow over. He made an appointment with my lawyer, after which my lawyer advised me that we had better get him to go for some psychiatric counseling before taking him into court. He suggested a motherly therapist who had a sign on her office door that read, "if you don't pay your bill, I'll let you go crazy." I doubt that Gordon ever paid his bill, but I don't think she let him go any crazier than he already was. She was able to bring him close enough to reality that he did not contest the action.

A few months later I was free. My sister and my friend, Judy Heisler, had agreed to be the witnesses to having heard Gordon make the required statement at a dinner party. The judge affirmed that I had witnesses present in the court but did not call either of them, basing his decision solely on my testimony. He commented, "It's strange how these very personal statements are so frequently made in the presence of dinner guests. Annulment granted."

Moving On

In the late spring, the release of inmates began at the rehab facility. There was no aftercare. Funding had disappeared. The original director, a charismatic black man, had left to continue up the career ladder to a higher post in state government. He was replaced by a former prison warden whose governing philosophy was punitive rather than educational. This man died of a heart attack before the end of the year. The facility remained open with a new leader, but I did not continue on as news of more and more overdoses and deaths filtered in.

Many of my students passed their GED exams, but as far as I know, most returned to their old lives and habits. A final blow to their good intentions came when one of their role models, a highly regarded counselor, was found to be addicted to drugs himself. If he could fall, what chance did they have? I went back to working for Kelly Girl, but decided that the idea was to reach people when they were still children, with a hope of doing something with their lives.

CHAPTER 15

Ned's Story

When I was writing this book, Uncle Ned's daughter, Darlene told me that for a large part of his life, he didn't think his family loved him. I can only believe he did know at some point, because I cannot see how someone who was so much loved could fail to know it. Throughout his life, Uncle Ned had the respect and love of his wife and children, although his strict religious beliefs made this a rocky trail at times

Uncle Bob Gets His Comeuppance

When Uncle Ned was in high school, he overheard Arthur Bernhoft, Aunt Gladys's husband, tell Grandma and Grandpa Cole that he would make a man out of Ned. Uncle Ned was subsequently sent to live with the Bernhofts for a time, and he did everything he could to rebel against their authority. He'd show them! He was returned home without much change in his demeanor, but he gained a strengthened sense of purpose by his resistance to Arthur's efforts, whatever those had entailed.

In the kitchen of the farm at Sandy Lake, there is a patched-up spot in the ceiling where Ned, goaded beyond endurance, shot at his brother with a shotgun. Bob's version of the story, handed down to his family, was that Ned was trying to kill him. Ned's version, handed down to his family, was that he was only trying to scare his brother into stopping the beatings, and that it was successful for a while before they resumed once again.

Whether it was the experience with Uncle Arthur, or just desperation that prompted him to take a stand against his brother Bob, I don't know, but the day came when Uncle Ned had enough of his bullying. Through the years they fought often, but Ned always came out on the short end, receiving brutal beatings from the bigger boy. Tucker said that his father told him, "When he was sixteen, he and Bob had a knock down fist fight in their barn. Dad told me that the fight was very bloody, but Dad beat Bob until Bob could no longer rise from the floor. Bob never confronted my dad again. Dad also told me that Bob often taunted him, telling Dad that he would never have any piece of the farm." Bob made good on that threat.

Darlene told me about the times Uncle Ned and Uncle Bob took their mother's homemade wine that was stored under the front steps. They replaced the wine they drank with colored water. Grandma Cole maintained that her dandelion wine was permissible in the Lord's eyes, as it was "just a little wine for the stomach's sake." She never noticed when it was a little weaker. As a young man, Uncle Ned sometimes drank to excess, especially when with his friend, Glenn Heasley. Ned always owned up to it and took the consequences, unlike his brother Bob, who sneaked away to the Stoneboro Hotel.

Uncle Ned's Motorcycle Diaries

When, in his late teens, Uncle Ned looked out over the fields one beautiful May day, and all he could see was the backbreaking, never-ending hoeing that they represented. He was a senior in high school, sitting in class next to an open window on the first floor of the school building. He looked out the window, and there was Glenn Heasley beckoning Ned to join him. It was like the Lorelei to a sailor.

Ned looked at Glenn, then looked at the teacher, then back at Glenn. He did this several times, then jumped out the window. Uncle Ned never did manage to graduate from high school. He and Glenn got on their motorcycles, and took off for the unknown.

The pair were young and adventuresome, out to see the world. They went to Cincinnati, Ohio, and passed through various towns to Longview, Texas, where the cheesecake incident occurred. Down to their last dollars, they pooled their money and invested in a large cheesecake, thinking it would be filling and offer nutrition as well. After eating half the cheesecake, they realized the folly of their ways. It sat like lead in their stomachs. I'm not sure either of them ever ate cheesecake again.

Many years later, Uncle Ned told Darlene about the time he and Glenn were picked up for vagrancy and sent to jail because they did not have the penny toll to cross the Covington Bridge. He wrote to his dad: "Dear Dad, no mon, no fun. Your son." My grandfather replied, "Dear Son, Too bad, so sad. Your dad." In his first response, Grandpa did not show his son the same compassion that his father, Augustus, had shown him when he had returned from his European tour, flat broke, to New York. Grandpa had wired his father that he needed funds to get home. Augustus wired him just enough money for a train ticket back to Pittsburgh.

Grandpa sent Ned nothing with his first message, but when her father told Darlene about this incident, it was with humor rather than malice. It seems that, after Grandpa had his little joke, he relented and sent Uncle Ned some money.

Uncle Ned told his son more details about that incident, that he apparently thought Darlene's ears too delicate to hear. He and Glenn "came to a small bridge at the edge of town. The sheriff was there and escorted us to jail for being vagrants. We thought this not too bad, because we figured that we would get a meal and have a good sleep in a bed. Instead, we were thrown in a cell with a homosexual, who propositioned us to let him give us a blow job for $1.00."

Ned said that he and Glenn were sorely tempted because they hadn't eaten for several days. They finally decided against the offer because they figured that it would take more out of them than $1.00

of food would put back. In the morning, the sheriff escorted them to the other end of town and told them never to return.

Uncle Ned had other stories about his adventures. Although they were penniless a good part of the time, they were nice looking, cheerful, and honest fellows, and often received food from farmers and ranchers who felt sorry for the two young lads. They would stay with a family for a couple of days, doing odd jobs to repay the people for their kindness.

When the boys reached Longview, Texas, they stopped for a longer stay with a family who had taken a liking to them. Uncle Ned got a job driving a local taxi, as well as helping out around the homestead. Whether it was his twinkling eyes or wing-like ears that caught her fancy, the young daughter of the family became smitten with him. After a few months, he proposed, she accepted, and a huge wedding was planned. On the day of the wedding, my ignoble uncle got cold feet, hopped on his motorcycle and quit Longview.

Many years later, Tucker and his wife often drove through Longview on their way between Albuquerque, New Mexico, and West Palm Beach, Florida, from one of their homes to the other. One summer, when Tucker was at his father's in Franklin, he played a great practical joke on him. Tucker told Ned that he was driving through Longview, and happened to stop early one morning at a coffee shop. He sat down beside an old guy and began to talk to him. Eventually, the old-timer asked him his name. When Tucker told him, "Ned Cole, Jr.," the fellow jumped up out of the chair and shouted in Tucker's face, "You are the son of that son-of-a-bitch, Ned Cole. I would like to see that bastard one more time."

When Ned heard this, his face turned beet red. Tucker could not help breaking into a big grin. "Gotcha," he thought to himself. Ned laughed and said, "You son of a gun." Ned always liked a good joke, even when it was on him.

Some time after his return to Pennsylvania, when he was nineteen, Uncle Ned was in a serious automobile accident. He was riding in the rumble seat in the back of a car when it hit a bus at high speed. Ned's legs and hips were crushed. He remembered nothing after the moment of impact until much later when he woke up in the hospital.

He spent several months there, and it took nearly a year before he was fully recovered.

The Gun

On his sixteenth birthday, his uncle Frank Henderson gave Ned a .25-caliber Colt. When he was twenty, his friend, Glenn Heasley, asked Ned to sell him the gun. Ned refused to sell it to him but said he would give it to him with the understanding that, if Glenn was ever finished with the gun, Ned would *buy* it back from him. That's the way Ned was. Many years later, at Helen Cole's funeral reception at the Cole farm, Glenn showed up. Ned's son, Tucker, thought of the gun and asked if he still had it. He did, and said that he would bring it back the next day. True to his word, Glenn returned the following day with the gun. Glenn explained to Tucker that he was honor-bound to give the gun back to Ned, and he proceeded to do so, along with the original bullets that Ned had given him. Ned then placed the gun in Tucker's hand. Tucker knew then that he would one day give it to his son, Benjamin.

The gun was forgotten for awhile, hidden away in the pocket of the briefcase that Tucker had with him at the time of his grandmother's funeral. It happened that a few years later he was at an airport security check point when the gun reappeared. It was in the pocket of the briefcase that he had grabbed to carry with him on the plane. Tucker heard one of the female guards say, "There is a gun in this case! Whose case is this?"

Tucker felt his heart drop to his toes. Quietly, he told her that the briefcase and the gun were his. The woman opened the case and passed it to a very old male guard who looked into the case, picked up the gun and said, "My, my! I haven't seen one of these in years." Tucker knew the gun was loaded and, without thinking, snatched the gun from the guard's hand to prevent an accident, removed the clip and bullet in the chamber, then handed the gun back to the guard.

Tucker soon found himself in a room with FBI agents. After some questioning, one of the FBI agents told him that he was one lucky guy because the Federal District Attorney was too busy to mess with his case. The county sheriff was not so forgiving. He hauled

Tucker off to jail and booked him. Tucker was released on his own recognizance.

A few months later, the case came up for hearing. By then, Tucker had obtained a talented young trial lawyer. The lawyer told the judge what had happened and convincingly pleaded that Tucker really did not know that the gun was in the case, which was true. The lawyer presented the facts that Tucker was an Air National Guard commander with top secret clearance, and that he had a very responsible civilian job. The lawyer used the legality that one had to be "cognitively aware" that one was committing a crime. That point is different from ignorance of the law, which is not an accepted excuse.

The judge agreed and dismissed the charges. The prosecuting attorney, a young black female, jumped up and shouted at the judge, "Judge, you cannot do this. We caught the guy red-handed." The judge turned to the prosecutor and informed her, in no uncertain terms, that if she did not sit down and shut up, she would be held in contempt. Tucker walked out of the courtroom, in another narrow escape.

Back in Pennsylvania Uncle Ned Gets Married

In July of 1939, when he was in his late twenties, Uncle Ned married the flamboyant Evelyn Murrin Cassidy, a widowed, Catholic lady from Pittsburgh. She wore elaborate hats, lace stockings and make-up. She was not beautiful in the classic sense, but she was a handsome woman, and exuded an energy that made hers an arresting presence. When he first took his bride to the Wesleyan Methodist Church in Sandy Lake, the shock of the ultra conservative congregation can only be imagined. Uncle Ned enjoyed their discomfiture, but he should have warned Evelyn about what kind of reaction to expect.

To complicate matters further, she had a small daughter, also named Evelyn. The child became known as Snooky. The family was dubious, wondering if Ned had bitten off more than he could chew. He was censured by his oldest sister, Gladys, who was not happy with his marriage, and let him know it in no uncertain terms. How could he marry a Catholic, and a widow at that, with a child? It took a while, but after some raised eyebrows, Evelyn's good character and

Uncle Ned in his thirties at Sandy Lake

down-to-earth nature won over every opponent. She and Ned made a formidable team.

And, of course, Snooky was adorable. She was certainly Uncle Ned's darling, and was always considered by him to be his first child. Although the couple proceeded to have two more children — Ned, Jr., known as Tucker as a child, and Darlene — Snooky never lost her place in her stepfather's heart. She was so much his own that he did not tell his biological children about her parentage until his other daughter was fourteen.

When his younger daughter Darlene, discovered the truth after coming upon Snooky's birth certificate by accident, she confronted her parents. Had she not found that paper, the truth might never have come to light. The community where they lived most of their lives was not informed until Aunt Evelyn's funeral when she was seventy-nine, when Tucker included that information in his eulogy.

Uncle Ned found a job at Dixmont, a home for "mentally deranged" people, taking care of the large plow horses and plowing the fields. In those days some of the better mental facilities tended to be farm-like, with some of the patients helping to grow the food as part of their therapy. In the course of time, someone with no knowledge of psychiatric treatment decided that the facilities were taking advantage of the patients in order to keep costs low, and the practice was stopped.

Ned was there plowing the field on April Fool's Day in 1940 when one of his colleagues ran up to him to tell him to go immediately to the hospital. Aunt Evelyn was about to give birth. Uncle Ned wasted no time in unharnessing the horse, and rode to the barn bareback. Ned, Jr. was already born when he arrived at the hospital, and Evelyn was smiling. Uncle Ned remembered that as one of the happiest days of his life.

Back to Sandy Lake and the Farm

Two years later, Grandpa Cole talked Uncle Ned into returning to the farm. Ned packed up his wife and two children, and his father-in-law drove them back to Sandy Lake. Ned rented a small bungalow at the end of the lane leading to the Heasley farm, just down from Grandpa's. Ned continued working on the farm for two years, but he wasn't cut out to be a farmer. Over and above his own lack of vocation for the work, Uncle Bob had grown even meaner and more surly. Grandpa was already having trouble with him.

Having no interest in farming and not being able to take his brother's cruelty any longer, Uncle Ned made a final break. He went to work on the railroad as had his uncle, James Cole, before him, landing a job on the Pennsylvania Railroad. Years later, the date that he retired from PennCentral in March 1976, was the last day that the railroad was known by that name. The following day, it became Conrail.

He worked out of Oil City, so he and Aunt Evelyn moved their family to Rocky Grove, on the outskirts of Franklin. Their first home there was a small bungalow on McCalmont Street. Uncle Ned was away from home for several days at a time with his work, but they had good neighbors who would lend a hand if Evelyn needed help with anything.

Life With Uncle Ned

Uncle Ned and Aunt Evelyn shared a singular, lifelong devotion. It was not easy being married to Ned; as my mother had said, "He was always cute. Never got over it." He was the darling of the neighborhood, and justifiably so, highly regarded by men and women alike. The men respected him for his ready willingness to lend a hand when needed and his fair-dealing ways. The women admired his willingness to help around their houses with little chores that their husbands kept putting off. He also gave a sympathetic ear to their problems. Aunt Evelyn sometimes complained, semi-joking, that he did more for the people of the neighborhood than he did at home.

Of the neighbors, one family stands out in my mind — the McCauleys. Snooky and their daughter, Janice, were good friends, and I remember going over to their house when I visited. Many years later, when I was in college in Meadville, I was with Uncle Ned and Aunt Evelyn when they visited the McCauleys, who had moved to that town. Shortly after that, Mr. McCauley had his mid-life crisis and left the family flat. Uncle Ned, true to his role as confidante and comforter of the neighborhood women, tried to help.

In the course of her early life, Aunt Evelyn had difficulty with her knee, which necessitated some surgery. The healing arts were not so refined then, and the result was stiffness in that leg for the remainder of her life. This injury became complicated by a stroke and arthritis in later years. Uncle Ned tended her at home, and the physical demands were heavy.

Sarah McCauley lived with Uncle Ned and Aunt Evelyn for a time in later years after Evelyn's stroke. The move was mutually beneficial, as Sarah could maintain her independence from her children and help the Coles at the same time. However, she left when she realized that she was in love with Ned, and did not want to cause any trouble in his family. Her presence had made Aunt Evelyn nervous, but I had no doubt that Uncle Ned's behavior was honorable.

Uncle Ned liked to portray himself to Evelyn as a stern disciplinarian. When he returned from a few days out on the railroad, she expected him to mete out any punishments the children earned in his absence. He would take them to the basement and instruct them to holler as loud as they could while he struck one of the support poles with a belt. He eventually told his wife that her practice of holding punishments for him to deal with would have to stop. She would have to address any problems as they arose, and not make him the bad guy.

When his son, Tucker, then age fourteen, accompanied by his friends, drove Ned's 1951 pick-up past the dead end of their road, into the forest, where he came to rest stuck on a log, Ned's friends came to the rescue to free the truck, only to encounter an active beehive under the log. When Ned returned, he was about to supply some real punishment.

Grandpa Cole said, "now, Ned — remember when you were young."

Ned looked at his shame-faced young son and said, "Well, don't do it again."

On Being Ned's Son

Uncle Ned was perhaps the most strict with his son when it came to imposing his religious views. I believe it was his deep love for Tucker that caused him to expect perfection. As Tucker told me, "We were expected to go to church every Sunday, then spend the remainder of the day in quiet contemplation and rest. Reading the Sunday paper was our only diversion. I did not like it.

"On my Mom's side, all were Catholic. Sunday was a day for fun, parks, movies and baseball games. When my dad was out of town on the railroad, and my Catholic Aunt Mary and her kids visited, Mom would let us kids backslide a little."

Tucker had other memories of his father's attitude. "I recall very vividly the last time my dad and I discussed religion. We were trimming trees at the Sandy Lake farm one summer after my freshman year at college. At the time, like any young man, I was searching for meaning to life. I asked Dad a question about the existence of God. Dad about took my head off, and told me to never again raise such a question in his presence. He got his wish. I turned my back on religion and never looked back. Dad died never hearing me again say a word about religion. Dad often asked painfully, 'Where did I go wrong with you kids?' I never had the heart to tell him. It was his intolerance of any religious view but his own."

Tucker resented the fact that his father forced his mother to give up her religion. Of course, she had been quite willing to do that out of her deep love for Ned. She never tried to sway her children's views on the subject, and was faithful in encouraging them to attend their father's church, even taking them there herself when he was away working. But it was not only Evelyn's religion that was to be denied, but also her previous marriage, and the fact that Snooky was a child of that marriage. As far as Ned was concerned, Evelyn's previous marriage and her dead husband never existed. Snooky was Ned's own child, and that was the end of that.

Uncle Ned also seemed to have inherited Mary Ann Cole's characteristic of intense concern about what the nebulous group known as "the neighbors" might think. Tucker remembered that he once received the worst of the few switchings he received for throwing berries at a girl on his way home from school. He liked her and didn't know what else to do. His father happened to see this from where he was sitting on a neighbor's porch. Tucker told me it was his father's embarrassment in front of the neighbor that generated the whipping.

Evelyn

Aunt Evelyn, on the other hand, was more reserved about showing her love for her children. I remember that, in middle age, her temper was shorter during one phase of her life, no doubt biological, and she would occasionally wing a plate at Tucker's head, which he found highly amusing. But when all was said and done, whatever her children did was okay with her. Darlene summed it up. "If any of us children would happen to murder someone, Mom would say that we had a reason and the person probably deserved to die." Darlene was not close with her mother as a child, but as an adult she came to value Evelyn.

Tucker added another axiom of Aunt Evelyn's. After they had grown up, she told them that "A parent has done their job if a kid graduates from high school and is not in jail." She was quite proud that all her children managed those two feats. She didn't pressure her children to achieve in school. She asked only that they get at least C's and graduate. Tucker was quite comfortable with that level of expectation — he remembers that he went from first through twelfth grade without ever doing any homework. He later went on to college, and eventually obtained an MBA, after giving up his "no homework" rule. He had only fond and loving memories of his mother.

My Home Away from Home

During my Allegheny College years, I frequently spent weekends and short vacations at Uncle Ned and Aunt Evelyn's house. After their early years, they had built a larger house just up the road from the little bungalow where they started out. Uncle Ned did most of the construction himself with the help of his son. By the time I was in college, Snooky was married, so only Tucker and Darlene were at home.

Since my family lived a day's travel away, Uncle Ned and Aunt Evelyn became my surrogate parents, faithfully coming to see me in the Playshop productions at college. One of my roles was Stella in Tennessee Williams's *A Streetcar Named Desire*. My parents had also made the trip to see that one. The setting is a steamy hot summer in an old section of New Orleans. The characters are sometimes in various states of undress to signify the sultry atmosphere. Stella is in her slip in one scene, and later puts on a dress during the course of the action. Uncle Ned's comment after the show was, "Now that was a perfectly nice dress. Why couldn't you be wearing it at the beginning of the scene?" In spite of that, he and Aunt Evelyn were always proud of me.

Pride and Prejudice

One of Uncle Ned's flaws was a strong prejudice against people not of his race. When Tucker and his wife, Carol, decided to adopt a racially mixed baby, Uncle Ned was adamantly against it. Tucker's three natural children were no longer babies and he and Carol felt they had room for more. Racially mixed children had a harder time finding homes. If they wanted a baby, that was the way to go. They adopted Jonathan, a biracial child, half African-American and half German-American, who was a beautiful dark-skinned little boy.

Shortly after Jonathan joined their family, Tucker took his family to visit Ned and Evelyn. Ned was greatly disturbed about having a "black" grandson. He would not even look at the baby. Tucker, now a mature man and father of four, drew the line in the sand. He told his father that he had only done what Ned had taught him was right. He gave him a choice: he could accept Jonathan as his grandson, or he would henceforth have NO son. Ned recognized his own stubborn will in Tucker and knew it was no bluff.

A couple of weeks later, Ned and Evelyn returned the visit to Tucker's family, then living in a new, large colonial house in Murrysville, just outside of Pittsburgh. Ned was still apprehensive, and a little hostile about Jonathan. But a short time before he and Evelyn were to leave, Tucker happened to walk by the entrance to the family room where Jonathan was in a floor crib. Ned was kneeling at the crib and talking, with tears streaming down his face, to Jon. He was telling him how sorry he was that he had thought the way he did, and that he would try to make it up to him. It was all over. Ned was Jonathan's.

Ned never knew that his son had witnessed this scene. In later years, some of Ned's proudest moments occurred when he introduced Jonathan and Tucker to his friends. For a man who was so concerned about what the neighbors thought, he must have been gratified when his friends heaped praise on him for being the grandfather of a black child.

From there, it was an easy jump to the acceptance of Benjamin, the next racially-mixed addition to the Cole family. Ben is half American Indian, one-quarter black and one-quarter Italian. Tucker used to joke to his Italian friends that everything except the Italian was fine. There was never another thought of discrimination against them by Uncle Ned who became their staunch champion.

When Jonathan was ten months old and discovered to be congenitally deaf, Uncle Ned did not learn signing along with the rest of the family, but he and Jonathan had their own special communication system. He showed Jonathan his own signs for the alphabet, different from the accepted signs. Jonathan's middle name was Ned.

Gertie

There was a young girl who lived in the neighborhood of the farm, who, as a young man, Uncle Ned had protected from the unwelcome advances of his older brother Bob. Gertie was still in school and had a difficult life. She was one of many children of a widow lady who was raising her family single-handed. Gertie could not help but love the kind and funny young man with protruding ears who was her protector, but Uncle Ned did not see her in romantic terms.

Gertie was married to someone else in the front parlor at the Sandy Lake farm, by my grandfather, who was also a Justice of the Peace. Uncle Ned had coerced the bridegroom into marrying the girl, as she was pregnant by that fellow. She later divorced that man, married another, and had children with him. Then her second husband eventually died.

In later years, she came to live with the Cole family to help Uncle Ned in caring for Aunt Evelyn. It was a godsend for Ned, but the two women developed a strong undercurrent of dislike for each other. For Ned's sake, they maintained a pleasant front, but the veneer of civility often wore thin.

Gertie considered Evelyn to be overly demanding of Ned's attention, and Aunt Evelyn was certain of Gertie's feelings for Ned. Animosity between the two women grew. On more than one occasion, Aunt Evelyn liked to tell me, with a smile and a wink, that she was spending all Ned's money so Gertie wouldn't get it. Aunt Evelyn also once confided to me that she knew what Gertie was after, and that she'd never get Ned. With a set and determined expression, Aunt Evelyn said that, despite her condition, with one touch, she could still keep Ned from straying. It struck me again what strength their relationship had.

Uncle Ned was a man, however, and thoughts will come. When my daughter, Julia, was a baby we were visiting my parents in Florida at the same time as Uncle Ned and Aunt Evelyn. We were at the beach when he and I had a private conversation. He didn't put it into direct words, but it was evident that he was skirting around trying to get my opinion about his developing a physical relationship with Gertie. He made it clear that his love for Aunt Evelyn was undiminished.

I could see that the situation must be very difficult for him, but I did not encourage him either way. He had to make up his own mind to do what was right. We hadn't spoken in definite terms and he didn't tell me his decision. I hoped he made the right one, but others in the family had their doubts. My mother, who was close to Ned, was certain that there was more going on. Long after Ned's death, my mother spent a lot of time with my daughter, Sarah, and spoke her mind about Gertie, saying that she knew the full extent of their relationship.

Darlene took Gertie's part in some of the disagreements with her brother and sister. She was supportive of her father in his difficult situation, and saw Gertie's presence as a benefit to her mother, enabling her to remain at home. Darlene was the only one in the family who remained in contact with Gertie after Ned and Evelyn's deaths, trying to ease her final years.

Tucker distanced himself from Gertie after settling the car on her, and the sum of money that his father had specified in his last wishes. Ned had already deeded the mobile home in Florida to Tucker, on the promise that it would go to Gertie after Ned's death. Tucker kept the promise. From that point on, Tucker and Snooky washed their hands of her.

Darlene felt differently. She was not thrilled by the situation either, but realized the value it had afforded both Ned and Evelyn. Gertie lived on in Florida for several more years, and Darlene and her husband, Craig, would fly there, take her out to lunch, and give her a Christmas present. She did this for her dad in appreciation of Gertie's help to her parents.

Gertie also benefited from the situation, as it provided her with a home for many years of her life — fifteen with Ned and Evelyn, then several more in Florida. When Gertie eventually had a stroke, her children would not help her, and she was sent to a rehabilitation center.

She was lonely and scared when she was discharged, and wanted to return to Pennsylvania to see her daughters. Darlene came down from her home in Atlanta to fly her back to Pennsylvania. Gertie wanted to break the trip at Darlene's house, and the doctor approved this plan. However, during the first night at Darlene's, Gertie suffered another stroke and was hospitalized in Atlanta. Her favorite daughter refused to take her into her house, and Gertie was airlifted to a rehabilitation center in Sharon, Pennsylvania. She was soon hospitalized with a series of strokes, the last of which was fatal. Snooky did go with Darlene to visit her there, but Gertie barely recognized them.

The Race Is Almost Run

When Uncle Ned was approaching his eightieth birthday, his children decided to have a party for him. It was to be a waterskiing party at Sandy Lake park. Uncle Ned had owned several motor boats in his life — mostly with lots of horsepower for waterskiing. His children and grandchildren had enjoyed many happy vacations together on the water, and he had taught his grandchildren how to waterski.

My sister and I attended the party with our mother, and were happy to see relatives we hadn't seen in years, and share the events of the intervening time. Some of us swam, some waterskied. I will never forget the sight of Uncle Ned at age eighty, getting up on those waterskis, and waving at the crowd of relatives as he sailed past.

Two months before Ned died, he was sitting on the back porch of his home with Tucker who said to him, "Dad, there is one more thing you need to teach me before you go."

"What's that?" Ned asked.

"Dad, you need to teach me how to die with dignity."

Two weeks later, Tucker was back, and it was time to make the decision to take Ned to the nursing home where Evelyn had been living for the last three years. Ned was reluctant to leave the house where he had lived so much of his life, and Gertie was still there taking care of him. Tucker pointed out how unfair he was being to Gertie and said that if he continued to remain at home, the burden of caring for him would kill her. Tucker knew this wasn't true, but he also knew that Evelyn was greatly troubled at not being with Ned during his dying days. He wanted his dad to be with his wife at the end.

Tucker made the unilateral decision, then dealt with the repercussions from Darlene, who was disturbed that he did not consult her first. He had not consulted Snooky either, but she was in complete agreement with his decision. He was not going to take the chance that anything would interfere with his mother's right to have this one small dignity. A few days later, he drove Ned to the nursing home.

By now, Ned was in a wheelchair much of the time, and in great pain from prostate cancer. On the way to the home, Ned asked Tucker to stop first by a store where a young man worked who was also dying of cancer. Ned wanted to say good-bye and say a few kind words to the man. That was the way Ned was, always kind, always thinking of the pain of others. Their next stop was the Dairy Queen for one last chocolate soda.

When they arrived at the home, Tucker pulled up to the front portico and proceeded to help his father out of the car. Ned, in a kind voice, asked his son to step aside. He would walk in under his own power. Ned got out of the car and walked the few yards to the front door. His eyes were filled with the pain it had cost him, yet

Uncle Ned and Mom at her ninetieth birthday party (Marian in background)

they managed to twinkle as he smiled with satisfaction and said, "Okay, we can go the rest of the way in the chair." He was still cute. Never got over it.

A month later, Tucker was visiting his parents at the home, and it was obvious that Ned's life was very near the end. Tucker was about to leave Ned's room when Ned said, "I would like to do this right." He slowly stood and took a step toward Tucker. He held out his hand, as was always their custom when parting, and shook his son's hand. Then he sat back down in the chair. That was the last time Tucker saw his father standing.

When Uncle Ned was dying, as the end drew closer, his children were all at his side. He described seeing lots of beautiful flowers in the meadow with his mother smiling at him, waiting for him.

At one point, Ned's other children stepped out of the room to give Tucker a few minutes alone with his father. Holding his hand, he told him in a quiet voice that he loved him very much, and that he had been a very good dad. Again, Ned smiled. Darlene and Snooky returned. Tucker was on one side of the bed, Darlene on the other, Snooky near the foot. Darlene and Tucker were holding Ned's hands. Ned whispered, "Mother, I'm coming. I can see you." Ned took a last gasp of breath.

The nurse was nearby and told them it was over. Tucker turned to her and said, "No, not just yet." He had his finger on Ned's neck pulse and could still feel his heart beating. His heart continued to beat for a few more pulses, then, thump...more quietly, thump, more quietly still, thump...silence.

Aunt Evelyn, too, had been at his side. On the last night, she left his room earlier and went to bed. She had stated many times during his last illness that she wanted to die rather than see him in pain. Darlene believes that, as Evelyn left his room that evening, she made a commitment to herself, willing her life to end.

The next time I was in Franklin, it was for Uncle Ned's funeral.

I went with the family to the viewing. Many of my relatives were with us, staying in the homes of kind neighbors. Aunt Evelyn was seated in an armchair near the coffin that Uncle Ned, himself, had picked out and paid for. He had prearranged his whole funeral.

When I approached Aunt Evelyn, she took my hand and insisted that I remain by her side throughout the evening. She introduced me to people I didn't know or scarcely remembered. She seemed to draw comfort from my presence. Perhaps it was because my mother and Uncle Ned had always been so close.

Being aware of her own impending death, and perhaps willing it to be so, Evelyn called an editor of the local newspaper with an addition to her obituary. Throughout her married life with Ned, at his insistence, she had denied her life prior to their marriage. She denied her Catholicism, her first marriage, and the fact that Ned was not Snooky's birth father — although a good father he had been. She wanted her past to be recognized, and this was duly added to her obituary. The editor was uncertain at first, thinking this was perhaps the rambling of a dying woman, and confirmed it with Snooky before printing it.

Four months later, Tucker received word from Snooky that Evelyn was near the end, and he traveled to the nursing home. When he walked through the door into the utter silence of his mother's room, he saw Snooky, forlorn, sitting at the foot of the bed holding her head in her hands. She looked up at her brother and said in a quiet voice, "Mom is gone." Evelyn died four months to the day after her husband.

Ned's Children

Snooky, now Evelyn Cole Karns, was special to me. She was one year older, a vivacious, popular brunette. One year is a vast gulf when one is young, and she could easily have treated me like the tag-along that I was, but she didn't. For some reason, I always thought of her as much older, and was surprised to find later that it was only a year's difference.

When we were young, we would finish dinner, then be off to range through the neighborhood, stopping to visit this friend or that. Everyone knew everyone else's kids on McCalmont Street, and everyone admired Snooky. She had blossomed as Uncle Ned's daughter.

Uncle Ned had made her adoption formal when it was time for her to enter first grade. She needed to use her legal name to register for school. Snooky remembers going into a judge's chambers with her mom and dad when she was almost six. The judge asked her if she wanted to be adopted and she said she did.

When asked by Darlene what she thought about this, Snooky replied that she had always felt there was something wrong with her because no mention was ever made of her biological father, or if it was, the subject was hushed and closed.

By the time Ned and Evelyn married, Snooky was extremely spoiled from living with her grandmother Murrin, and difficult to handle. After they moved back to Sandy Lake from Pittsburgh, to a small cottage near the farm, Ned would take Snooky with him to the fields where she would ride on the tractor all day with him, giving Aunt Evelyn a much-needed break from the lively child. It also served as a time to forge the strong bond between Snooky and her new father, that would last a lifetime. She was fond of Grandpa Cole, and her father was always close to his dad.

Snooky's first father, Eugene B. Cassidy, had been struck by a car and killed when she was three months old. Her uncle and aunt on his side tried to communicate with her but were quickly rebuffed by Ned and Evelyn. They had turned Evelyn and Snooky out of the house they had lived in with Eugene because they owned it. Evelyn took her baby and moved in with her own mother. This situation caused a lot of resentment between the Murrins and Coles against the Cassidys. After Ned and Evelyn died, Snooky's sister encouraged her to contact the Cassidy branch of her family, but she would not.

The effects of secrecy carried down to the next generation. When Aunt Evelyn died, and Tucker gave the eulogy, Snooky's original parentage was mentioned. Her son, Mike, had not known that Ned was not his biological grandfather. Darlene was stunned when he told her that day, and asked if that meant she wasn't his aunt. Of course she was, being Evelyn's daughter.

When I was a student at Allegheny, Uncle Ned and Aunt Evelyn became my parents away from home and Tucker became my brother. The difference in our ages had become less important now that we were older teen-agers, and I was caught up in his energy field.

Ned, Jr. was known as Tucker as a child. He later ditched that name, but he was always Tucker to me. He was very much like his father, with mischievous eyes and ears that stuck out. I didn't hang out with him when he was younger, and it was Snooky that I was closest to growing up. But I do remember that he was always in trouble.

One of Tucker's favorite places was the barn at Grandpa Cole's farm. During our annual summer visits, there were times when Uncle Ned's family came out to the farm while we were there, in addition to the time we spent at their house. Tucker would disappear into the barn and not reappear until it was time for them to go home or to eat a meal. Very often, Grandpa would be in the barn, too, and Tucker stayed close to him, forging their special bond. There were always cows and various chores to keep them busy. Behind Grandpa's back, Tucker delighted in leaping out of the hayloft to the floor below.

We arrived at Uncle Ned's house one summer when Tucker was ten, only to find him with a cast on his leg. I always thought it was the result of a jump from the hayloft, but Tucker later told me the real story. The young boys of the neighborhood were in the habit of crawling on top of a garage belonging to his friend's father. It was a one-story building, and Tucker liked to jump from the roof to show off to his buddies. He did this once too often, and on the last occasion, landed badly and tore out all the ligaments in his knee. He spent the remainder of the summer and part of the school year in a full leg cast.

He has continued nursing that knee for his whole life. Even now, with a wrong twist, it slips out of joint and he falls to the ground. No big deal — he just has someone grab his leg and jerk. With a pop, he continues on his way. As I remember, he did get a lot of mileage out of that cast — the whole neighborhood visited him regularly, and he held court like a young rajah while they signed it. There wasn't room for another signature by the time I saw it.

Tucker was a member of the Rocky Grove Boy Scout Troop No. 28. He and the other scouts went on a winter weekend camping trip, where they stayed in a cabin. On Saturday, they went hiking. When they returned and were within a hundred yards of their cabin, a large group of boys from another troop accosted them and started a vicious snowball battle. Tucker found himself on a small rise, surrounded by the other troop. His buddies abandoned him and ran to the safety of the cabin, leaving him to his fate. He was angry beyond reason for what he felt was their disloyalty and cowardice. He drove off the other troop, but never forgave his buddies — he "held it without mercy with no thought of forgiveness."

Teddy Bears

When seeking refuge from the arguments with Uncle Bob at the farm, Grandpa Cole slept over at Uncle Ned's house. Grandpa would catch the bus to Franklin, where he got off at the drugstore. The druggist was a neighbor of Uncle Ned's, and drove Grandpa to Ned's at the end of the day. Grandpa always kept extra clothes at Ned's for these visits.

The family was still living in the small house, and Grandpa had to share Tucker's double bed. It was Tucker's habit to sleep with a multitude of stuffed bears. Aunt Evelyn insisted that he could not have the bears in his bed when Grandpa was sleeping over, and she removed them every time. When Grandpa was ready to get into bed, he brought back all the bears, then crawled into whatever space was left. Sleep was uncomfortable, but he knew the bears were important to Tucker, and he loved him. This memory drove Tucker's future goals.

During these visits, Grandpa Cole told Tucker many stories about his life. He told him about times on Neville Island, his travels in Mexico, his Colorado mining days, the farm in Sandy Lake, his European adventure, and the days when he worked on Ohio and Mississippi riverboats. Most importantly, he told the young Tucker about his dreams of recovering what the government had taken from him. The memory of Grandpa's dreams and deep disappointments became the defining drive of Tucker's life. When he grew to manhood, Tucker vowed that he would get back Grandpa's fortune for him.

Getting Grandpa's Fortune Back

After college, and a meteoric rise as an Air Force officer, due partially to his cleverness in bypassing red tape, Tucker pursued his goal of getting Grandpa's fortune back. He began with an MBA from University of Pittsburgh and soon landed the first of a series of prestigious positions in industry, culminating at ABEX Corporation, Railroad Products Group. He and some colleagues, in a leveraged buyout, bought the company, turned around and sold it to another company. Within two years, Tucker retired at age fifty-two.

He had not forgotten his Grandpa Cole. After he submitted his first federal tax return that showed more than $1,000,000 of income, he flew to his dad's winter vacation home in Florida. Tucker and his dad took a walk along a beach near St. Petersburg. As they walked on that moonlit, warm evening, Tucker held the tax return up to the sky and said, "Grandpa, we made it back."

The collective reaction of the cousins to Tucker's accomplishment was, "How nice for Tucker." We all admired his brilliance and determination in making his fortune. Nancy and I were mildly impressed, the Bernhoft cousins the same. I don't know about the other Cole cousins. My mother, on the other hand, was extremely impressed, and was disappointed that the largesse didn't extend to her; I have no idea why she expected it to, other than she saw that Tucker was very generous to his mom and dad. She did ask him, several times, to contribute to Houghton College, and he showed an understandable lack of interest in that. I don't know that Grandpa benefited much, having died some years previously, and I don't know that his far vision was strong enough to see the tax return.

China

Geared for retirement, Tucker received a call that help was needed to negotiate a joint venture contract between the company that had purchased ABEX and the Chinese. Instead of relaxing between beach and desert, Tucker found his time filled with trips to China and meetings in the U.S. A joint venture contract was concluded and Tucker was ready to really retire.

The new company, however, had no assigned project manager and no general manager. A reluctant Tucker agreed to take on these obligations in Datong, China. For the next two years, he lived there until the plant was finished. In China, Tucker (Ned) is affectionately known as "Neda." The Chinese could not quite end a word with a hard "d."

Jonathan

Tucker loved all his children, and tried to be the father that his father was, but without the flaws. One child was particularly close to his heart and affected him deeply. He and his wife, Carol, were raised in an almost all-white, small, western Pennsylvania town. There had been no black children in Tucker's entire school district and only a handful in Carol's. To them, race was not an issue. In their Sunday School days, both had been taught the little homily "red and yellow, black and white, they are precious in His sight." It had become part of their attitudes about people of different races. Neither sets of parents had expressed any prejudicial remarks during their childhood years.

Tucker had made some black friends in the Air Force, and again on his first job in Philadelphia, and had only then understood how poorly black people were often treated in the U.S. Tucker and Carol were brought up to believe that they truly lived in the land of the free.

When they started talking about having a fourth child, they decided to look into adoption, as Carol had had some difficulty with her last two pregnancies. Tucker was busy with his work, so left the task of dealing with the adoption procedure red tape to Carol, who was up to the job. When it became clear that the blue-eyed, blond baby, who was the supposed ideal, was out of reach for a couple with three biological children, they had no reservations about adopting a biracial child. Such babies were plentiful and, to them, a child was a child. They did not see their decision as a crusade or a cause. Little did they realize they would be stirring up a storm of family controversy.

After surviving the endless interviews and forms, they were invited to visit the Children's Home of Pittsburgh to see the available children. Tucker will never forget the first moment he saw Jonathan lying in his crib. The child was the most beautiful little boy Tucker had ever seen. Partly in jest, he said to the head of the home, "I will take that one right there." It was the head of the home who would make the decision.

By the time I saw Jonathan, he was an energetic little boy with a penchant for running around the house at night. I was visiting with my husband and daughter, and we were forewarned that he might pop into our room at any time during the night, and we should not to be alarmed. He did. We were not. He was a handsome, smiling child with dark skin and Caucasian features — a heartbreaker in the making.

At the age of ten months it was discovered that he was totally deaf. Carol became active in state organizations concerned with deaf children, and when the time came, Jonathan was given the advantage of special schools and a special college. At the age of twenty-six, he came to live with his parents in their house near the coast of Florida. Jonathan was their rock, always helpful, always compassionate. He was alone in the house one night after arriving home and garaging his car. Unable to hear the engine, he accidentally left it running. He could not hear the carbon monoxide alarm when it went off, and died in his sleep. His beloved pets died as well. There were thoughtless, painful rumors that Jonathan had committed suicide, but his parents and others who knew the sunny young man well knew otherwise. It was later officially ruled out. His tragic loss was greatly mourned, and Tucker's pain was unbearable. He has never really stopped crying.

Tucker has a fierce family loyalty, as evidenced by his vow to his grandfather. When his father lay dying of cancer, Tucker was determined that he should not suffer as his Uncle Arthur had suffered. Uncle Ned was haunted by the memory of Arthur's screams of pain in the night when he had visited during that time. Close to the end of his father's life, Tucker was beside himself with anguish. He told the poor nurse that if she let his father suffer, he would come back and kill her and her whole family.

Hopefully, she understood that it was grief talking and not the man. Tucker would never have carried through such a threat. In any case, the nursing home staff was enlightened about pain control, and Uncle Ned died peacefully.

Where Are They Now?

Tucker and his wife, Carol, eventually retired to Florida to a house on the East Coast. There he bought himself a yacht which, a few years later, he proceeded to sink. He accepted the loss of his boat with a casual outlook. He was getting tired of it anyway. He built a small ranch with more land, then built a barn, started raising horses, and now whiles away his time taking care of them, along with a multitude of dogs and cats. Friends visit frequently, they play golf, and attend an occasional play or concert. Just one more turnover.

16

Finding a Husband

Germans and Italians

After leaving the rehabilitation facility, I was sent to a succession of jobs by Kelly Girl. My social life took a new direction as I was taken into the circle of my friend, Judy, and her Democratic liberal associates. We marched in a parade for integration, and attended a party to celebrate a victory for Mayor Koch. On my own, I joined a neighborhood group that was collecting funds to support the Poor People's March on Washington, D.C.

My idea of teaching went to the back burner when I met Jurgen. I was collecting for the march and came across him in the brownstone next door to mine. He was charming and attractive, on the order of Michael J. Fox, and was in New York on temporary assignment at the home office of Intercontinental Hotels, while waiting to take his new post as food and beverage manager at a new hotel under construction in Dusseldorf, Germany. He had worked for them in the past, had left to come to the U.S. with Sheraton Hotels, and was now returning to Intercontinental in his homeland. He was leaving in six weeks, and, after a whirlwind romance, we decided that I would follow some weeks after his departure. My plan was that I would find work teaching English at a Berlitz school in Dusseldorf.

Meanwhile, Kelly Girl landed me at the Italian company, Olivetti, in its Numerical Control division. When I accepted the assignment, I had no clue as to what its product was. I knew Olivetti only for its typewriters. The numerical control machines were Auctors — huge computer-driven, precision metal-working machines, used to make parts for aircraft and artillery as well as other items. They looked like space monsters. The office was on Park Avenue in Manhattan, but was soon to be moved to a warehouse near LaGuardia Airport. It wasn't far from Kennedy International Airport either, allowing for more convenience when receiving the machines that were imported from Italy. There they would be modified to fit client specifications by a team of Italian technicians, before being shipped to their final destinations to U.S. customers.

At the head of this office was an executive vice president from Italy, Renzo Castellini, a university-trained engineer. The other leader was an elderly American gentleman from the New York office of Olivetti, Vice President Len Bowen. The third member of administration was an American accountant who frantically tried to keep track of the division's finances. An American sales manager, George Britto, and an American engineer named Lloyd Kagley, who wore cowboy boots, headed the next level. Under Lloyd was a team of Italian and American technicians.

My job was to assist Mr. Castellini's executive secretary, Mary Davidson, soon to be Mary Minogue, as she capably handled his correspondence, fielded phone calls and organized his busy schedule. I was to do more of the grunt work and assist Mr. Bowen when needed. I was also to cover for Mary when she went on her honeymoon. Apparently, I accomplished these tasks efficiently because I was soon invited to join the company permanently.

Here was a dilemma. This was pretty much a fun place to work with the wide variety of personalities involved: the temperamental Italians, the harassed accountant and the flirtatious Executive V.P. However, I made no secret of the fact that I was leaving soon for sunny Germany. The next day Mr. Bowen called me into his office and told me that, after conferring with Castellini, they wanted to hire me anyway. Was this a premonition? Did they have some inside psychic information? On those terms, I accepted their offer.

Meanwhile, Jurgen's sojourn in New York was coming to an end. We had seen plays with his boss, who was also his friend, and his boss's wife. We had often gone to dinner in elegant restaurants, and I ate food I never thought I would try, such as snails (escargot). I learned a lot about food. I learned how to cook calves' liver so that it actually tasted good. Too soon the idyll ended, and it was time for the shipboard farewell. Jurgen decided to make a vacation of it and sail on an ocean liner. His boss, his boss's wife and I piled into a taxi with all his luggage and accompanied him to the ship. His trunks had been sent ahead. We saw him to his cabin, and after a hug, a kiss and some champagne, Jurgen said he'd see me soon.

Olivetti

However, one cannot remain sad for long around a bunch of Italians. Outside of work I made preparations for my upcoming trip. At work, I was fast learning the ropes and becoming part of the office culture. There was a frenzy of activity as we prepared for the move to the new site. Support staff was hired for the additional foreign crew that was coming, so there were several more of us by the time the first day arrived.

Our new digs were not elegant, but were clean and new, having been recently renovated. Mary had her own office between Castellini and Mr. Bowen. The frenzied accountant, with his new assistant, Lila Lindaberry, was around the corner on the other side of a new office manager. Lila was a pleasant, smiling older woman. Beyond that were the sales offices and a small reception area. Margaret was hired as receptionist. She was in her forties and dressed seductively, believing herself to be glamorous and irresistible to men, having been a showgirl in her younger days. She soon decided that Lloyd — with his cowboy boots — was the latest love of her life. However, she was not his and he spent a good deal of time and effort avoiding her.

Additional technical engineers and assistants had arrived from Italy, Germany and Scotland and their offices were on the inside hallway, close to the vast warehouse area where the machine work was done. The female staff now consisted of Mary, me, Lila, Little Mary (a gopher), Margaret, Barbara, Elaine and Martha.

Mary was an interesting girl with an ivy league prettiness. She called her father, an advertising executive, Jim in a fond manner. She often met him for lunch before the office moved to Queens. During her college summers, she, having been a student of the Italian language, and had gone to Italy as an au pair, helping with the children of the Castellini family. From that contact, she had obtained her position with Olivetti after graduation. She had a good sense of humor, and communicated well with the Italian technicians, whose English was sketchy. One of our favorites was Giorgio Vinciguerra, and Mary often called him by the English translation of his name — George Win-the-War. He would blush with shy amusement.

Among the influx of foreign men was Tullio Bortoletto, an Italian engineer and friend of Castellini. Tullio was the only man who was shorter than Castellini, and some of us thought that was the reason for their friendship. I, at five foot four, was only slightly below eye level with Castellini. Tullio was a stocky fellow with red hair and beard, and a pugnacious personality. He had a way of showing up when he wasn't expected, and one always had a feeling he was eavesdropping. He probably was, since Castellini seemed to know much of what was going on, although he wasn't often there himself. He spent more and more time out playing golf in nice weather, or on ski trips in the winter. He could seldom be found when the salesmen needed him to help close a deal.

Farewell to the Italians

The day arrived for my departure. I had put my few sticks of furniture in storage, given up my apartment, and moved in with my friend, Rita, for the last week. My dog, Sebastian, had gone to live with my parents, a good companion for my father. I brought all my luggage to the office in a taxi that morning, planning to go to Kennedy Airport from work that evening for my 9:00 P.M. Icelandic Airlines flight. I had little work to do that day, so spent most of it chatting with friends, saying goodbye.

On this day, I also became acquainted with Ugo Boggio, an Italian engineer who was new to the staff. He had recently joined us from a company in Detroit. In the past he had worked for Olivetti Numerical Control in Italy, troubleshooting in many parts of the world, but had left the company to accept a position with an American engineering firm. He had now left the latter to return to Olivetti, but was hired in the U.S., involving a different visa status. He would be traveling to Italy soon to obtain the required visa and resolve the legalities involved. My first impression of Ugo was that he was stuck-up. He went around with his nose in the air as he acquainted himself with his new surroundings. He was tall and slim, and although his hair was dark, he had green eyes and fair skin. Some people compared him to the German actor, Max Schell.

As the end of the workday approached, everyone slowly disappeared. I was summoned to the accountant's office, which was one of the largest rooms. There they all were, and a present sat on the table in front of them. My eyes filled with tears and my friends began teasing. The moment passed into smiles and laughter. Not only had

Ugo

they arranged this little farewell party, it continued to the airport. Those who could, piled into cars accompanying me and my luggage to Kennedy. Once my luggage was checked, we repaired to a bar with a view of the runways. Several more drinks were consumed. Margaret had been busy propositioning Ugo, and attempting to sit in his lap. He did not look thrilled.

During this time, George Britto, the sales manager, took me aside. He was an outgoing, outspoken sort of fellow, often the teller of risqué tales. He played the office lothario and was fond of teasing the girls with outrageous propositions that were taken in good spirit. To our knowledge, he never followed through and was not serious. I suppose today he would be accused of sexual harassment, but no one saw his banter in that light. This evening he was very serious when he spoke with me. He said that, if things did not work out in Germany, I should come back to Olivetti and there would be a job waiting. He told me to call him if I ever needed anything. I never doubted that he meant every word. Castellini was out of town that evening, but must have been in agreement with this promise.

It was now time to say goodbye to my friends and head for the plane. Amidst hugs and tears, they went as far with me as they were allowed to go.

German Interlude

I will not dwell at length on the two months in Germany. I arrived in Dusseldorf anticipating my reunion with Jurgen. He was nowhere to be seen. After an hour, I called him at the hotel where he worked. He had forgotten that I was arriving that morning. We were off to a good start. He dropped everything and picked me up, then took me to a boarding house where he had stayed when he first arrived. He had arranged for me to stay there until I got myself settled. Then he left. There I was, alone in a strange city, left to fend for myself, knowing only a few words of German.

I dug in my heels and headed out the next day to find a job. I did so at the Berlitz school, as planned. I also had to locate certain German agencies to obtain the necessary papers to live and work in that country. I found my way to various parts of the city by bus and streetcar, and somehow made myself understood by bored clerks. I coped with the bureaucracy that involved the post office among other places, in the process of obtaining the necessary permits to work.

The next the thing was to find a room. I didn't want to stay at the boarding house forever, and I wasn't on its meal plan. Fortunately, some of the other teachers at the school were either American or Canadian and had already been in Germany for awhile. They knew their way around. One Canadian, Celine, was in somewhat the same situation I was, with a boyfriend she rarely saw. She helped me find a room near the trolley line, and, with other girls, we mastered the ins and outs of shopping.

It wasn't a bad life except that I never saw Jurgen. He always had some excuse connected with his work. Finally, he invited me to dinner at his hotel. It was a beautiful place, and the Belle Epoque dining room that he had planned was impressive. I got up my nerve to ask him a direct question about what was going on, and the truth came out, about his other girlfriend — a chambermaid. His excuse for not telling me was that he had taken it upon himself to decide that I was better off in Germany than in New York. He hoped that I would eventually make a life for myself here — without him — once I settled in. I was appalled at his nerve. The evening ended after a few well-chosen words from me.

The next day, I made my reservation to fly home, with George Britto's promise in mind. Fortunately, I had had the foresight to buy an open-ended round-trip ticket when I came to Germany. I didn't even tell my parents I was coming. I would be leaving the next day, and would call them when I arrived. I packed hurriedly, and a shame-faced Jurgen took me to the airport. We waited in near silence until time to board.

Hello to the Italians

After what seemed like an endless flight, the plane arrived at Kennedy Airport. I collected my luggage and cleared customs. Then, thus encumbered, went in search of a phone. It was just about 5:00 in the evening. I called George.

"Stay right out front. I'll be there within the hour." No questions were asked, but I had no doubt he would be there.

In approximately one hour, George pulled up to the curb and loaded my luggage into his car. During my wait, I had been wondering what I was getting myself into and hoping I could handle any moves he might make if I had misread his motives or his character. I didn't anticipate any real problem.

As we drove away from the airport, George still asked no questions, but proceeded to tell me the plan. I would spend the night in a room that he kept reserved at the Holiday Inn near the office. He lived a couple of hours from the office and often stayed at the hotel rather than drive home. He had another room lined up for himself for the night. (I was glad he cleared that up.) First he would provide me with dinner. In the morning, he would drive me to the office and I would begin my new job — as Executive Secretary to Castellini. George had been busy while I was waiting for him.

During dinner I gave him a brief explanation of what had happened, expecting an, "I told you so." He didn't say anything, just nodded wisely. I was still a little self-conscious about what I might expect that evening. He dropped me at the door of my room and left. After making a call to my parents to let them know I was home, and a call to Rita to arrange to stay with her temporarily, I settled into an eventless night. I marveled at the kindness of this man who had helped me with no ulterior motive.

The next morning, George met me in the lobby, bought me breakfast, then drove me to the office. The situation was that Mary, now Mrs. Minogue, was moving with her contractor husband to another state and was, therefore, leaving Olivetti. My return was providential. She would still be at the office for another week or two, and would orient me regarding her job.

Mary was wonderful. She was relieved that she could turn over the responsibility for Castellini's life to me. He was married with children, but behaved like a bachelor playboy. Mary gave me a little insight to the experience she had while working in his home in Italy. It seemed that there was a lot of animosity between him and his wife, which often resulted in flying crockery. No one was ever injured in these displays, their aim being poor. However, it was quite hard on the crockery.

Ugo Returns

Shortly before my return from Germany, Ugo had come back from Italy, his new visa now in order. We both had the task before us of finding places to live. We were discussing this a day or two later, and Ugo suggested that we should look together since he had a company car. I agreed to the practicality of this, and we began our hunt, which continued over the next few weeks. I was again staying with Rita in the meantime. Ugo and I went out after work, looked at a few places, then had dinner. This pattern repeated itself evening after evening.

A week or two later, Ugo invited me to go out with him to Greenwich Village on a Saturday evening. I went, and romance ensued. We changed the focus of our apartment search to a place for two, assuring each other that it would be much more economical. We found a one-bedroom apartment in Flushing, Queens in a nice new

Ugo with Julia and Sarah

building. Of course, this had to be kept secret at the office, which led to several humorous instances in the following months.

We thought ourselves very clever, pulling the wool over the eyes of our coworkers to avoid office gossip. We rode to work separately, Ugo driving, me taking the bus and walking several blocks to the office (hmmm!). Some of the other secretaries lived not far from our neighborhood, and one morning as I was leaving the building, I saw them at a little distance, coming down the street. I ducked back inside until they passed, then proceeded on my way. They never saw me.

My parents presented another problem. They thought I lived alone. We invited them for dinner one Sunday after they had already met Ugo. I was busy in the kitchen and he was entertaining them in the living room. My mother disappeared and Ugo quietly suggested I find her. I found her in our bedroom in front of an open closet door. She gave me a wide-eyed innocent look and asked, "Where do your guests put their coats?" Hers, as she well knew, was hanging in a coat closet next to the front door. Nothing more was said by her or us.

At Christmastime many of the Italians returned to Italy for the holidays, leaving only a skeleton crew at the office. It was an easy matter to get the time off for a vacation. Of course, Ugo and I were planning one together, but could not let that be known. Ugo got to tell his true destination — that he would be taking a whaler cruise in the Virgin Islands in the Caribbean for the week. I got to make up a story about going to the Baja Peninsula in Mexico. We congratulated ourselves on our cleverness as we arrived at Kennedy Airport and, after the usual waiting around, boarded our plane.

What we did not find out until many months later, after we were married and I was working elsewhere, was that Castellini was also at the airport that day in the departures terminal seeing Tullio Bortoletto off to Italy for Christmas. He heard our names being paged to report to the gate for seat assignments. He was quite amused and gratified. During the past months, he had often suggested that Ugo and I should get together — what a great couple we would make. I had turned these admonitions aside, brushing them off, pretending lack of interest. Ugo had done the same. How Castellini must have chuckled to himself when he found us out! In the months that followed, he hoarded his secret knowledge, deflecting any suspicion that we might know that he knew, by making occasional suggestions that he and I should get together since we had so much in common. I'm not sure what it was that we had in common.

Another Visit to Marian

At the time they married, Marian's husband, Bob, owned an old farmhouse called The Crest, on a mountaintop in the Adirondacks. It had character — and an outhouse. Family gatherings were held there until it burned to the ground one spring during their absence. The outhouse was spared. A new house was built on the site and, although it was a pleasant one, it lacked the ambiance of its drafty predecessor.

I visited them in the old house over the Washington's Birthday holiday. It was the first time Marian and Bob were meeting Ugo, with whom I had lived for almost a year. We left our apartment in Queens, New York, after work on Friday and arrived late in the evening, tired and cold. I hadn't been specific about the relationship between Ugo and me and had left it for Marian to figure out. We exchanged amused smiles when she guided us to two separate bedrooms. Then we found out about the outhouse. It was February.

The next day was spent on the Gore Mountain ski slopes with Marian and her husband, and my cousin Don. I was barely a beginning skier so they led me to the bunny slope for a lesson, and left me while they headed for the expert trails. My cousins had extensive skiing experience as did Ugo, who grew up in the Italian Alps. I spent the day on the bunny slope, and they returned, glowing, from their invigorating runs from the top of the mountain. They bonded with Ugo and I found myself almost an outsider.

Back at the house, we prepared fondue for an afternoon snack while Don played the piano — self-taught and by ear — and others chatted. The atmosphere was warm and relaxed. It was the usual Cole get-together. I hadn't seen them in years, but it was like yesterday. I sat back and imprinted the comforting scene on my mind. It remained with me and I recalled it on a similar occasion in the future.

Chicken Marengo

One week, the big wigs from Italy were coming for meetings with Castellini. By this time, Ugo and I were settled in our apartment in Queens, but, as far as the office knew, he lived there alone. He wanted to invite Castellini and the brass for dinner one evening but the problem was how to do it without letting on about our relationship. Ugo came up with the idea that we would just say I was helping with cooking and serving the meal.

We decided on a new recipe we had just tried for Chicken Marengo. We had liked it and thought it would made a good presentation. Our kitchen was a small galley-type with little room to maneuver. The gentlemen were around the corner in the living room, enjoying their cocktails and canapes, when I summoned Ugo to the kitchen. In transferring the finished chicken and its rich sauce from the sautee pan to the serving platter, the whole thing had slipped to the floor. After a hurried conference, we scooped it up onto the platter from the well-cleaned floor, and carried on as if nothing had happened. The dinner was a success.

Teacher

Time to Become a Real Teacher

After our return from the Mystic Whaler vacation in the Virgin Islands, Ugo and I decided that one of us had to leave Olivetti. It could not be Ugo, as he had the career job and his visa was tied to it. It didn't really matter to me, so I was elected and quickly found a position in Manhattan as secretary to the editor of Motor Boating Magazine, a Hearst publication. I had recently resurrected my idea of becoming a teacher, and would have to take some night courses to complete the undergraduate requirements. Working in Manhattan would be convenient.

My decision was precipitated by an article in Atlantic Monthly about the work in Open Education being done by Lillian Weber at City College. This was not elementary school teaching as I had envisioned it — it was alternative teaching, it was creative. I had avoided the idea of teaching, not wanting to follow a family pattern, escaping into the world of drama at Allegheny. But this was different. This was what I wanted to do, and perhaps I could influence some child — even if only one child — to take a positive direction with his life and prevent the fate that I had seen in my year with the Narcotics Commission. This would be important work.

There had been a teacher shortage and it was possible, with a degree in anything and twelve credits in education, to take an exam for a provisional certificate. After that, requirements for permanent certification had to be fulfilled within a certain time frame. I enrolled at Hunter College to complete the necessary undergraduate credits, then applied and was accepted at City College for the desired master's program under the guru, Lillian Weber.

My first teaching job, once I had acquired the provisional certificate, was obtained by attending an open call for teachers at the District 7 office in the South Bronx. I was selected by an assistant principal from P.S. 1 to be an above-quota teacher. This involved reporting to the school each morning and being assigned where I was most needed. If no classroom spot was available, I would have been put to work in the office doing clerical work, but that never occurred. There was always a call-out from the teaching staff, sometimes for a day, sometimes for a week.

After a one-day orientation about the school, during which I met my fellow new recruits, I was ushered to a fifth grade class whose teacher had suddenly become ill after the first day. She would be out for two weeks. The grades were divided into classes by tracks, and this class was next to the bottom level. I had no student teaching experience, but I had my twelve education credits and the provisional license, plus my degree in drama. Armed with these inadequate tools, I was placed in front of a wild pack of Puerto Rican and Black children, all of whom seemed bent on either jumping out of the second-story windows, running out the classroom door or doing each other bodily harm. I was ignored. Their antennae told them when the assistant principal was approaching, and they raced for their seats, sitting lamb-like. Once she had surveyed the room and left, they were at it again. During her brief visit, I did not want to show my panic, as I was afraid she might think I was inadequate to the job. After she left, I renewed my futile efforts to maintain order.

Lunchtime came. I remained in the classroom, put my head on the desk and sobbed. I sobbed through the whole lunch period, stopping to wash my eyes with cold water and achieve some semblance of dignity before the afternoon onslaught. The afternoon was no better. At the end of the day, I sobbed again. I sobbed all the way home in the subway, avoiding the mildly interested stares of fellow passengers. Overnight, I decided to approach the class with resolve the next day and turn the situation around.

With my new plan in mind, I rode the subway back to school the next morning, ready to take charge. It was not much better, and I discarded Plan A. But I was now able to at least put names to some of the faces so I could direct my entreaties on a more individual basis. "Stop that Jose," instead of just "Stop that."

I'm not sure how I stumbled through the next two weeks, Plans B, C, D, etc., all failing, but at the end of that time, I did know all their names and had actually had conversations with some of them. I had taught them nothing, but they were less chaotic. We had gained some regard for each other, and it was with a little sadness that I turned them back over to their original teacher.

I was still completing the required undergraduate education sequence at Hunter College. I was taking methods of teaching math and social studies, both from a retired school principal who had apparently taught in better days, when students listened when a teacher spoke. During those first two weeks, I spent a lot of class time staring, glassy eyed, into space, shell shocked from my day on the front lines.

Kindergarten Briefly

The Monday following my adventure with the fifth grade, I reported to the principal's office to see what was in store for me next. This time, my assignment was a kindergarten class. Their teacher had pneumonia and would be out for a month. I considered it a reprieve, although I knew little about teaching kindergarten. The office assured me there would be a teaching assistant to guide me and lesson plans to follow. I could relax and maybe even teach something.

That month was a haven in the storm. The assistant was a jewel, and the children adorable. The assistant guided me through the routines that were designed to acculturate the children in school life, and they obligingly cooperated. The mothers came in the mornings to bring them in and collected them again in the afternoon. I felt comfortable. The only snag was that I couldn't count on being in the kindergarten on any given day. If a greater need arose in another class, the kindergarten was split up among the other classes and I was thrown to the wolves.

So, in between the days of joy, the nightmare continued. I was insulted, ignored and rendered voiceless by trying to make myself heard above the din. At times I was bruised, but usually not on purpose. I was also regarded with increasing scorn by the assistant principal for my lack of disciplinary toughness. I had been informed by other faculty members that the assistant principal's car had been set on fire by the students during the previous year because of their intense hatred and fear of her. The culprits had not been caught.

The children in the school were wild, but most were not evil. I looked forward to occasional respite in the kindergarten classroom, but that came to an end. Claire Selletti, their teacher, returned, recovered from her illness, and I was once again completely at the mercy of chance. Until now, I did not know Claire, not having remembered her among so many on orientation day. But I made it a point to go to her classroom and introduce myself. She was a kind, pixie-like young woman. We became friends, and she gave me some excellent advice during my time at P.S. 1. Our friendship continued beyond that time, but we lost track of each other after she and her dentist husband moved away.

Teaching on the Front Lines

At P.S. 1, my next assignment of any length was two weeks in a fourth grade, situated in a trailer annex outside the main building. It had been made over into two interconnected classrooms. I was replacing one of two teachers who were notorious for sitting in teachers' meetings, carrying on their own conversations with no effort to subdue their voices, while the principal tried to conduct the proceedings. They were rude, and I didn't like them. The other half of this pair was in the other classroom, and she offered help if I needed it. I was to learn what kind of help this would be.

It was November, almost Thanksgiving. I had a little more confidence by now, being further along into my methods courses, and having had some experience with the children. I had learned that, although I couldn't appeal to all, I was able to establish good rapport with some, and that, whatever else they learned from me, they learned that I cared. Caring was a rare commodity at P.S. 1 in those days.

Things were far from perfect in that fourth grade class, and the children got out of hand from time to time, but they were at a nice age, and we got along. Their teacher had created lovely, manicured teacher bulletin boards, but there was no place for the children to display their work. Thanksgiving would be over before their teacher returned, so I allowed them to take down her decorations and hang up their artwork and their gold-star papers. I allowed them to work in groups rather than doing everything by rote. That involved talking. Sometimes they became a little loud, but usually responded to a reminder. I thought things were going well.

There was one little boy in the class who required a lot of attention. He was a cute, chubby little Puerto Rican child, and I was very fond of him. But this one particular day, he was whining and getting on my nerves, so I decided it was time to take the other teacher up on her offer of help. I sent him to her class to cool off, expecting him to return, contrite, in a short while. I took him to the connecting door and she signaled to send him in. He was reluctant to go, but he had no choice.

The rest of the class, now subdued, went back to the matter at hand. A few minutes later the connecting door burst open. The boy ran through the room as if devils were after him, and they were. The students from the other class came racing behind him and chased him out the front door to the schoolyard. I had gotten up to go after him when the other teacher appeared at the door. She ordered me to leave them all alone, not to go out. She went back into her classroom and closed the door.

I sat down on the edge of my chair, but the screams from the schoolyard brought me right back up and I raced to the door. The boys from the other class had my boy down on the ground, pummeling him. Hearing his screams and cries, I disregarded the order from the other teacher, and I went out after him and chased the other boys away. The girls from the other class had been looking on. They went back to their classroom by their outside entrance, grumbling, glaring at me over their shoulders. I gathered up my student and helped him back inside. We were both in tears by now. I calmed him down, washed his face and hands, and found that, aside from a few tears in his usually neat clothing, he was basically unharmed, at least physically. I promised him and the rest of the class that I would never send them to the other room again, or allow such an attack.

Word of this occurrence spread among the other students, through siblings and friends. The boy's brother had been in my first class — the disastrous fifth grade — and he had been one with whom I had some reasonable conversations. Among the students I was developing a reputation for caring, but that earned me no regard from most of the teachers. For one thing, I had committed the cardinal sin of allowing the students to touch the teacher's bulletin boards. It seems that they were sacrosanct. Then I had disobeyed the order of a senior teacher and interfered with the peer discipline that she had allowed. I let the children talk in class. I made them feel like worthwhile people, rather than like little animals. The younger teachers, particularly the new ones who had started with me, did not share those views with the old guard, but they were hesitant to go against the tide. The old guard was ranged against me, not overtly, but covertly in looks and sly, demeaning comments. To them, I was an outcast, a pariah.

Hand-to-Hand Combat

Later in the fall, on parent-teacher conference day, there were meetings in the afternoon, so the children would only be present in the morning. One sixth grade class was all boys, with a male teacher who had a knack for handling behavior problems. He called out sick that day, and I was designated to take his class. I knew the boys were pretty rough, but one had quite a reputation. The previous year he had been expelled from school for throwing a girl down a staircase, resulting in her breaking her leg. I could not believe that, with my inexperience, the administration would have me take this class, but I saw no way out. Other faculty members who were in the office when I received my assignment, gave me pitying looks — even the old guard — and I believe they started taking bets as to whether or not I would come out alive.

On my way up the stairs I devised my plan. I had seen it in a movie somewhere. I would zero in on the boy whose reputation had preceded him, and make him my helper, in charge of the other boys. I would not fight him, I would make him my ally. It worked — at least until 11:00 in the morning when he announced it was time for the class to go to gym. Not knowing their schedule, I didn't argue with him. My "helper" lined them up and we went to the basement where an impromptu gym with some play equipment was set up. That was the last I saw of them. They scattered to the winds. I was alive, they were alive. I reported to the office amid clapping and cheers from the teachers and staff who were there. No thought was given by anyone to the fact that the boys had run off. No one thought I would last as long as I did. But I had made it through and survived the worst class in the school with no injuries sustained. It was an accomplishment.

My Own Class — and Roberto

A week before Christmas vacation, I was assigned to the bottom-level fifth grade, just below the class with which I had begun my career at P.S. 1. Two male teachers of this class had already fallen by the wayside. One had become ill with Hepatitis and the other had thrown up his hands in disgust. This could become a permanent assignment. I entered the class that Monday prepared to love these children and to make the proverbial difference in their lives.

They looked back at me, questioningly, patiently waiting, sizing me up. They knew a little about me already, but I knew nothing about them. They were quieter than the other fifth grade had been. These were the dregs, the not very bright, the emotionally disturbed, the children for whom there was little hope in the educational world. This was the challenge I had been waiting for. In my own mind, I bonded with them. The vice principal's attitude was that anything I might accomplish with them would be a step up, and if I failed, nothing would be lost.

I made my plans along the traditionally expected lines, but knew that I would adapt them to the children as we went along. I had read Sylvia Ashton-Warner's *Teacher*, and here was my chance to practice her theories about organic learning. By Thursday, we had not accomplished much academically, but had established a mutual respect and a little trust. One girl still spent time hiding in her coat locker, a tough-looking boy still sat sullenly in the back, and another sly boy was still looking for angles to get away with small transgressions. But the others were there, waiting to see. They knew how to react to authority with quiet fear but were not sure about this new-found acceptance. They could become boisterous at times, testing the limits.

And so it was this Thursday afternoon, when it was time to get their coats and leave for the day. I was trying to get their attention and quiet them so we could accomplish this in an orderly manner, but I was not having much luck. By day's end, they had expended their ration of restraint. The assistant principal, hated and feared by the students, entered the room and immediate silence ensued. She glared at me and boomed out, "This is not the way to get ready for dismissal. I'll show you how it's done!" She took up her position at the front of the room like a martinet, with me cowering behind.

The children were by now cringing in their seats with fearful eyes fixed on this woman. "First row get your coats," she barked. In dutiful silence, they got up, and followed in a silent line to the lockers. When they were seated, she repeated the routine with the second row, and so on, until all were sitting in their coats, belongings on their desks in front of them, waiting to escape.

She turned her malevolent stare to me. "That's how it's done!" She snapped her head around and marched out of the room, leaving me fighting back tears of humiliation.

When she was gone, David, one of the older boys, stalked purposefully up to me and confronted me. "Did she make you cry?" He asked in an angry and outraged voice, sounding much like the knight who is about to save the princess from the fire-breathing dragon.

David's concern outweighed his anger, I couldn't hold back the tears. They rolled down my face, and that was answer enough for him. "Don't you worry about a thing. Roberto and I will take care of everything. We'll help you."

At that moment, the bell rang and they were gone. Roberto had not been present during this episode, as he preferred to run around the school on his own adventures, a free spirit.

The next morning was Friday — assembly day. The whole school regularly descended on the auditorium, each class to its own assigned section, for whatever enlightenment awaited. There was a prize for the best-behaved class. It was beyond my ambition that my class would ever be selected. I would have been happy just to not have them thrown out.

When my students entered the classroom that morning, Roberto was with David as they marched to the desk. He had heard what happened with the assistant principal the previous day and was indignant. He was eager to work with David to maintain good behavior in the other kids.

The pair proceeded to line up the class, pulling and prodding this one and that one into position. I had to intervene only a few times to prevent excessive roughness. The other kids were slightly owlish about the methods, but they cooperated. Smiling with satisfaction, Roberto and David led the others across the hall and down the stairs, while I followed behind, then moved forward to lead the class into the auditorium. With a minimum of fuss, the children found their seats.

The program of the morning was inconsequential to the little drama that was occurring in our rows. Every squeak and whisper was greeted by a poke or nudge from my two helpers, or others that they designated to act for them, to deal with misbehavers along the row that they couldn't reach themselves. My job was to keep the helpers from getting too carried away with their good work, and I was glad that my children were doing so well and acting creditably. The end of assembly came and the winning class was announced. It was us! We had won!

This success was too much for the kids to accept calmly. Fortunately, in everybody's rush to leave the auditorium, their lapse in decorum was overlooked. Roberto and David were elated. I hoped we could build on this success and really pull the group together as a class. However, I overestimated the ease with which such a task could be accomplished, and was disappointed that the children relapsed into their old ways once back in the classroom. No matter. We would work on it.

Christmas vacation loomed, and we planned a party for the last afternoon. I had gotten little gifts for the children, brought in some Christmas records, and arranged for a few refreshments. The party was not a great success, as their idea of a party was a free-for-all. It did not include remaining in the classroom. Roberto disappeared entirely, and others came and went, trying to see friends in other rooms. If I stood by the door, there would be a commotion in another part of the room. I could not be everywhere. David tried, but he had already done his bit to help, and he was more interested in having fun himself. Besides, I would not let him and Roberto continue to pinch, poke, and prod the others to induce them to behave.

Over the vacation, I regrouped and came up with a new approach now that I knew the children better. Roberto and David were both bright, and I was sure I could train them to help the others in a responsible way, rather than simply control them. When I returned to the class, I was greeted with the information that David was gone to live with his father in Brooklyn. That left me with just Roberto. David was a big loss to me because Roberto by himself was more volatile. He was bright, but very restless in the classroom. He thought that, because he helped at times, he earned the privilege of running out of the classroom and around the school as he chose. I finally called his father in for a short conference. The records stated, "parent cooperative."

Roberto's father was a quiet, well-mannered man and listened respectfully as I related the problem with his son's behavior. I made sure to emphasize Roberto's potential. When I finished, he turned sorrowfully to Roberto who was standing by with his head hanging, and said, "Well, Roberto, I guess we'll just have to take you home and chain you to the radiator like we did the last time."

I was shocked. This was not the outcome I wanted. Now I understood what was meant by "parent cooperative." I tried to intervene and explain to Roberto's father that I just wanted his support and influence in correcting Roberto's behavior, not physical punishment. I repeated that Roberto was a bright boy who had a chance if only he would focus his attention on learning. His father looked at me patiently as if I were a well-meaning child who needed to be humored and reassured. But the message was that he would deal with Roberto in his own way.

After his father left, I tried to apologize to Roberto for what I saw as a vast communication failure, and to make him understand that I did not want him beaten or chained to a radiator. He, too, looked at me as though I was a simple child to be humored and said, "It's all right."

It wasn't all right with me, but I had no chance to make amends. The term ended a short time later, and I was called to the principal's office. There were budget cuts and the above-quota teacher position had been dropped. A tenured teacher from another district was being transferred in to take my class. I was reassured that it was no fault of mine, it was just the system. I could go to the district office and hope to find another position. Good-bye and good luck.

I was devastated. I had put a lot of effort into the children. I had gotten the sullen boy to smile, the sly one to be a little more trusting, and the girl who had hidden in the coat locker to come out. A few were actually doing a little reading and learning. These were my children. I left the building and walked the few blocks to the District 7 office. My heart was crying.

Once again, my timing was good. I was immediately snapped up and offered the one remaining position in a Title I project to help slow readers in the parochial schools in the district. The basis was a phonics program written by a former nun who would be training us. There were four other teachers already on board. Training would begin immediately so we would be ready to begin with the new term. One window closes, another opens. At last I might actually be able to teach something, and to children who were well disciplined and interested in learning. There was one more thing I had to do to put closure to the P.S. 1 situation.

With new confidence — I now had a real position — I walked back to P.S. 1 and into the office. It was just before lunch, and I explained that I wanted to meet with my old class to let them know where I was going, and that it was not their fault that I was leaving. I didn't say it, but I particularly wanted to make them understand that, because I was afraid the assistant principal would try to make them feel at fault, reinforcing their feelings of worthlessness. Permission was granted, and I went to the room just as they were putting on their coats for lunch. The little girl emerged from the coat locker.

Their new teacher, a man, was considerate and went out of the room, leaving me alone with them. After I explained the situation to them, and told them how much I would miss them, the bell rang and they went with me down the stairs, Roberto sliding down the banister. He was crying, and there were a few muffled whimpers among the others, as well as a loud wailing from the closet girl. I explained to them that I would be working in the Catholic schools nearby.

"B-b-but I don't want you to become a nun," sobbed Roberto.

I assured him that would not happen — that not everyone who taught in the Catholic school system was a nun, or even Catholic, as in my case. Roberto was mollified, and the group followed me out of the school to my car that I had left parked there (I had acquired it during the semester). They continued to follow my car down the street until I turned the corner. Perhaps I was not a success as a disciplinarian, but I had imparted something that most teachers in that school did not — a sense of self and value in my students.

I saw Roberto a time or two after that when I was teaching at St. Adalbert's, a few blocks up the street. It turned out that the school was located on the street where he lived, and when he played hooky, he guarded my car. He didn't really need to because the families of my new students did a good job of that. But it made him feel good. He said the new man teacher wasn't bad, and had them doing some interesting projects. I can only hope that he treated them with humanity and encouraged the growth of their feelings of self-worth. Roberto promised that he would try to stay in the classroom and learn. I hoped things were starting to look up for him.

CHAPTER 18

Teaching in the South Bronx

Teaching Reading

Teaching in the phonics program was the best of both worlds. I had well-behaved children in the parochial schools and the pay scale of the city public schools. There were only ten students in a forty-five minute class, and I had a pleasant and competent teaching assistant, Mrs. Falcone. The remainder of my first year of teaching was idyllic, once I became comfortable with the program itself.

The purpose was to give a boost to those students who needed just that little bit of extra help to increase their reading proficiency. It was not an in-depth reading program for children with clinical reading disabilities. It was clear-cut and left lots of room for enhancement and creativity. A library of children's literature and suggestions for additional projects were provided along with it. I was gaining ideas from my course work at Hunter College, and was even able to bring in some things I had learned in my children's theatre course at Allegheny. A favorite activity of the second graders was acting out the story of *Three Billy Goats Gruff,* which they did with gusto.

As the last teacher hired, I covered two schools, one in the morning, and one in the afternoon. In the morning, I was at a larger school and had sixth, seventh and eighth grade classes. Some of the students were quite tall, but they lived in fear of their principal, Sr. Rachel, and did their best to avoid any confrontations with her. She was a short, stocky lady who resembled Queen Victoria, and her students held her in the same awe as they would the queen.

Every class has a clown, and I had the one from seventh grade. He was a pleasant boy, tall and thin. One morning he was pushing just a little too far, and the others were starting to join in his spirit of fun. Before they got off-track and began clowning as well, I decided to remove the instigator and send him to Sr. Rachel. He went with some reluctance. The next morning, the clown was back in class, smiling ruefully.

"Please don't send me to Sr. Rachel again," said he as he rubbed the top of his head in remembrance.

"What happened?" Too late, I remembered the little boy at P.S. 1 whom I had sent to the neighboring fourth grade teacher for respite.

"Just the usual. She stood on a chair and pulled me up by my hair."

He had a black, nappy head and his hair was short, but one could get a good hold from above. His scalp was obviously sore and he rubbed it absentmindedly during class. But, he took the punishment in stride, holding no malice. I apologized, and he accepted with good grace, making an effort to keep his humor in better control during the course of the semester. I didn't send him to the office again.

In the other school, I had the younger grades that first year. The principal, Sr. Justine, was a younger, forward-thinking nun with whom I developed a good rapport. In the second grade there was a little Hispanic girl named Frances M. One morning, Frances came in and announced that she wouldn't be in class the next day, as she was going to see the school psychologist to find out what her "proglem" was. I made a note of her planned absence, and the day she returned, my assistant, Mrs. Falcone, asked her if she had found out what her "proglem" was. We had been amused by Frances's terminology.

Frances stated, with great seriousness and the facial expression of a wise old woman, "my proglem is Sr. Roberta."

Mrs. Falcone and I could not hide our laughter. Frances, thinking her statement must have been really funny, laughed with us. Sr. Roberta was Frances's teacher, a dour, elderly nun of the old school. The word was that she was not above using corporal punishment on her students, although it was no longer condoned by school authorities. I never saw her do this, but heard several reports of it. Verbally she was certainly very strict and not popular with her students. We could see that this sweet but lively girl might well have a "proglem" with her.

The school year passed, and I was content. During the following summer, I finished my undergraduate education sequence at Hunter College. I was now ready for graduate school and exposure to the ideas of Lillian Weber and was looking forward to her classes. Of course, there were courses taught by others as well, but she was the guiding hand.

Marrying Ugo

The other event that occurred that summer between undergraduate and graduate school was that Ugo and I got married. His future with Olivetti was looking uncertain as Castellini appeared to be running the American branch of the Numerical Control division into the ground. Ugo felt it was time for him to move on. However, he was still an Italian citizen, which could make finding another job more difficult. We had also started looking at houses out of the city, inspired by friends, Judy and Arthur Heisler, who had bought a summer place in the Catskills where we were frequent visitors.

We just weren't sure what we wanted to do, but decided that our plans would go better if we got married. We started looking into it, and found that, because Ugo was still an Italian citizen, the easiest path would be to get married in Nevada where there were no reciprocal agreements with the Italian government. We had acquired a cat named Samantha, along with a vacation cabin in the country, not far from Judy and Arthur. We arranged for our cat to stay in a cattery and made our plane and hotel reservations.

The least expensive fare was a package promoted by the gambling casinos. We boarded the plane with the gamblers, and got into a conversation with our seatmate. He was a middle-aged postal worker who saved up for this annual vacation gambling at Las Vegas. Ugo and I thought that a rather silly goal, but we developed a fondness for the poor fellow.

We arrived at the Aladdin Hotel along with our seatmate. Ugo and I proceeded with our plans, obtained a license, decided where to have the ceremony, and dressed up for the occasion. The third day of our trip was D-Day. Meanwhile, we had been dropping into the Keno parlor on a regular basis to check on our friend. He was all wild eyed with excitement about how wonderful it was that they gave him all these free meals and free drinks. He hardly saw the inside of his room, practically living in the Keno parlor. He had lost a bundle and could not see our point when we explained to him that all those meals and drinks were anything but free. He had paid well for them.

On our wedding day, we set out in a taxi for the courthouse, that being the only place that presented any dignified environment. We didn't want to be married by Elvis in one of the overly ornate wedding chapels that dotted the city. When we told him our destination, the taxi driver asked, "Are you sure you know what you're doing?" He thought Ugo was the big winner and I was the cocktail waitress from the night before. We assured him that our plan was not spur of the moment. The judge who performed the ceremony scarcely looked at us and mumbled his way through it quickly. Then it was over. We were married.

Another taxi ride brought us to Caesar's Palace, with its impressive columns and rows of fountains. Inside, we found one of the many cocktail lounges and, while I staggered off to a ladies' lounge to vomit, my nerves having caught up with me, Ugo found a table and ordered champagne. He finished his glass as he awaited my return, and ordered another round for both of us. There were now three full glasses and one empty on the table. The waitress asked him if he was celebrating something or just lining up glasses.

"Actually, I'm celebrating. I just got married."

"Oh, you poor stupid fool!" she exclaimed.

"Have you ever been married?" he asked.

"Yeah! Three times."

"In that case, who's the more poor stupid fool?"

That shut her up, and she stalked off just as I was returning, feeling much better and ready for my champagne. We had our wedding dinner that night on Cleopatra's Barge, floating on a man-made canal inside Caesar's Palace. When we were finished with dinner, the evening was still young, and Ugo wanted to find something to do. He suggested we visit the gaming tables. This was about the last place I wanted to spend the evening, but he was eager to try his luck. Parsimonious by nature, he did not want to risk losing much money. His suggestion was that we return to our hotel and that he take $30, go downstairs to the tables, and gamble until it was gone. I would remain in our room, guarding his wallet from him, not giving him another penny no matter how much he might plead, should he want to gamble more. That is what we did, and he was quickly back at the door, minus the $30. He did not ask for more.

My gambling consisted of taking fifty cents of the dollar in change that he had given me on arrival, to play the slot machines, playing and losing it, then pocketing the other half of the money. Period. Apparently, I did not inherit Grandpa Cole's weakness for "just one more turnover." That was the beginning — and end — of my gambling career.

It was obvious by now that neither of us was a gambler, so we had to find something to do for the remainder of our package trip. We rented a car and drove out to Lake Mead — a beautiful man-made lake above Hoover Dam. We took a picnic lunch and rented a motor boat, returning in the evening to the hotel to get ready to attend a dinner theatre where David Frost was playing. He was one of our favorite television personalities. We had some time beforehand and decided to take the external glass elevator to the top of the building and enjoy the view of the city. This was when I knew I had acrophobia. I crawled as close to the building as I could get, and closed my eyes. I knew it was the end. We would crash to our doom.

However, it was not the end; we emerged safely and enjoyed our evening. The next day, we prepared to leave for home. The bus to the airport was at the front of the hotel, and our bags were on it. We looked around for our gambling friend. We tried the Keno parlor, and there he was, eyes red-rimmed with lack of sleep, hunched over his Keno card. With some difficulty, we extracted him from the room and helped him out to the bus. His bag was there — he had traveled light, and I don't think he even unpacked. We dragged him onto the bus and poured him into his seat. He slept the whole flight home.

The next day, we collected our cat and began married life.

Using My Theatre Training

Lillian Weber was a middle-aged, grandmotherly woman whose short hair was still dark, with wisps of gray. She was bulky but agile, full of energy. Her mind worked constantly, jumping from one brilliant thought to another, and I loved listening to her whenever I had the opportunity. She came to know me. I was shy about speaking up in classes or meeting with her, but when I did speak, she usually liked what I had to say. I felt validated and actually bright for the first time in my life. When I graduated, it was with a 4.0 average. I now knew what I was capable of when my interest and admiration were engaged.

Returning to the South Bronx, my second year of teaching began well. One of the teachers had dropped out of the program over the summer, having gotten married and moved away, so I was no longer low man on the totem pole. A new person had been hired, and I chose to stay the full day at St. Adalbert's. The school went up to the eighth grade, as had the other one, but my classes were drawn from no higher than the sixth grade.

My classroom was also the staff room and the teachers assembled there for lunch. It was a large, sunny space and easily accommodated tables for the teachers and a large area for my students, including all my supplies and books. Now that I had a home base, I felt that I could really expand on what I was learning in my graduate classes in individualized education. I was fascinated by the new ideas I was exposed to by my professors and Lillian Weber, and began gathering recruits for the program among fellow faculty members at school. Although I still technically worked for and was paid by Title I, I was very comfortable with the other teachers and Sr. Justine. I felt like I was part of the school. One of the third grade teachers, Maria Proskurenko, was especially interested and soon entered the same graduate program. I was in an enviable collegial situation.

Now that I was teaching the older children at St. Adalbert's as well as the young ones, I found a way to put my drama training to good use. In my searches through college bookstores, both at City College where I was enrolled, and Columbia Teachers' College that had an excellent selection of teaching tools, I stumbled across a book entitled *Shake Hands With Shakespeare*, and its sequel *Push Back the Desks*. These two volumes contained simplified, but not watery, versions of a number of Shakespeare plays. The feel of the storyline and language remained. During that year, we performed *Romeo and Juliet*, and *Hamlet* for the whole school at assembly. I adapted the plays still further as the versions in the books remained too long as they were, but the end result was a success in many ways.

At Christmas, the fourth grade performed the play of *Amahl and the Night Visitors*, based on the Giancarlo Menotti opera. The fifth grade acted out *The Night Before Christmas* to the music of the song version.

I was fortunate that a new boy had come into the sixth grade that year from public school. His reading scores were just a hair below what they should be, and he was placed in my class. He was a Black boy named Tom, and had a bright, inquiring mind. The first play we did was *Romeo and Juliet* and of course he was Romeo. A pretty but shy Hispanic girl played Juliet, and there were good parts for everyone who wanted to be in the production. Rehearsals were held during class and after school.

In my spare time at home, I made costumes and props with some help from Mrs. Falcone, who was wonderful with these projects. The music was the Prokoffiev ballet piece. I had had fencing at the American Theatre Wing and still had my fencing foil, so was able to coach the fight scenes. We borrowed a second foil. Our sets were simple, using what we found at hand. I had to spend some extra time coaching Vilma on her Juliet lines, and there were a few tearful moments, but she came through believably in the end. The performance was well received by the other students and the parents who attended.

Riding the crest of success, I dove right into adapting *Hamlet*. Vilma had had enough of starring roles after playing Juliet, and Yvette was selected to play Ophelia. Tom was Hamlet. No one else was eager to play leading roles, and everyone was happy. Again, I made costumes, coached fencing and planned music. The music this time was from Olivier's movie version of the play. I had seen it and loved the ending where Hamlet's friends carry his body aloft up the winding stone stairs to the roof of the castle, after Horatio delivers the eulogy. I wanted to incorporate this dramatic moment, with all its feeling, into our production.

I went to the eighth grade teacher and asked to recruit some of her biggest boys. I selected four and coached them on what they were to do. Tom was not aware of the plan — he would not be aware until the time came. I told him only that there would be a surprise and to just go with it.

The day of the performance came, and the play drew to its close. Hamlet had been slain and lay on the stage. The ending music began, and I signaled the selected boys who gathered as a cadre and marched up the side steps to the stage. There were glances at me from my group of actors, but I just smiled and nodded reassurance to them that this was planned. As if they had been rehearsing for a month instead of not at all, the boys knelt as one and lifted Tom to their shoulders, turned with him aloft, marched down the steps and out through the center aisle as the music swelled. It was just like the final scene of the movie. I had goose bumps then, and have them now as I remember that moment. I was not the only one. The applause and praise that my students received from so many others, including the older students, made them feel ten feet tall. That day, they were stars and soaked up the accolades. They had earned their place in the sun.

My Own Classroom

The phonics program was successful and the students did well on their post-tests at the end of the year. Most of them were ready for mainstreaming back into their regular classes for reading. There was a question as to whether the program would continue at St. Adalbert's, because there was not another pool of potential recipients in the small school. I could be transferred to another school if the program was to be funded again by Title I for another year.

However, I was no longer interested in continuing with that program. I was well into my graduate course work. and it covered more that reading. It was all about the integrated day. I wanted something more to integrate. I wanted to teach all the subjects so I could intertwine them and make them into a meaningful whole. Sr. Roberta, the one who was Frances's "proglem," was retiring from teaching and taking up a position as assistant to Sr. Justine in the office. I applied for her job and got it. I would be the new second grade teacher. Of course, now that I would be working directly for the school and no longer in the New York City system, there would be a major cut in salary. No matter.

There were actually two second grade classes, the other taught by another elderly nun of the old school. I began making teaching materials and planning my classroom around individualized principles. There would be art, music, animals, cooking, writing and all kinds of reading. I would keep St. Justine happy and follow the formal reading and math materials, but I could expand those as I wished, and she gave me latitude in everything else. I was losing Mrs. Falcone as she belonged to Title I, but I gained a mother, Mrs. Jones, who volunteered her help three days per week. She was younger, but not as well trained as Mrs. Falcone. However, she was enthusiastic and eager to learn.

The Camelot Year

The first year in my own classroom went well. I loved the children, and we did outrageous, educational things. We took a trip to the Museum of Natural History on Central Park West. Some of my students had never been out of the Bronx before. As an elementary school child, I had hated class trips. I would look forward to them, then be bitterly disappointed by the reality. We all marched in rows and couldn't move at our own pace. We had to look at boring things because someone else wanted to, or be torn away from something that caught our eye if no one else was interested. The cafeteria always smelled of old bananas. I had fleeting memories of this museum as a child, but knew it well now, having lived around the corner from it for a couple of years not long before. My class was going to have a different experience.

I lined up several mothers to go with us, including Mrs. Jones. The students were divided into groups and assigned to Mrs. Jones, the others and me. The ground rule was that we would go separately into the museum, entering by different doors so the officials wouldn't know we were a school group, as the rule still existed that school groups must proceed together in a pack as I so unhappily remembered from my own school days. Under my plan, each group of five students would see what they wanted to see, traveling quickly through the exhibits, and meeting across the street on the rocks in the park at noon for lunch. The children loved the conspiratorial mood of the trip.

Once we were off the subway, we went our separate ways. My group wanted to see the dinosaur bones, among other things, so we headed there first. Next, it was on to something else. We moved quickly without a whole herd to slow us down, going on to room after room, their interest soaring. Once, we glimpsed one of our other groups across a long exhibit hall. Both groups pretended not to know each other. At noon, we emerged from the front door, and from the top of the massive staircase, we could already see the others gathering across the way. My group zoomed down the steps but waited, at the curb as instructed, until I could cross them. At lunch, they shared experiences, all talking excitedly about what they saw. I don't remember ever having such a feeling after a school field trip when I was a child. We milked that trip for the next few weeks, writing experience stories, and making up social studies and science projects.

As the year wore on, we put on an assembly about the six wives of Henry VIII. The PBS series was running then, and what I told them about that king piqued their interest. Some of the kids actually watched several of the episodes at home with their families. What they liked was the Blue Beard aspect — all the beheadings. The more gore, the better they liked it. There was a comedy song recorded by Elsa Lanchester (wife of Charles Laughton, who played Henry VIII, but not in that series). It had to do with Ann Boleyn and began, "With her head tucked underneath her arm she walks the lonely tower. With her head tucked underneath her arm, at the midnight hour." We made a papier mache head and dressed one of the girls with the neck of the dress over her head so she would appear to be headless. Another child played Henry's ghost. They mimed the song and it brought down the house when presented at assembly.

One Saturday, with Ugo's help, I took a group of interested girls to the Metropolitan Museum of Art. None of the boys opted to go. Not all of the girls were allowed to go, some of the families being culturally over-protective, but about five accepted the invitation. The goal was to see the Egyptian exhibit and mummies. I don't remember just how we got onto that track, but something had ignited their interest. We read in an encyclopedia about the embalming techniques, and these girls were eager to see the results. More gore. They raced through Egypt, then on through the Hall of Armor, which they found equally fascinating. Then on to some of the reproductions of homes in early America, federal, etc. They fed their eyes on the exhibits. There was no lesson plan to follow, no goal except to satisfy curiosity and drink in new and exciting experiences. It was exposure to something they had never seen or dreamed of before. It opened new doors of inquiry and possibility.

There were animals in the classroom: a hamster and guinea pigs. One of the suggestions I had learned in my graduate work was to encourage a slow reader to read to the class guinea pig, because the guinea pig will not laugh if you make a mistake. One little boy was slow at everything; he had a slow walk, a slow smile and a slow speech pattern. Of course, his reading was slow, and very hesitant as well. He would take forever to get through a passage in the group. I suggested he read to the guinea pig and he did — on a daily basis. Next he was volunteering to read in his group. Then he began writing little books about the guinea pig; actually he wrote very large books covered by giant pieces of construction paper, and containing illustrations that he drew. He became famous in the school for his books.

He was sent to the office to read them to Sr. Justine. She sent him to other classrooms. He was a hit. He grew, he beamed. By the end of the year, he was not only a reader — he was a writer, an author.

Science and math were learned through cooking as well as other activities. In the school basement there was an old unused kitchen area from the days when the children's meals were prepared on the premises. Now the meals were premade and delivered daily. I had a children's cookbook written by one of my professors, with recipes and the math/science concepts that could be learned. I bought baking equipment and made large waterproof recipe cards based on the book. I trained Mrs. Jones in the concept of using cooking as a learning experience and what the possible objectives and benefits were. I sent the students, under her guidance, in rotating groups to the basement to cook.

Mostly they made muffins. We wrote experience stories about the cooking and discussed the concepts they had discovered. The measuring was math, and science was involved with the chemical change during baking. The next step was to sell the muffins to other classes. We didn't have that many muffins — maybe a dozen or so each session. We limited our sales to the first grade to give them a little practice with money as well. The object was to return with the correct amount of money for the number of muffins sold. They were sent off on their own to carry out this task.

There was one boy, bigger than the others, who had come in from public school that year. He was a wise guy, and not academically as advanced as Tom, the sixth grader, had been in the phonics class. It was this boy's turn to lead the muffin sales. He saw everything as a big joke and paid no attention when instructed about how much to charge, how to make change, etc., but he deserved his turn.

When he came back to the class with his crew to give the sales report, there was grumbling among the members of his group, and their faces were angry. He was seriously short of the required sum. His group knew he was doing it all wrong, and he would not listen to their advice. I never had to say a thing. When the rest of the class heard his report — they all knew by then how to figure out how much he should have brought back — they reproached him and upbraided him for the shortfall. The smile fell from his face, and he became crestfallen. He realized that he had seriously overstepped and his classmates took a dim view of his attitude. Peer pressure had its effect, and after that day, he was more subdued and not so quick to make light of the class activities.

One day at lunchtime, I planned to leave the school and received permission to take several girls with me, up the street to the local supermarket to buy muffin ingredients. Some of them had never been to the supermarket, although it was in their neighborhood. Their mothers must have felt it was easier to leave them at home with older siblings and enjoy a few moments to themselves. We made a list of the ingredients we would need for the next batch of muffins, counted the money in the muffin kitty, and we headed off. The girls chattered among themselves during the short walk. Once at the store, we located the items on our list and were about to check out when one girl spied an advertising banner that read, "PRICES CUT TO THE BONE!"

"What does that mean — prices cut to the bone?" she asked.

I explained that it meant the prices were reduced as low as possible so the store could move some slow items and still make a profit. The girls thought that was the funniest thing and the more they repeated the phrase, the funnier it became. By the time we were out on the sidewalk, they could hardly contain themselves. They linked arms and started skipping back toward the school, all the while chanting, "Prices cut to the bone! Prices cut to the bone! Prices…" until they reached the building, which they entered, flushed and laughing.

I never talked down to my students, using language that was presumably what a second grader could understand. The real world isn't like that, and I had read books by other teachers who frowned on watering down the vocabulary in the classroom. I was comfortable with using my normal speech pattern of occasional three- and four-syllable words with the kids. One episode validated this practice. It was lunchtime, and my class usually waited, lined up in the hallway, next to the other second grade class, for the signal that it was their turn to go to the lunchroom. This day, the teacher of the other class, the elderly nun, was obligated elsewhere, and I was in charge of both groups.

In the course of a typical conversation with my class, I happened to use one of my common words. I didn't realize until that day just how much their comprehension had grown. Several kids from the other class asked, "What does that mean?" and they repeated the word.

Almost as one person, my group turned to them and in a chorus, gave the definition. I was surprised and gratified that more of what I had learned in my reading and classes, had been proved. Children were obviously able to figure out the meaning of long words far beyond their previous experience, subconsciously using context clues. Once I was aware of this phenomenon, I noticed other words that I used that my class seemed to understand with ease.

London

In February of that year, during the school break, Sr. Justine and I had arranged to travel to London with a group of teachers from Westchester County who had invited the Archdiocese to send along any interested professionals as well. We would be visiting the schools there to see how they applied open education techniques. This was a wonderful opportunity to obtain ideas firsthand and for Sr. Justine to see how well the approach could work school-wide.

It was a whirlwind tour and, disappointingly, did not include the inner city schools whose results had been most dramatic, and where Lillian Weber had done her research, because they were closed for their break as well. However, suburban schools had been lined up, and the faculties there were eager to receive us and share their success. Each morning, the bus waited in front of our hotel to deposit us at a different school. On the whole, it was inspirational, and I gathered new ideas to apply at home. One thing that impressed me in one particular school was the kindness of the teachers. We were given a hot lunch from their cafeteria. The food was terrible, but we were glad to have something to eat and made the best of it. The other schools had prepared special lunches for us. We mumbled some disparaging comments among ourselves, then learned that the teachers at the school had given up their own hot lunch for us and had to scrounge for themselves or go without. We hoped none of our rude comments had been overheard, and made more of a show of appreciating the meal, looking around us sheepishly. We did not want to appear as the "ugly Americans."

In the evenings, Sr. Justine and I, and sometimes a priest from the archdiocese, Brother Robert, who was also in our party, went to dinner and then to the theatre, trying out the restaurants of different nationalities. London was (and is) a cultural center for a multitude of ethnic groups. We had been warned against strictly British restaurants, the one in our hotel being a good example, where food tended to be mushy and tasteless, overcooked and under-seasoned.

One evening we ate in an Italian restaurant where the owners still remembered my husband Ugo, from when he had spent some months in London years before with Olivetti. I had to describe him, but they remembered right away. In a second-floor Indian restaurant, Veeraswami, we had curry, then steak at an American steak house. On our last night, we went to Simpson's for traditional British food, but geared to tourists who had read Dickens. Roast beef and Yorkshire pudding were the staple fare, with Trifle for dessert. Not like what is served in the typical British kitchen, it was as good as it sounded in Dickens's novels. The dining room was in a second-floor drawing room, and the ambiance was perfect, with a fire glowing on the grate.

We saw a play a night, including the long-running *Mousetrap*, by Agatha Christie. Sr. Justine and I ventured in the rain on a free morning to the British Museum where we, like the girls from my class, were enthralled with the mummies. Of course, we did Westminster Abbey, but not the Tower of London. I saw the tomb of Elizabeth I, my idol, and was awed by the experience. She was a woman who had survived by her wits against heavy odds, but was not afraid to show her humanity as well. She took a weak, bankrupt country and made it the strongest and richest in the world at that time.

The worst thing I remember from that trip was the rudeness of one of the salesgirls in the London University Bookstore. Sr. Justine and I had been looking forward all week to the last Saturday, when we planned to indulge ourselves in buying some of the many titles available there on open education. We had saved room in our suitcases.

Unfortunately, I had been having some digestive difficulties for several days and it came to a head while waiting in line. My face felt hot and I was suddenly perspiring profusely. I was dizzy and nauseated. I had to find a toilet soon or be terribly embarrassed. I dragged myself to the counter and finally got the attention of this girl. In a barely audible voice, and with great effort, I asked where the bathroom was. She looked at my miserable, sick face and laughed. She then pointed the direction. I turned and headed the way she had indicated. I heard her behind me say to her colleague, "She ahsked where the bahthroom was. You'd think she wanted to take a bahth!" Then laughter.

My face was flaming hot but I could do nothing but get to the toilet as soon as possible. I was almost crawling when I got there, but I was in time. My stomach emptied, I was much relieved. I washed my face with cold water and felt better. Now my thoughts turned in anger to the rude snip that had been so insulting. Refreshed, I headed back toward that desk, but she was nowhere to be seen. Just as well, or I might have said something that would create an international incident. I found Sr. Justine and chose my books, and we went on our way.

Back in the Bronx and Goodbye to Teaching

The population of St. Adalbert's had been dwindling. It was a little like *The Bells of St. Mary's*, except that there was no Bing Crosby to save the day. The next year there would be only one second grade. The elderly nun had retired, and I would be the sole second grade teacher. This meant more students in the classroom, but I was moved to the larger room. It was also my last semester of graduate school, and I had a minor research study to complete.

By November, I also knew that I was expecting my first child, and by December, I was nauseated every day, all day. Ugo and I planned to move to New Jersey, having bought my parents' house so that they could move to Florida. I would be a stay-at-home mom for the next few years at least. I gave my notice that I would be leaving in January at the end of the semester. I finished my graduate degree, oriented my replacement at school, packed our belongings, all through a haze of nausea. We moved to the distant suburbs of New Jersey and that was, essentially, the end of my school teaching career. There would be one brief return years later, but it would not be the same. These had been the golden years of teaching for me.

Many years later, I received a letter from a student at Cornell University. It was from Sandra, one of the girls in that second grade class. I had had a conference with her father after I realized how pressured she felt to succeed at school. She was a bright girl who always did her work but with an air of tension. She had been the only one who seemed uncomfortable with the relaxed atmosphere in our classroom. After my talk with her father, at which she had been present, she was able to enter into the spirit of learning for the sake of learning and seemed to enjoy the rest of the year.

She had sent the letter to thank me for that year, and for what she felt I had done for her. She was excelling in her college studies at Cornell University, and doing so with the spirit of inquiry she had gained in my classroom. For me, that made it all worthwhile.

CHAPTER

19

Gains and Losses

Florida

When my parents retired, they moved to Lebanon, New Jersey, then decided the winters were too much for them in the cold, snowy climate. They had visited Aunt Gladys in Florida and liked it there. Uncle Ned and Aunt Evelyn were also wintering in Florida by then. Tarpon Springs was on the Gulf Coast, and my father could once again have a boat — the dream of his life after giving up his beloved *Vagabond*. He missed the wooden sloop which he had sold to invest in the shore house. They sold the house in Lebanon to me and Ugo, and moved to Tarpon Springs.

My father retired to enjoy his ham radios and spent much of this time chatting with friends around the country. My mother joined every group possible at her new church, the Friends of the Library and sundry others. Not content to be just a member, she became an officer in most of the groups she attended. She was as busy as any executive. And, of course, the preoccupation with big houses and people with status continued. My phone conversations with her invariably dwelt on what tea was held at what house, what was served, and how opulently the house was decorated, as well as the pedigree of the owner. The church she joined also had its society element.

Gains and Losses

I was to live in the house in New Jersey for the next thirty years. My parents were still there when we moved from an apartment in north Jersey in January. Their furniture was rearranged to make room for our few sticks. We had come from two rooms with a dining alcove and kitchenette.

My mother had been diagnosed, erroneously it later turned out, with colon cancer and was facing surgery in late winter. At first, she was sure she would not live to see my baby, but her usual optimism returned and her spirits improved. The plan was that they would stay until she was recovered, then move south to their new home.

She made an amazing recovery and was soon up and around. There was no follow-up chemo or radiation treatment and I thought that odd at the time. I wasn't told until after her death at age ninety-five that the cancer had been a false alarm, but other family members knew it well before I did. She had not sought a second opinion. This was before the surgery was reversible, and the price of her haste was living with the unnecessary colostomy for the rest of her life.

Julia was born in August 1974 — a Leo, like me — and Alexander was born in 1977. He lived for only an hour. I firmly believe that it was the swine flu shot that killed him, the one the doctor had approved. After other such incidents occurred around the country, I heard the following year that the flu shot was no longer recommended for pregnant women.

When Julia was a year old, I started taking piano students, first from the neighborhood, then from the surrounding area. My clientele grew. Eventually, I went back to college, at Trenton State this time, for courses in music theory, advanced piano pedagogy and more lessons, in order to keep up with my students. We added Saturday workshops and, of course, recitals.

Sarah Arrives, and I Lose My Dad

My father died in Florida just at the time our daughter Sarah arrived in our lives in 1980. My mother often asked me to share memories with her of my father, but I could say nothing to her and shrugged her off. She thought I didn't love him, and I didn't care that she thought that. When he was in the hospital, I had made and cancelled plane tickets several times when first she said I might want to come right away, then that he was better and would be coming home soon, then worse, then better. One evening I returned from the big piano recital that my students had worked toward all year. My cousin, Tucker, and his wife, Carol, were with me when the phone rang. My father was gone. My mother had advised me not to come once too often. I could only hope he knew I loved him.

The cause of my vacillation about going was that, a day or two after his stroke and my mother's first suggestion that I cancel the plane reservation, I received the long-awaited call from New Jersey's Division of Youth and Family Services (DYFS). They had a child for us. Not just a child — a four-day-old baby girl. It was Sarah. If I had flown to Florida, I would have missed the call, and she would have grown up in another family. That has been my comfort. Ugo was in Europe at the time, setting up the European office of Wasino, a Japanese company with whom he had just started a long career. I had no one to leave the new baby with if I went, and didn't feel comfortable taking a newborn on a plane.

Sarah Catherine, named after my father's Aunt Sarah Valentine, and Catherine the Great of Russia, came into the family in the same way as Snooky, Jonathan and Benjamin — she was adopted in. I first saw her in a desk drawer at the DYFS office, having been brought from the hospital that morning. She was four days old. I picked her up. She stared at me for a long moment with gray-green eyes, then promptly went back to sleep. She was a tiny mite with her head of strawberry blonde curls. Julia, then age five, and I had learned of her existence only a few hours before, when our caseworker called.

Julia was in kindergarten, and when she came home from school at noon, she told me about a cat she had seen that was hit by a car behind the bus. We rushed out to find the cat and if it had been alive we would have taken it to the vet. The cat was dead. We arrived back home just as the phone was ringing.

Our caseworker, Miss Callahan, started the conversation on a casual note with pleasantries. I thought at first that she was just calling to touch bases with us as she had been out of the office for some time taking courses. But then she got down to business. "I have something for you."

She proceeded to tell me about the baby that was now available. She was four days old, racially mixed, with a Polish-American mother who had been in love with a Black American father. When he refused to marry her, she came home from California to her family in New Jersey and had been going for Lamaze training to prepare for the birth. She was not the usual unmarried mother, being older than the norm and having some college education. The father was reported to be a nursery school teacher and former track star in college.

When she had finished telling me about the baby she asked, "Do you have any questions?"

I replied, "Yes. How soon can I get her?"

She replied back, "How soon can you get here?"

My only concern was that Ugo was then in Paris and would be for some weeks more. That would be no problem, as Miss Callahan told me that she already knew that he would prefer an infant to an older child who might already have some emotional baggage. Not only that, but this child did not have any physical handicaps. We had been led to believe that we could expect something along those lines and had filled out a questionnaire about what we could and could not accept. It was a given that the children that were currently available would be racially mixed. Sarah was considered handicapped because of this, nothing more. That was no handicap to us.

Miss Callahan went on to explain that, when this child came up for adoption, she was considered a plum by the social work staff, and several others had wanted her for their clients. She had been allowed an hour to find me, as we were at the top of the list. If she had not, Sarah would have gone to the next in line. If the cat had been alive, we would not have had Sarah.

After telling Miss Callahan that Julia and I would be there as soon as possible, we jumped into the car and raced over to Lynne Simms across the street. She didn't answer my first knock but I pounded on the door. Her car was in the driveway, and I knew she was home. I opened the door and yelled, "I have a baby!"

She came down the stairs sleepily, but waking up fast. She had been resting because she was a week past due for baby number six. As soon as she heard my tale, she offered her infant seat for the trip home. While I was off picking up the baby, she went out and bought me a small supply of infant clothing and blankets. Expecting a toddler, I had given away all my baby things.

Julia and I got back into the car and went on to the A&P for Pampers, then on to New Brunswick to the DYFS office. When we first saw Sarah, Julia and I fussed over her for awhile, held her, hugged her, examined her. She was perfect. She smiled at us — or so we believed — and went back to sleep while I completed the paperwork

It was a new thing with the state that infants could be placed in their permanent adoptive homes immediately, if it was determined that the birth mother was not going to change her mind. Legally, she had six months to do so, and it would be cruel to place a child, then have to return it to the mother. The child usually went to a foster home for the six months, where the foster parents were more attuned to children coming and going. Sarah's birth mother had stipulated that she wanted her to go directly to her adoptive parents, and our caseworker, Miss Callahan, and the birth mother's caseworker, concurred that there would be no risk of a change in her decision.

The paperwork completed and thank yous said, we placed Sarah in the borrowed infant seat and headed home. We had just gotten in the door when the younger Simms kids descended on us to see the new baby and to bring the items their mother had bought for her while we were gone. Another neighbor's son, John Vierow, who mowed our lawn, arrived for his afternoon's work. When he walked in and saw the infant, he fell back against the wall with shock. Lynne arrived with some food for me and Julia, knowing I'd be too excited and busy to cook.

That night, I put the baby in bed with me. She was smaller than Julia had been and I couldn't part with her for that night. I had a fleeting jolt of realization about the enormity of what I had undertaken, and wondered how Ugo would take the news. I didn't have a direct phone number for him in Paris, but had called his office with the message about Sarah's arrival.

The next morning he called. "I got this message that we have a four-day-old baby but that can't be right. She must have meant four years."

"No, she's actually five days old now." A pause.

"Well, I guess it can be done. My parents did it," and he laughed. His father was fifty when he was born.

I told him more about the previous day and the miracle of timing that had allowed it to happen. He was thrilled. Unfortunately, he would not be able to leave Paris for two more weeks, as he was in crucial negotiations there for the new division he was creating for the Japanese company.

Sarah was accepted by the whole extended family, particularly by my mother, when she finally saw her. Sarah was a sunny, smiling child, and Mom adored her. All the maternal feelings that she was never able to show, if indeed she had them for Nancy and me, were showered on Sarah. She was even willing to go out of her way and put aside her own multitude of activities for Sarah's sake as Sarah got older and I needed the help.

When Ugo returned home three weeks later and saw the new addition to the family, he was enchanted. A few days later, we all boarded a plane for Florida to help my mother, who was having a hard time adjusting to my father's loss. Many people had attended the memorial service that she held for him, and my sister had been with her, so she had plenty of support at that time. She was always practical and understood the circumstances that delayed my trip.

Mom was now living in the second house they had bought in Florida. They had sold the first one and bought one that was on a canal and had a small swimming pool behind the lanai. My mother enjoyed watching the water birds in the early mornings. We were seeing this house for the first time.

Our arrival worked out well for Mom, because she was just starting to dig through the financial paperwork that my father had left behind. He had taken care of everything monetary, and the woman with the master's degree, who had been an officer in innumerable organizations, had no clue how to read a bill. Ugo led her step by step through the bill paying and banking routines she would have to master, as well as principles of budgeting. My father had put their investments in Merrill Lynch, and my mother came to rely heavily on the wisdom of Richard Ray, her financial adviser. Many years later, when I inherited what was left of those accounts, I, too, relied on Richard.

Ugo taught Mom how to handle her everyday finances but could not instill any long-term savvy. A few years later, she sold her house and moved into a condo. It was large and airy, and saved her having to do yard work. She had plenty of room to continue to entertain family and friends.

In the summers, Mom would drive north to stay with us. When Sarah was very young, Ugo's niece visited us for a couple of weeks. It was decided that a trip to Washington, D.C., would benefit her and Julia both, and Mom agreed to care for Sarah in our absence. I think this is when they developed their special bond that Mom was never able to establish with her own daughters or Julia.

Julia

Julia was a remarkable child from the beginning. She was beautiful, even as a child, and self-assured from birth. She was named for her paternal grandmother Giulia, and Queen Elizabeth I of England. Perhaps that foreshadowed where she would live her life.

For several years, first Julia, and then Sarah and I had season tickets to the New York City Opera on Sunday afternoons. Julia was seven, then eight at the time. We would go into the city early and have lunch at one of the nice restaurants in the area. Julia already had gourmet tastes and knew how to behave in elegant settings. One Sunday during intermission, the elderly lady sitting in front of us turned and complimented Julia on her excellent behavior for one so young.

Just then, the woman's eye was caught by movement in one of the boxes where someone was entering. "Oh, look! There's Bubbles." Bubbles was a fond nickname for Beverly Sills, former opera star, then artistic director of the company. The elderly lady encouraged Julia to go around and get Ms. Sills's autograph. Without a qualm about venturing off alone, Julia left her seat, program in hand. I was glad not to go with her as I was not as undaunted as she about meeting someone of Ms. Sills's eminence. Julia was too small to hide behind. I anxiously watched the door of the box to see if Julia would find her way; otherwise, I would have to go in search of her. She had to make a circuit of half the theatre in the outer hallway. Sure enough, Ms. Sills admitted her to the box. I saw her laugh as she signed the autograph, then turn and wave to me when Julia pointed me out. A smiling Julia returned to her seat, quite pleased with herself.

Mom Moves Back North

When I subsequently divorced, and my sister and I prevailed on Mom to move back north where we could better help her, Mom agreed but would have to sell the condo first in order to buy something close to us. The market in Florida was slow, but she suddenly announced that the condo problem was solved and she would be closing soon on a new townhouse that she had picked out in Lebanon near me.

Mom

Some years later, after Mom had gotten herself into an assisted living facility at Heath Village in Hackettstown, she became seriously ill and was hospitalized. Nancy and I decided at that time, to move her out of the apartment section of the assisted living and into the main building where she could be better monitored. Nancy was going through Mom's papers as we had to dispose of much of her belongings for the move into one room, and she found that Mom had signed the condo over to Houghton College for some lifetime monetary settlement. Just one more turnover.

Mom had always maintained her connection with that school, faithfully attending reunions, and donating inordinate amounts of money to the alumni fund. She enjoyed playing the lady bountiful. She also felt she owed the school a debt of gratitude for offering her the long-ago opportunity for a college education. It had always been a thorn in my father's side, but he allowed her this caprice. Over the next few years, whenever Mom would mention that representatives from Houghton were expected to call on her, Nancy and I made sure at least one of us was present.

We were gratified on their last visit to find that they wanted to modify the agreement and have Nancy, who had power of attorney, take over the management of the money while they retained the principal. Nancy could see no benefit in that and had no interest in taking on the extra burden. It seemed that our mother had lived longer than Houghton expected — she was now over ninety — and the deal was costing them money. The agreement was iron clad, and they couldn't get out of it entirely, but they hoped to rid themselves of the costly portion while keeping the profit. Their request was denied, and we never had any contact with Houghton representatives again except to notify them of our mother's death.

Divorce and Beyond

After the loss of Alexander, Ugo and I grew apart. We couldn't communicate with each other through our sadness. I have since read that marriages can go either way after the loss of a child, but often do not survive that loss — due to the way each parent perceives and feels it. If I had known that at the time, perhaps I could have made an effort to prevent the drift. As it was, whatever our conscious reasons at the time of our divorce — our myriad of complaints about each other — the actual unbridgeable gap was the loss of our son. We had each suffered our pain alone, and it had built a wall between us that no counseling could tear down. My grandparents had weathered two infant deaths, but it was more common then, as medical knowledge was less advanced. People were expected to just deal with it.

It took years to get to the point of separation. Julia was twelve and Sarah six when that point came. It was painful all the way around, but we got through it. We devised an awkward shared custody arrangement, but a year later, Julia elected to live with Ugo, at his insistence, to benefit from the advantages he could offer. She attended private school and traveled internationally. Her first car was his old Mercedes. I could never have provided those things for her.

After Julia graduated from Villa Walsh Academy in Morristown, New Jersey, Sarah followed the same route. She did not have Julia's self-assurance, although she had intelligence and beauty in her own right. To compound matters she found it more difficult living with the stepmother, that her father had meanwhile provided, than Julia had. Julia was ever the self-assured, independent being. But Sarah was another matter. Life was not as easy for her, even with the advantages. When Ugo was away on business, I would receive sobbing phone calls from her. Her stepmother may not have intended to damage my daughter, but the result was the same.

Be a Nurse

It was necessary for me to once again earn my living and to maintain a home for my children. I could not go back to teaching piano. That had been a good and enjoyable supplement when the children were growing up, but I didn't have the qualifications to charge top dollar for the lessons. I tried sales, but that was not my forte. I dreaded making cold calls. I had my own business for awhile, and although it was a financial success, I made the mistake of choosing something I didn't enjoy and eventually the aggravation outweighed the income. There were some years of floundering. Teaching was not the best option because, by then, there was an oversupply and jobs were scarce. I found a teaching job briefly, in a New Jersey city, but it was quite different from my Camelot days at St. Adalbert's. I had been spoiled and could not go back. The policies set forth by the principal in my new school were rigid, and I was expected, once again, to be a disciplinarian.

Throughout my years in the Lebanon house, I was fortunate enough to have an exceptional friend and neighbor in Lynne Simms. She was the mother of six and a nurse with a degree in English — an odd combination. Almost as odd as mine. She was the soul of kindness and put up with me through almost thirty years of ups and downs. She was a strong and determined woman. In the afternoon, I would occasionally stop by and have a cup of tea with her in her kitchen. I was lamenting about my employment options and she put down her cup and presented her solution to my problem.

"Why don't you become a nurse"?

"What? Are you crazy?"

Me – the nurse

"It's not like it used to be. The salaries are higher, and there are more opportunities. You could become a nurse practitioner. It's like a doctor. With your personality, you'd be a natural."

This sounded interesting, so I looked into it. I registered for a local LPN program to try out the profession. I was never a science person, and my math was off the low end of the charts, but my memory for detail was excellent, probably thanks to all those years of recounting the movies at the dinner table. I graduated as valedictorian at last. My mother was so pleased.

By the time graduation rolled around, I was already accepted at Rutgers, College of Nursing for the Bachelor of Science program. Although they accepted some credits from my old Allegheny College transcript, it still took four years to complete the program while working part time and summers as an LPN in a subacute nursing facility. When I graduated with high honors, Mom was still living and was there for the answer to her lifelong question. I wasn't salutatorian, but it was a larger class.

Unfortunately, it was not what I liked doing, but it was what I could do. I went on to graduate school, gaining a master of science degree, but did not know what direction to take next. Management filled the void and sucked me up. It almost sucked the life out of me. I floundered in that for awhile, 24/7, then stuck my toes into psychiatric nursing where I should have been in the first place, if I had to be a nurse at all. That has provided a satisfactory living in the ensuing years.

As a young adult, Sarah returned to me while she struggled to find her own way and get out from under what she perceived as Julia's shadow. After college, she worked for a year with me at a state psychiatric facility in New Jersey, getting a taste of what some people's reality was. Her problems paled in comparison. When I bought an old house and moved to Maine, she moved with me at the last minute. We renovated it into a unique and beautiful home that Mom would have liked.

Mom's Later Years

During her two years in the Lebanon condo, Mom was very helpful to me with my girls. She cared for Sarah while I worked, and continued the close bond with her. Not so with Julia, who was in seventh grade at this time, a difficult age. She returned home from school one afternoon to find herself locked out of the house by her grandmother. Mom found it hard to cope with Julia's creative energy, and they frequently locked horns. When I came home from work, I would find them thus entangled. Mom decided that she wasn't going to deal with Julia on this particular afternoon, and, since the weather was good, the child could just stay outside until I returned. But Julia was an enterprising girl and found a way to get in through a window.

Of course, once she arrived north, Mom again resumed her practice of joining. Now she was at the Lebanon church. It was not as fancy as the one in Ridgewood or the one she had attended in Florida, but it had an active congregation. The meetings and teas commenced anew.

When she ultimately arrived at the retirement community, she wasted no time before joining groups there and taking office. She even received some press when she taught French to preschoolers at the facility's daycare center. The New York Times wrote an article about her, including her picture. She also enjoyed the clientele she met at the community, once again favoring those with a claim to fame and/or fortune. She particularly liked the Friday evening wine and cheese in the elegant front lobby that had influenced her decision to move there.

She gave up driving her car at age 87, giving it to Nancy, who was in need of one. For Mom's ninetieth birthday, Nancy and I held a surprise party for her in my backyard. We rented a tent, tables and chairs, contracted a caterer to provide the food, and a DJ to play golden oldies. We invited all the relatives and as many friends from her past as we could muster.

The best present was the last visit with her brother, Ned. She had always said that he was cute and never got over it. He was still cute, although age had bowed his legs farther than they had been throughout his life. Ned told her that it was probably the last time they would see each other, a bittersweet reunion. Aunt Gladys was already dead of breast cancer, and Uncle Bob was long gone, but

Gladys's children were all there. Darlene and Snooky accompanied Uncle Ned. Four out of five grandchildren were present, Sarah being in Italy for the summer. Some of my father's nieces and one nephew were there as well. Of course, none of Uncle Bob's children came.

Our mother had influenced both Nancy and me during our childhood, harping on the Neville Island house and its grandeur. She was often critical of Nancy's efforts, but recognized that "she had a difficult row to hoe." A few years later, when she retired from her teaching career, through her own efforts Nancy was able to buy a new and elegant house near the Jersey shore. She had denied herself many things over her life in order to accomplish this goal. Mom would have loved the shore house.

Mom died at age ninety-five in a small nursing home near both Nancy and me. She had some dementia but could still speak French, and could still do many of her own activities of daily living. She walked with a walker. One day she told the staff she didn't feel well and was going to her room to lie down before lunch. When they called her for the meal, she was gone. As in life, she orchestrated her death well. Her wishes were expressed in a letter to me and Nancy, and were easy to carry out. Direct cremation, small memorial service. No fuss. Done.

There is one more person whose story has not yet been told. I did not forget her. She will come forward now, and you will come to know her. She was a tiny little elf of a girl.

CHAPTER

Darlene

It was only recently that Darlene and I formed a closer bond. I had, of course, seen her and spoken with her at family functions over the years, but there hadn't been much opportunity to get to know her one on one. I knew many things about her from Aunt Evelyn and her usual praise of her children with our Dunnie this, and our Dunnie that. But I didn't get to know her until she and her husband, Craig, came up to visit me in my newly renovated house in Maine one summer. It was shortly after that visit that I had the inspiration to write this book and Darlene became my strongest ally and supporter.

Darlene — Dunnie as a child — was a tiny little elf of a girl, with black hair and big dark eyes. There was a sprinkling of light freckles over her upturned nose. She was cute. She also had an obstinate streak and a temper, inherited from her mother, and probably from Mary Ann Cole, that stood her in good stead against the merciless teasing of her older brother.

In spite of his teasing ways, Darlene idolized Tucker. She remembers, "He was the only person in the family who read to me when I was little. Many a night I would crawl into his bed and he would read stories to me, and when the light was to be off, he would make up stories. My favorite was, *Bambi*."

Darlene was close to her father, and every year on her birthday, he would tell her about how he was on the train for work and received word that his wife was in labor. Ned told her he was so excited that he jumped off the moving train and hopped another headed back to Oil City so he could get to the hospital for his wife and the birth of their child. In Darlene's case, he made it just in time and it was another of the happiest days of his life.

Ned later had to face his superior for breaking the rules by jumping off a moving train, and face the possibility of dismissal. He told his boss that under certain circumstances in life, one will do most anything to accomplish what must be done. This had been one of those circumstances for him. The boss smiled and gave him only a mild reprimand. Darlene's husband now repeats that story to her every year on her birthday. Ned had a way of making each of his children feel special.

Growing up, she was smart, popular, and accomplished in athletics. As an adult, she studied piano and learned to sew in an effort to emulate her grandmother. Nevertheless, it's hard to follow an act like her brother, and it took many years before she realized that she cast a pretty big shadow of her own, and need not be daunted by his. There was another more ominous shadow hovering over her from her childhood, one that would take years to conquer.

Darlene remembers Grandma Cole as being kind and loving, although other grandchildren saw her as stern and lacking in affection. Grandma made clothes for her, and later, she would see scraps of the fabric from her dresses used in the quilts Grandma made. She remembers Grandma's smile, and the pleasure they had in each other's company when they baked sugar and molasses cookies, or made popcorn on a Saturday night. Darlene was possibly Grandma's favorite because the child was loving and compliant, and did all she could to please. Some of the rest of us were "snippy," not unlike my mother toward her Grandmother Cole, Mary Ann.

When Grandma was staying at Ned's, she frequently commented how appreciative she was of being in a nice warm house, whereas the farm was always cold. Aunt Evelyn made sure the thermostat was turned to high to keep Grandma warm and happy — at the expense of the comfort level of the rest of the family.

Darlene knew how Grandpa Cole had felt about his older son, Robert, our Uncle Bob. Ned, her dad, told her that his father sometimes cried to him about the person Uncle Bob had become and the situation in which he now found himself because of it. There was an old farm down the road from Grandpa called the Heasley place, where Grandpa and Uncle Ned raised several acres of Christmas trees. Grandpa bought that farm and gave it to Ned to make up for the fact that he hadn't gotten a fair share of the homestead. Bob's refusal to share was a continuation of the bullying he had inflicted in their early years. By the time he was older, Ned had given up any interest in a share of the family farm.

When Darlene was a young girl, she, Tucker and Snooky used to help their dad by pruning Christmas trees. It was arduous work for the ten-year-old she was when she first began. She admits that she grew tired and sat down, hidden in a row, and continued to make snipping sounds with the blades, in order to get a rest. As she grew older, she became stronger and more dedicated to the work.

Instead of pay, Darlene and her brother used to be allowed a load of trees to sell. That was the reward, as they were expected to work for no pay. At first, they set up a little stand by their house, but their

Darlene

road dead-ended just beyond, so there was no traffic. They changed their approach and drove the trees around the neighborhood, selling them door to door. They were soon sold out. It was a lucrative business, and they each made a couple of hundred dollars — a nice profit. This was big money to the two young kids.

When Tucker went to college, Darlene continued on her own. By now, Uncle Ned had sold the tree farm to a family who are just remembered as the Russians. Now Darlene was working for pay, and it was up to her to gather her crew. Always a popular girl, she had no trouble rounding up several boys, loading them on a truck, and heading for the farm early in the morning to prune the trees. The Russians paid them all $1.00 per hour. One by one, the boys would quit. Darlene carried on alone until all the pruning was done. Even when she was in college, when she was home for the summer and working a summer job, she would get up at 4:30 in the morning to prune, hurry home, shower and go to her other job at Polk State School, get home from that, shower again and go out on a date.

She married a local boy, but, three sons later, it failed. Meanwhile, she had met Craig Coberly, a nice farm boy from Kansas. His farm consisted of thousands of acres, and he used a small plane to keep in touch with all corners of it as well as to travel to town. Most importantly, he was Darlene's soul mate, and he loved her. Her parents received a letter from her telling them that she was divorced, remarried, no longer living in Albuquerque, and living in Texas. Her father would not speak to her at first, but her mother, true to form, accepted whatever Darlene did. As Darlene said before, if any of her children happened to murder someone, Evelyn would say they had a reason and the person probably deserved to die. Or be divorced.

Of course, Uncle Ned came to accept Craig into the family, and confided stories about his own boyhood that none of the family had ever heard before. Uncle Ned had not relinquished his baby Darlene over to James Riddle, her first husband, but he confidently handed his "Sunshine" over to Craig. Darlene remembers two songs Uncle Ned had for her: *You Are My Sunshine,* and *There Was a Little Girl Who Had a Little Curl.* Craig lived up to the trust.

It was with Craig that Darlene was able to face her demons and realize her worth. He supported and encouraged her in whatever adventures she sought. He is like Uncle Ned in many ways — a gentle man who thinks all men are equal, and your word means everything.

I had attended Uncle Ned's funeral. Tucker had decided he could not deliver the eulogy for his father. He had nothing to say. He had loved and respected Ned, but Tucker could not bring himself to stand before his father's friends and family and say what was expected — that he was a great man. He would also have to tell them the other side of his father — the intolerant side. He explained that to his sister beforehand. When it came time to deliver the eulogy, Darlene stepped up to the podium and, although she also struggled with her emotions, rose to the occasion and gave a moving tribute to her father.

Near the end, when Evelyn was in a coma at the hospital, Darlene had taken off from work and flown up from Georgia to be with her, she and Snooky relieving each other at the bedside. Their vigil was interrupted by a call from Tucker's son, Jeff, that Jonathan had died so tragically, and Darlene left to be with her brother and his family in Florida. It was only days later that the summons came to return to Franklin because Evelyn was gone. Aunt Evelyn was seventy-nine when she died.

A year or two later, Darlene and Craig hosted a family reunion at their Atlanta home. It was Darlene's way of honoring her father and putting closure to his death on a happy note. He would have enjoyed the comaraderie of his family. Craig had prepared lineage charts and t-shirts, with a replication of the lineage, were given to the attendees.

Craig had also uncovered descendants of Milton Cole, Augustus's brother, who had gone to Wisconsin to make his fortune. Eight or ten of them came to the reunion and told about life in the logging camps and how Milton had acquired his wife. It may have been that she first belonged to another man, who did not take well to having his wife stolen.

Family members were asked to bring memorabilia of the Coles. I brought a booklet of my mother's memories, coaxed from her in her nineties. Darlene had Grandma Cole's pearl-handled revolver. This was the first I knew that my demure grandmother owned such a weapon. As far as I know, she never used it, but from what I know of her now, I can picture her aiming at a victim with grim purpose. Uncle Ned had given the gun to Darlene several years before.

The weekend was a celebration of all that was the best of the Cole family. The last time I had seen Darlene was at Uncle Ned's funeral. I would see her again in three years at my mother's memorial service.

CHAPTER 21

Realizations

The kitchen in Grandma Cole's house smelled like new, raw milk that they brought in from the barn for the family, and for making freshly churned butter. Once in a while, I'll get just a whiff of something that reminds me of that smell and I'm immediately transported for a moment back to that clean, bright place, and I'm a child again.

I remember the farm smells in the little mudroom outside the kitchen door. There was a sink where the men washed up before coming into the house. Their manure-covered boots were left out there, their sweaty jackets hung in a row by the door. The mudroom smelled like the musky barn, sweat and strong yellow soap.

My sister's memories of the farm are more from the time after my grandparents left. Although Norine disagrees, Nancy's impression was that the house was dingy and it smelled bad. The toilet didn't always work. The living room, now devoid of the green horsehair furniture, was forlorn and shabby. Children's fingerprints dotted the walls and their few toys were scattered about. Nancy and my father couldn't wait to leave and go to Uncle Ned's, where everything was clean and airy.

Norine told us that her father eventually repaired and renovated the farm. He replaced the barn roof, built a new silo, and resided the chicken coop. Major repairs were made to the house, including a kitchen renovation and the addition of a half-bath to the downstairs bedroom. Norine, an adult by then, painted and wallpapered the entire interior.

As my grandfather grew old, he became more bitter and depressed. His life's hopes were slipping away. He had managed to lose both his family homes as well as whatever other assets and real estate holdings he had. His eldest son was ruled by greed and warped by religion, inflicting cruelty on his wife and children.

Grandpa was now dependent on his other son and eldest daughter for his own and his wife's existence. Norine assures me that her father sent his parents a monthly check, as did my mother, to supplement their social security. Other than that, my mother might as well have lived in another world, a more sophisticated world, a world he didn't understand. This was a world he almost knew as a young man traveling to Europe and to the West, the son of a wealthy businessman and landowner. This world had eluded him, slipping through his grasp like the dust of Neville Island.

He was not alone in this bitterness. According to Norine, my grandmother became a carping instigator, creating tension between Uncle Bob and the rest of the family. At every opportunity, she threw it up to him that his sisters had the ambition to make successful lives for themselves, while everything around him fell into disrepair and ruin.

By that time, Grandma wore the pants in the family, and her word was law. She had learned the lesson well from her mother-in-law, Mary Ann. My grandmother would lay down that law for Uncle Bob and my grandfather, then leave for Gladys's for months on end. It was during that time that Grandpa took to seeking refuge at his son, Ned's, in Franklin.

After they left the farm, my grandparents constantly expressed their unhappiness about not being able to live out their days at the Sandy Lake farm. It had been their home for so much of their lives. Nancy remembers when she was sixteen, and spending the summer at Aunt Gladys's, that Grandma told her of her resentment. I remember Grandma complaining no matter where she was. Nothing was the same again.

My grandmother lost two children, yet remained married to my grandfather. Divorce was not an option at that time, as society was not supportive of women divorcing in those days, no matter what the cause. Most women were financially dependent on their husbands and not prepared to make their way alone. They could not afford the luxury of standing on principle, not even to protect their children and grandchildren. However, if she could have done so, she had other, more serious cause than I did. Women learned to live with aberrant behavior in their men, guarding others from it as best they could.

When my grandfather lost the Sandy Lake farm, whether by putting it up as collateral on another of his stock market deals gone sour, or due to his son's avarice, Bob's bitterness continued to fester and soon spilled over to his mother as the farm progressively deteriorated. Even she could no longer forgive him, who had once been her favorite, her darling boy. My grandmother mourned what Uncle Bob had become.

Toward the end of her life, although my grandmother's mind remained sharp, she became frail in body, and Gladys, ill with cancer herself, could no longer care for her. My grandmother was sent back to the farm and to Uncle Bob, accompanied on the plane by her granddaughter, Marian. Uncle Ned was at the airport with Uncle Bob and Norine, to drive her to the farm. My grandmother didn't recognize Bob, but Marian remembers her greeting her other son, "my little boy, Ned."

Aunt Jeanne was still living at that time, and it fell to her to care for her mother-in-law. Her daughter, Roberta, remembered our grandmother once saying to Aunt Jeanne that she hoped never to be in Jeanne's care in old age because she had not treated Jeanne kindly. Grandma was now at Jeanne's mercy — and merciful she was. With true Christian charity, Jeanne turned the other cheek as she had always done, and made her mother-in-law's last days as comfortable as possible.

While looking out the dining room window from her wheelchair, Grandma said, "Well, Bob, I've come home to die." Grandma died at the farm on June 10, 1975 at the age of ninety-six. Darlene, who always held a more positive image of her grandmother, was glad to know it wasn't in the winter when the atmosphere would have been more dismal and gray. Grandma was very aware of her surroundings.

Darlene observed the effect that the strong religious beliefs and practices of our grandparents had on their descendants. Uncle Ned tried, with honesty and integrity, to live by the same rules as his parents, retaining the rigidity of their beliefs. It created friction between him and his son. Aunt Gladys lived by those beliefs through her ministry to others but was also overzealous when it came to her own children.

With Uncle Bob, the rules became warped as he applied them, shaped by his own shortcomings of selfishness, bitterness and greed. My mother maintained the rules at heart but sought a form of her religion that would allow her to apply them in a gentler guise, thus accommodating her more romantic and worldly leanings.

The end result is that half of us in our generation are fallen-away Methodists, and the others have modified their beliefs. We've each gone through our own reconciliation with the way we live our lives. Both Grandma Cole and my mother would exhort us periodically to "accept the Savior as our Lord," and we all went through our struggle to do so. Uncle Ned exhorted Darlene as he was dying.

There is more to the story of the Cole family. One more element needs to be brought into the light. Where did the fault lie for what happened to one little girl? Clearly, the perpetrator was to blame. Did the loss of fortune so turn Grandpa's moral reason that he allowed himself to think of doing the unthinkable? But what about others? Others knew what he had done before, but gave no warning to the child. Some things were not discussed in the best of families.

When I was a child, I spent a lot of time sitting in front of our large, floor-model radio, listening to my favorite programs; *Let's Pretend* on Saturday mornings, *Tom Mix* and *Captain Midnight* on weekday afternoons near the dinner hour. When Grandpa visited, the radio had to be relinquished to him for his news and stock market reports during my prime listening time. He was still looking for "one more turnover."

I was not allowed to disturb him and cast sidelong, dark, sulky looks while I waited to resume my place in front of the radio. I remember once seeing him coax my little sister over to sit on his lap with her golden, corkscrew curls. Something struck me as odd as she trudged over with reluctance. He lifted her onto his lap with a smile, she with a look of discomfort. She doesn't remember it.

I didn't think more of it until we were adults with grown children. I don't know how it came up in conversation, but with an awkward suddenness, she said, "You know, Grandpa wasn't so wonderful."

"What do you mean?" I replied. I didn't like to hear negatives about the Cole family.

"Do you remember the summer that Mom and Dad went to France and sent me up to Aunt Gladys's while they were away?"

I did remember. I had driven up with a new and very temporary boyfriend for an overnight visit.

"I was sixteen. He pulled me onto his lap and wouldn't let me go. I was yelling at him and Grandma came and reacted vehemently. I thought at the time that she was overreacting, but after that, Grandma always tried to see that I wasn't alone with him."

"I'm sure you're just imagining things." I envisioned the portly old man with his red, jowly face, plain round spectacles, balding head and large paunch. The thought that came to mind disgusted me. I rejected it. "That's ridiculous!"

That was the end of the conversation. When I later learned something from a cousin, I reopened it with Nancy. She then said that she hadn't understood the implications of the situation at the time, but that years later, our mother told her that when she was in her later teens, she'd been warned by our grandmother to stay away from him. Mom never knew just what had happened, only that her mother was very upset because something had happened with Gladys. Soon after, Gladys and Mom were sent to live with relatives.

As I was writing this book and talking to family members, the truth emerged, indisputable. I didn't try to elicit any information from others. The story came out spontaneously when my cousin asked me if Nancy had told me anything about an experience with Grandpa. I replied that she had. My cousin asked if I knew anything else about him. I remembered that Nancy had visited this cousin not long before and had mentioned something about her having had a traumatic experience with him as well. Nancy hadn't given me any details, and again I had brushed it off. I could no longer deny the truth when my cousin told me her story.

I could no longer deny that my sister was not the only innocent girl who caught Everson's eye, nor was Aunt Gladys. After my grandparents left the farm and lived with the families of their children, one granddaughter was singled out for his secret attention. She was a tiny little elf of a girl. He lived in her house six months out of the year.

Families didn't talk about such things, living in a conspiracy of silence. No one thought to warn such a little girl, a little girl who looked like my Julia at the same age. Perhaps Grandma thought he was only attracted to teenage family members.

To overcome the little girl's reluctance, he offered her money and kept upping the ante as more demands were made. Finally, the demands reached the point where she knew it was wrong and she refused to continue further. When she finally got up enough nerve to tell her parents that Grandpa was making her uncomfortable, they simply advised her never to go upstairs alone again to her grandparents' room. She hadn't given them details, being too embarrassed, and her parents never dreamed what the man was actually doing. Nothing was said to the girl about the wrong being on the part of her grandfather. For years, she thought herself at fault.

When she was an adult and learned that he had attempted to molest other females in the family, my cousin hoped her mother hadn't known this part of Grandpa's history, and therefore, had not known to warn her own child. From what I've learned of Aunt Evelyn's fierce love for her family, I believe this to be the case, otherwise the woman would have been upstairs with a meat cleaver!

As an adult, Everson's granddaughter continued to seek validation for what she felt about the wrong that was done to her. When she confided her experience to various men in the family, they disbelieved or dismissed her account as impossible. They had always loved their grandfather and looked up to him. He had loved them and had been a generous father to his sons, and a generous grandfather to his grandsons. He had his faults, but the revelation of his dark side was beyond what his grandsons could accept.

This little girl suffered on into adulthood for the family's sin of omission. One of Gladys's sons, a psychologist, commented that it was just what men did in those days. This was probably true, and from my psychiatric nursing experience, I have seen that it is true now, more than we would care to believe. But that is scant comfort to the victim, who needed the reaffirmation that she was okay. Her brother disbelieved her. The grandsons rallied around the memory of their grandfather and were not willing to see the truth, or give comfort to their sister and cousin.

When I discussed this information with Marian, who had not been approached by him and had been unaware of this side of his nature, she thought this might explain her memory of a certain coolness in our grandmother's relationship with him. Marian recalled seeing him sometimes come up behind Grandma at the kitchen sink and put his arms around her affectionately. She would shrug him off, a scowl on her face.

The first known incident with Grandpa occurred after they left Neville Island. Was it due to a twist of mind caused by his losses? Some need to prove his manhood as he approached his middle years and beyond? Or was it just what men did in those days, and which they still do? But wives and daughters, and society at large, perpetuate this outrage by keeping silent.

It did not stop there. Uncle Bob may have known what his father had done. No one spoke out against that behavior, and Bob may have felt that meant it was condoned. According to Norine and Roberta, he did not touch his daughters, but considered his granddaughters fair game.

Norine had gained strength from her life experiences and was not afraid to confront her father. One Sunday after church, she informed him that she must speak with him. When the time came, she laid it on the line.

"I know what you have done to Marsha's and Roberta's daughters. I know that you have exposed yourself to them, and have put your hands on them. It will stop or I will put you away." Her mouth was set in a grim line.

"No, I never…" He struggled to deny.

"Say what you like, I know you did it. I will put you away if it happens again."

By now, Norine was a formidable adversary, no longer a vulnerable child, and Uncle Bob knew his daughter would be true to her word. From that day forward, he gave his granddaughters a wide berth.

Uncle Bob was stopped, but again, nothing was spoken about in the family. None of us knew what he had done until I asked my cousins directly if he had carried on any of his father's behavior. A hue and cry is set forth when such things happen with the children of strangers, but the family is sacrosanct.

Uncle Ned, who was the optimist, the one who created a happier life for himself and his family, who did not allow bitterness to creep into his heart, did not turn to such emotionally destructive behavior.

Life Goes On

Throughout my life I wrestled with the trickle-down effects of the Cole family's fall and with my mother's influence on me, for good or ill. The story of the later years and what comes after will be told another time. But, at the end of the day, one thing remains of the Neville Island story and the Cole family.

My generation has fought the dragons and re-created themselves. Gladys's children, with strong Bernhoft influence, built fruitful lives in the education and health care professions. They each regained Mary Ann's status of being a person in his or her community who was looked up to and admired.

Robert's children, escaping from the lives of debasement that their father had tried to force on them, each found a way to build a life that was pleasing to him or herself. It was not easy for them, their father not having given them the tools to cope with the larger world away from the farm. But each one struggled and survived, and found a measure of happiness.

Corinne's children, my sister and I, like our Bernhoft cousins, found callings in the professions along with the inherent status. We both followed a more difficult path to career success, but we also found outlets for our creative drives. Early on, in college, I made a failed attempt to follow my interest in theatre, but gave it up for the security of a steady paycheck. Nancy made some stabs at writing and was paid, before she opted for life as a history teacher. It wasn't until our older years, backed by the security of pensions and retirement money, that we both found ourselves happily in the writing business.

Ned's children each struggled with the challenges of their growing-up years. Snooky had to fight the shadow of thinking there was something wrong with her because her father tried to keep her adoption a secret, as if it was a shameful fault in her. He thought he was doing the right thing out of his love for her, but he made an error in judgment. In spite of that influence, Snooky made a good marriage to a man who loved her, and stood behind her own children when they faced problems. She devoted her spare time to the local fire hall, becoming a leader in its civic activities.

View from the Neville Island Presbyterian Cemetery
(the farm was about where the distant tower is seen)

Tucker accepted life as a challenge from the beginning, seldom having self-doubts. He knew he would make it up to his grandfather for the loss of the family fortune, and that goal ruled his life. Perhaps his own family had to fight for their share of attention against Grandpa's ghost — Grandpa who put the bears back into Tucker's bed. His goal accomplished, the millions made, Tucker then had leisure to draw his family back around himself, finding out who these people were who had lived in his shadow for so many years.

Darlene's doubts and insecurities were superimposed from outside herself from a darker source when she was a child, and it took much of her life to quell them.

It would be the next generation, the generation of our children, that would produce the full flowering of the creative seeds. Nancy's son, Jim Gallagher, in his late thirties, finally gave in to his desire to become an actor and to write screenplays, and his brother, Chris, designs websites and writes songs and screenplays. Darlene's son is a successful film editor in Hollywood.

Julia, married a British filmmaker and wrote the screenplay for his first film. She herself is a successful photographer in London. She garnered excellent publicity for their careers when she put the video of their first dance at their wedding on YouTube for friends and relatives in the United States to see, and received over three million hits. Their first dance was the last dance from her favorite movie, *Dirty Dancing*. Her email said, "Nobody puts Baby in the corner."

Within months, this led to Julia and James being invited to be interviewed on the acclaimed *Oprah Winfrey Show*. She and James were just re-creating the dance when the audience suddenly started screaming and clapping. Patrick Swayze had walked out onto the stage. He came up to the couple and took over James's part in the dance, continuing on with Julia, who was in shock by then. The star had made it a policy never to make guest appearances related to his famous movie, but had put it aside after seeing Julia and James on YouTube. He was taken with what they had done.

My other daughter, Sarah, manages a premier six-screen art house cinema in Maine, and assists in selecting the films to be shown. She has ambitions of continuing to build her career in the theatre industry. This fascination with things theatrical first appeared as home entertainments, but Mary Ann, who "ran the show," never dreamed where it would take future generations.

When I spoke of Neville Island, I said that only the hardiest weed could push its way up through cracks in the pavement. My generation of Coles has bloomed like dandelions, making it through the cracks. The generation beyond us has flowered in undreamed-of ways.

We know little of our great-grandfather, Augustus, but we know much of Mary Ann. We know our grandparents, Everson and Helen, well. With their strict religious fervor, how would they have viewed the outcome of the line they progenerated. Mary Ann, Everson and Helen all ended their lives in bitterness and despair. If they could have seen into the future, they might have felt contentment and pride instead.

My grandmother told my mother that she was ugly, and my great-grandmother frowned on her snippy ways. Both women liked her older sister, Gladys, better. Mom bore it well, her self-esteem surviving. However, she forever carried the burden of "What will the neighbors think?"

My mother never told me I was ugly, but she never praised my appearance. She never called me stupid, either, but the mantra I lived under implied it. I was stubborn, willful and didn't match the standard that Mom had set for how her children should be. I never received praise for accomplishments until I was a middle-aged adult, but was criticized for failures early on.

With each emotional slam to the ground, I popped back up like a Joe Palooka doll, buoyantly optimistic that eventually I would meet the mark. I still kept having and following new ideas. The effects, however, were felt internally, and there has been in my nature a hesitance, a shyness about daring beyond some invisible point. My mind surged forward, but my body hung back, not always able to clearly express the ideas I had or exhibit a confident presence. I could do brilliantly with a prepared speech or learned lines of dialogue — I could be someone else — but could not extemporize. I had trouble looking people in the eye for fear of criticism. I doubted my self-worth. Mom was always carping at me to straighten my shoulders, but it was an emotional impossibility for me. And yet, I did well enough.

I have accomplished much in my life — not all of my original goals, but enough to answer my mother's question, the litany of my childhood: "I was valedictorian of my high school class and salutatorian of my college class. What happened to you?"

Epilogue

For the rest of his life, Everson Porter Cole pursued satisfaction from the government for the loss of the Neville Island homestead. He did not find it. Had he looked, he might have found that satisfaction in his own children and grandchildren. His wealth lay in the line he begot.

Everson lived to be eighty-nine years old. At the time of his death he was living with his daughter, Gladys, and her husband Arthur who was dying of cancer. On November 11, 1966, Everson Porter Cole got up in the night. He had not been confused, nor had he appeared distraught during the previous day. He drank Pine-Sol and died at 4:00 in the morning. The immediate cause of death given on his death certificate was arteriosclerotic heart disease. The day after his death, Gladys found a great many of the pills that had been prescribed for his high blood pressure, stuffed under his mattress. He was survived by his wife, Helen, all of his adult children, and all of his grandchildren.

Tucker vowed that he would make back the fortune that his grandfather lost — "For Grandpa." With Cole stubbornness and determination, he did that and then some. He did it with the railroad.

After Gladys's death, Marian was the mainstay of her family.

Donald found the secret of happiness within himself and retained it throughout his life.

Darlene conquered her demons and lived well.

Norine and Roberta remained near Sandy Lake and found solace in the religion that had overshadowed their lives.

Nancy earned her master's degree in history, and retired to the new house in Barnegat where she can proudly invite all her relatives and friends. She writes mystery novels and runs a writers' group with an iron hand.

I bought an old house, made it beautiful, then wrote this book.

The green horsehair furniture changed its color, did some traveling through eight states, and now resides in Florida, partly with Darlene and partly with Tucker. It may soon change its color back to green.

Just one more turnover.

Acknowledgments

I would like to thank all the people who helped me along the way with this book. First, my cousin, Darlene Coberly, who held my hand via email every step of the way, who trusted me to tell her part of the story, and who made me feel for the first time that I was truly a writer. Second, I thank another cousin, Marian Bernhoft Morse, who, with her late husband, Robert, did the original research in Pittsburgh and Neville Island. Her brother, Don Bernhoft, gave me his blessing to write the best book I could. My cousin, Tucker Cole (Ned, Jr.) contributed much of his section to the book, added to my knowledge of the Henderson side of the family, and spent the whole day of his fortieth wedding anniversary reading the manuscript. Evelyn (Snooky) Karns gave me encouragement and hospitality during the writing.

I never would have made it through without the help of all the wonderful folks at 1106 Design, particularly Ronda Rawlins and Michele DeFilippo.

I thank my cousins Norine Cole McGill and Roberta Cole Clayton who so generously shared what must have been very painful memories with me, and for their understanding.

My sister, Nancy, deserves accolades for working tirelessly on the first editing, and guiding me to make the book a viable whole.

I also thank my first readers: Wilma Welch, Mary Figliozzi, Phyllis Lee, Carolyn Laux, Laura Evans, Linda Powell, Norb Nathanson, and Marian Fletcher for their useful comments, their patience and encouragement.

About the Author

Jean Boggio is a graduate of Allegheny College in western Pennsylvania, with a BA in Drama. She went on to earn an MS Ed. in Education from City College in New York City, a BS in Nursing from Rutgers, College of Nursing, and a MS in Nursing from Rutgers University, both in New Jersey.

She grew up in Ridgewood, New Jersey, lived in New York City for many years, then moved back to New Jersey to Hunterdon County to raise her two children, Julia and Sarah. From there she moved to Maine where she now lives and writes with her six cats.

Sources

Newspapers
      Burgettstown Home Monthly
      October, 1900

      Fitchburg Daily Sentinel
      March 12, 1919
      (Massachusetts)

      Chronicle Telegraph
      December 16, 1921
      (Pittsburgh)

      Pittsburgh Tribune
      February 8, 1900

      The Bulletin Index
      Thursday, August 20, 1936

History of Allegheny County, 1899
and History of Allegheny County II – A. Warner
(Revised)

Family Accounts
      Corinne Cole Frith
      November, 1985
      June, 1999

The Coles of Neville Island
Prepared by Marian and Robert Morse for the Cole Family
Booklet – December, 1984

Harvey Henderson's papers and court documents provided by
descendant Chuck Henderson
and Letters from Chuck Henderson to Ned Cole, Jr.

Helen Henderson Cole's Bible

Cole Cousins
> Darlene Cole Coberly
> Ned Cole, Jr. (Tucker)
> Evelyn Cole Karns
> Marian Bernhoft Morse
> Norine Cole McGill
> Roberta Cole Clayton
> Nancy Frith Gallagher

Order Form

Fax Orders: (Number). Fax form.

Email Orders: (will be business email address)

Snail-Mail Orders: Colerith Press, Jean Boggio, 175 Dickey Mill Rd., Belmont, ME 04952, USA. Telephone: (business number)

Via Website: *http://www.jeanboggio.com*

You may pay by check or credit card using this form. If credit card, please sign below where indicated and include your card number. You may return the book(s) for any reason, for a full refund.

STOLEN FIELDS: A Story of Eminent Domain and the Death of the American Dream:

No. of copies: _____

Please send FREE information on:

Other Books _____   Speaking _____

Name: _____

Address: _____

City:_____ State:_____ Zip: _____

Telephone: _____

Email address: _____

Credit Card Type:_____ Credit Card #: _____

Signature: _____

Sales tax: Please add 5% for books shipped to Maine addresses.

Books will be shipped by ground unless otherwise requested. There will be an additional charge for shipping by air or international shipping.